GOD AND EVIL

God and Evil

A Unified Theodicy/Theology/Philosophy

David Birnbaum

Ktav Publishing House, Inc.
Hoboken, New Jersey
1989

COPYRIGHT © 1989
DAVID BIRNBAUM

Library of Congress Cataloging-in-Publication Data

Birnbaum, David.
   God and evil / David Birnbaum.
     p. cm.
   Bibliography: p.
   Includes index.
   ISBN 0-88125-307-3
   1. Theodicy. 2. Good and evil. I. Title.
BT160.B47   1988
296.3'11—dc19   88-39878
                                                  CIP

Manufactured in the United States of America

['Foreword' appears in editions commencing with the Fourth Printing.]

To

Rafaella

and Jordanna

ACKNOWLEDGMENTS

Professor Lawrence Schiffman

Rabbi Marvin Tokayer

Rabbi Yaacov Lerner

I will betroth you unto Me forever;
I will betroth you unto Me in righteousness and in justice, in kindness
  and in mercy.
I will betroth you unto Me in faithfulness; and you shall know the
  Lord"   —Hosea 2:21-22

In 1942 the medical service of the Revier [Ravensbruck death camp]
were required to perform abortions on all pregnant women. If a child
happened to [be] born alive, it would be smothered or drowned in a
bucket in front of the mother. Given a newborn child's natural
resistance to drowning, a baby's agony might last for twenty or thirty
minutes.   —Tillion[1]

The Lord, the Lord is a merciful and gracious God,
slow to anger and abounding in kindness and truth,
He keeps kindness to the thousandth generation.   —Exodus 34:6-7

According to the West German arrest papers, Dr. Mengele was accused
of the following crimes, among others: sorting out arriving prisoners,
particularly old people, children and pregnant women, for immediate
gassing; throwing the Zyklon B poison gas into the gas chambers;
throwing children alive into fires; conducting medical experiments on
living prisoners, especially twins, by injecting their eyes, spines and
brains with camphor and other chemicals; shooting children in order to
perform autopsies on them; exposing healthy prisoners to yellow fever
and extreme X-ray radiation for study; sterilizing and castrating
prisoners; draining the blood of children for study, and cutting off body
parts of female prisoners for tissue cultures.   —New York Times[2]

For He will give his angels charge over you
to guard you in all your ways
The Lord shall keep thee from all evil,
He shall keep thy soul
The Lord will guard you as you come and go,
henceforth and forever.   —Psalms 91:11, 121:7-8

FOREWORD

David Birnbaum's **God and Evil** is a bold and highly original synthesis which attempts to provide an overarching metaphysical solution to the vexing problem of radical evil in a world created and sustained by an all powerful, all knowing, benevolent God. Birnbaum's treatment of the highly intimidating and emotionally wrenching problem of a Jewish theodicy in a post-Holocaust world is audacious yet sensitive, traditional and yet highly innovative. The work ranges over a multitude of traditional and contemporary (Orthodox and non-Orthodox) Jewish sources, draws inspiration from the likes of Gersonides, Isaac Luria, Rav Kook and Rav Soloveitchik, but also from such unexpected quarters as Aquinas and Irenaeus, and yet somehow manages to stay within the parameters of an authentically Jewish, *halakhic* point of view. Birnbaum's book is an intellectual odyssey, yet it is also, as becomes very clear as one reads on, a highly passionate and emotional quest. The author is himself deeply troubled (as we all should be) by the stark contrast between his abiding *faith* in a God who is betrothed to (Hosea 2:21-22) and promises to guard the Jewish people in all their ways (Psalms 91:11), and who keeps kindness and mercy to the thousandth generation (Exodus 34:6-7), and the *realities* of newborn infants "immersed" unto death, and children being thrown alive into fires and having chemicals injected into their eyes, spines and brains, to name but a fraction of the atrocities experienced by God's people in Nazi Europe.

The originality of Birnbaum's approach is evident in his philosophical point of departure. Instead of first focusing on God's attributes, and the possibility of reconciling these attributes with manifest evil, Birnbaum begins with the question of the "purpose of man," a query he believes can only be answered by conducting a far more radical inquiry into the ultimate purpose and, indeed, the origin of God. Birnbaum, like the kabbalists of old, dares to raise the question of the origins of the Creator of the universe, a question which, in his view, must be raised on the grounds that its correct solution is a necessary propadeutic to genuine inquiry into the problem of evil.

Birnbaum's proposed solution to the question of divine origins, to the mystery of the kabbalists' *En Sof* (the infinite theistic principle giving rise to the God of Israel) is that "Holy Potential is at the epicenter of the Divine," that God is, by His very nature, *potential and possibility*, "transcending, space, time and cosmos," and ever-surging towards greater actuality. Birnbaum bases his thesis, in part, on the name by which God first became known to Moses and Israel: *Eheye Asher Eheyeh*, "I-will-be-that-which-I-will be" (Exodus 3:13-14) which he sees as a prooftext for his claim that *potential* is the holiest state of the Divine. Birnbaum sees the kabbalists' *sefirot* as "primal quests for potentiality" which bridge the gap from "emptiness" to "somethingness," and thereby become the vehicles of creation.

The significance of "Holy Potential" as the primal thrust of the universe, is that man, created in the image of God, has as his cosmic purpose the fulfillment of his own potential, encapsulated in the first Biblical command, *peru u'rivu*, "be fruitful and multiply" (Genesis 1:26). Birnbaum sees mankind's potential displayed in two possible, but mutually exclusive, sets of dynamics that were laid out in the Garden of Eden. The first of these, the dynamic of the "Tree of Life/Bliss" promises a gilded cage existence, dependence upon God, eternal life, tamed evil but a limited potential for growth; the second, the dynamic of the "Tree of Knowledge/Potential" promises a life of challenge, freedom, privacy, responsibility, independence, untamed evil and mortality, but an infinite potential for growth. The two of these dynamics are, according to Birnbaum, mutually exclusive, in that insofar as one participates in the first, he cannot participate in the second, and vice versa. A life of infinite freedom/potential is logically incompatible with dependence on God and personal immortality.

Given the fact that man, like God, has as his core essence, the realization of his potential, it is an essentially foregone conclusion, written into the very act of creation, that man would eat of the fruit, be banished from Eden, and fulfill the dynamic of the Tree of Knowledge. As such both natural and moral evil would forevermore both plague and challenge mankind. Indeed, the very possibility of man's fulfilling his potential for good, both on the individual and collective levels, is predicated on the possibility of both natural evil (as a challenge to man's resources) and moral evil (as a challenge to his freedom).

The closer mankind comes to fulfilling his spiritual, intellectual and other potentials, the closer he comes to fulfilling his purpose on earth via his role as a partner with God in creation. In doing so, however, man must maximize his privacy, independence and freedom. As mankind then moves closer to its own self-actualization, God must, of necessity, retreat further and further into "eclipse." Mankind has, over the centuries, indeed ascended greatly in knowledge, implicitly demanding greater and greater freedom. For God to intervene directly in human affairs at this late stage in mankind's development, as he did, for example, for the Jews in Egypt, would reverse the very development of both His and mankind's essence, and in Birnbaum's terms, threaten to "unravel the cosmos."

Sanford Drob
Editor-in-Chief
NY Jewish Review
February 1990

TABLE OF CONTENTS

PART II
The "Quest for Potential" Unified Formulation

GLOSSARY[3]

Dualism. The view that two ultimate and irreducible principles are necessary to explain the world, and evil in particular. Opposite of monism.

Emunah. Faith.

Halachah. Literally, "the Way," the legal parameters of Judaism.

Kabbalah. The esoteric teachings of Judaism and Jewish mysticism, especially the forms which it assumed in the Middle Ages from the twelfth century onward.

Man of Halachah. Jewish religious man of reason (note: our term diverges slightly from Soloveitchik's definition of *Halakhic Man*).

Masorah. Corpus of Jewish canon and explication; thus, the body of authentic tradition connected with the biblical text.

Midrash. A particular genre of rabbinic literature incorporating biblical exegesis, explanation of biblical texts from an ethical and devotional point of view (including related sermons delivered in public), and forming a running commentary on specific books of the Bible.

Mitzvah (pl. mitzvot). A Divine ordinance/precept in the Halachah.

Monism (from Gr. *mones*, "single"). The view that everything can be reduced to one singularity or principle.

Talmud. Composed of the Mishnah and the Gemara, the Talmud essentially records the exegesis, debate, discussion, and conclusions involved in the illumination of the Oral Law, as opposed to a totally literal reading of the Pentateuch. There are two Talmuds: the larger and more comprehensive Babylonian Talmud (*Talmud Bavli*) and the smaller Palestinian Talmud (*Talmud Yerushalmi*). In the absence of a qualifying description, the term Talmud generally refers to Talmud Bavli.

Tanach. Acronym for *Torah/Neveeim/Kesuvim*, (Pentateuch, Prophets, Writings), the three divisions of the Hebrew Bible.

Tefillah. (Jewish) prayer.

Theodicy. The problem of reconciling God and religion in the face of evil or (an attempt at) reconciling God and religion in the face of evil.

Note to reader:
On page 245 there are "snapshot biographies" of individuals cited.

PREFACE

This work is divided into three parts.

Part I has two major components. The first is a review and treatment of the subject of theodicy. The second portion reviews some major philosophical underpinnings of Judaism related to intellectuality, which have a direct bearing on our study.

Part II presents the major contribution of this work, my "Quest for Potential" formulation, a solution of the age-old problem of theodicy. Its nine points are numbered 100 through 900 for easy citation and reference. Though based on Jewish sources, its orientation is universalistic, and it presents a cohesive alternative to several classic philosophical formulations.

Part III contains a summary, and addresses the applicability of this study on a personal level.

*

PURPOSE

Jews today who reject agnosticism and choose a religious approach to life are reaching out for the spirituality of Jewish religious life, which will hopefully satisfy both their spiritual striving and the demands of their intellect. This quest for intellectual rigor in Jewish philosophy is basic in Judaism.

Thus, if one takes the step of choosing a generally religious approach to life, one must still seek to examine the religious and philosophical parameters of this life.

The purpose of this work is to present a unified theological formulation palatable to religious "man of reason" but falling within the framework of Jewish theological tradition.

xix

This work will support the credo that there is no necessary conflict between the heart and the mind, between faith and reason, between tradition and truth.[4]

Unde malum? "From whence evil"[5]—if there be a God?

The first known formulation of this paradox in Western philosophy was that of Epicurus ca. 300 B.C.E.[6] Eastward, and approximately four hundred years earlier, a thundering prophetic voice cried out:

Therefore is justice far from us,
Neither doth righteousness overtake us;
We look for light, but behold darkness,
For brightness, but we walk in gloom.

—Isaiah 59:9

How can we reconcile an all-powerful, all-merciful God with the existence of evil?

The question is indeed almost as old as mankind.[7] To phrase it another way: How can we affirm the validity of a sincere religious commitment in a world where we ourselves have witnessed such prevalence of gratuitous, gross evil? The problem goes beyond the issue of the suffering of the innocent, and beyond the question of the suffering of the righteous. It involves the fundamental issue of whether there is any higher moral order at all to the cosmos.[8]

The purpose of this study is not to make the case that a religious approach to life is a logical imperative, nor to expound its glories. Rather, the purpose is to offer a unified philosophical structure for those examining, considering, sympathetic to, or practicing a religious approach.

Our study will focus initially on the theodicy question. As the work progresses, and as components of our approach to the theodicy question begin to fall into place, we will address several other difficult philosophical/theological issues:

How can man's freedom be reconciled with God's omniscience (all-knowing), His foreknowledge, or His possible intervention?

If God is omnipotent (all-powerful), why does evil exist at all?
From whence eternal God?
What is the purpose of man, the cosmos?
Is there an underlying motif to the cosmos?

PART I
Theodicy, Theology, Intellectuality

10.00   THEODICY/THEOLOGY

10.01   Definition

The accepted name for the entire subject comprising the problem of evil and its attempted resolution is *theodicy,* from the Greek "θεός, "God," and δίκη, "justice.""[9] The word is a technical shorthand used several ways. *Theodicy* is a shorthand for the problem of evil in the face of God. It is also a shorthand for a formulation of a resolution of the problem of evil. A common definition of the word *theodicy* is "a defense of (the justice and righteousness of) God in the face of evil."

Some maintain, however, that it is ludicrous, if not sacrilegious, to defend God. Whether it is or not, we will in any event be using the following definition:

Theodicy: reconciling God and religion in the face of evil.

There are implicit major and minor themes in the theodicy dilemma, namely:

1. If God is omnipotent, omniscient, and all-merciful, why does (gross) evil befall the innocent, e.g., infants?
2. If God is all-merciful and omnipotent, why does evil exist at all?

Answers to the first element of the dilemma will lead us to follow up and inquire as to the ultimate purposes of man; answers to the second element of the dilemma will lead us into inquiries regarding the origins of the cosmos.

10.02   Discussion

Many people, from venerable scholars to schoolboys, compartmentalize the problem of evil. That is, they recognize that aspects of evil present a theological problem, and, having recognized that, move on to other matters.

However, theodicy, as hitherto approached and explicated, remains for many, if not most, a weak link in the chain of a religious approach to life. Writings and discourses on theodicy by the Jews, Greeks, Christians, and Eastern religions have graced our planet for thousands of years.[10] Theodicy is a problem not for all religions, but rather in particular for monotheistic religions proclaiming a God who is all-powerful and all-good. This clearly encompasses the major Western religions.

The goal of theodicy has generally been a modest one, namely, that of defending the validity of an existing faith. We suspect, however, that unraveling the knot of the theodicy problem will force the resolution of related theological issues and will yield a more dynamic and coherent theology.

Theodicy has been treated by many as somewhat independent of other philosophical issues, and consequently some formulators of theodicies have been justly reproached for operating in a vacuum. At the same time, most theologians would maintain that the formulation of a theodicy must conform to the commonly accepted religious philosophy. However, the problem is of such magnitude that we may have to modify some of our basic philosophical assumptions.[11]

Theodicy actually does not pose the same problem to all, even for those who share a common religious tradition. Different thinkers have different thresholds at which the issue of evil becomes a serious philosophical problem. In all probability, an individual reared during the Black Death in Europe would have had a different threshold than one reared in the 1980s in Europe. Camus said: "I continue to struggle against this universe in which children suffer and die."[12] Doestoevsky's Ivan Karamazov protested: "There is no justification for the tear of even a single suffering child."[13]

The gamut of Jewish responses includes the grossly sardonic. The writer Elie Wiesel tells the story of a small group of Jews who were gathered to pray in a little synagogue in Nazi-occupied Europe. Suddenly, as the service proceeded, a pious Jew who was slightly mad—for all pious Jews were by then slightly mad—burst in through the door. He listened silently for a moment as the prayers ascended, then slowly said: "Shh, Jews! Do not pray so loud! God will hear you. Then He will know that there are still some Jews left alive in Europe."[14]

This story combines two theodicy themes: a non-Jewish theodicy of a God turned evil, and a fundamentalist Jewish theodicy of God punishing all Israel for sundry transgressions.

The task of theodicy may include defining and hypothesizing on the origins of evil, goodness, and God, as well as the purpose of man. Divine omnipotence, omniscience, and omnibenevolence must be defined. Approaching the problem precisely as it has been tackled for several millennia is unlikely to yield a sudden flash of brilliant insight. Reorientation is necessary. Yet we must first proceed with certain basics.

10.03   Nadir and Refinement

There are those who argue—and we are sympathetic with the thrust of their argument—that the Holocaust represents a new extreme in evil, by dint of its intensity, magnitude, organized structure, and overwhelmingly diabolical nature. There are others who argue that the Holocaust was essentially just another atrocity, albeit on a larger scale, in a long line of ignominious atrocities perpetrated against the Jew and mankind.

Regardless of which of these two general lines of reasoning is employed, no one can argue that our generation has not come face-to-face with gross abomination and evil. Our generation has counted the corpses of the tortured and brutalized; we may encounter survivors of Hell on a personal basis. We do not operate in the abstract. As a consequence, we exercise inherent rights of observation, analysis, and, if necessary, refinement of Jewish philosophical doctrine. With all due respect to the claims of abstract intellectual and historical analysis, the qualitative and emotional differences yielded by the present-day encounter with evil must lead us to scrutinize theological doctrine in our own light. Doctrine is always cogent in the abstract, but only attains validity when it succeeds in the face of harsh reality. And if philosophical doctrine cannot handle challenge, including the challenge of experience, reformulation within the bounds of dogma may be in order.

> The Holy One, blessed be He, rejoices in the dialectics of Torah. Read not here "dialectics" *(pilpul)* but "creative interpretation" *(hiddush)*.
>
> —Soloveitchik[15]

In the post-Holocaust environment, in particular,[16] there is a growing body of respected thinking which welcomes aggressive inquiry and legitimate reformulation/refinement of Jewish thought.[17]

> To avoid Auschwitz, or to act as though it had never occurred, would be blasphemous. Yet how [can we] face it and be faithful to its victims? No precedent exists either within Jewish history or outside it. Even when a Jewish religious thinker barely begins to face Auschwitz, he perceives the possibility of a desperate choice between the faith of a millennial Jewish past, which has so far persisted through every trial, and faithfulness to the victims of the present. But at the edge of this abyss there must be a great pause, a lengthy silence, and an endurance.
>
> —Fackenheim[18]

The fact that one contends with the common theological formulations does not mean that one is contending with God. To put matters in further perspective, it should be noted that Jewish tradition gives wide berth to aggressive inquiry.[19] Occasionally God reveals His approval of those who contend with Him directly, as He did in the case of Job. He rejects the well-meaning defenders of His "justice" toward Job in the words which He addresses to Eliphaz the Temanite:

> My wrath is kindled against thee, and against thy two friends: for ye have not spoken of Me the thing that is right, As my servant Job hath . . .
>
> —Job 42:7[20]

The Holocaust shakes modern man's confidence and many of his basic assumptions. While it may be philosophically true, and even possibly provable, that the death of one innocent is as great a philosophical problem as the death of several million innocents, it is the latter which unnerves the mass of humanity. It is the latter which opens the gates for a communal introspection and theological reassessment.[21] For it is when the foundations of the entire community are still shaking, as opposed to the foundations of the immediate circle of a singular innocent victim, that the philosophical wisdom of the community is energized to creativity.[22]

Many theodicies, including many Jewish ones, are so philosophically subtle or inscrutable that they are explicable only by suggesting that the perplexed inquirer study the entire body of works of the formulator and his sources, if not the bulk of the collected works of the *Masorah* (corpus of Jewish canon, explication, and authentic tradition). A theodicy, however, must be understandable and acceptable to most people in order to be effective. It is not sufficient for a theodicy to be simply emotionally intriguing to a few ivory-tower theologians. Abstruse profundities should not play key roles for a "people of the book," which prides itself on its intellectual primacy. As man is a key protagonist in religion, the philosophy of man's interaction with God should be within reach of man.[23]

10.04   Ramifications

Although several thousand years of traditional explication, redaction, exegesis, amplification, and *chiddush* (new insight) may give the impression that Judaism is generally averse to loose ends, this is not the reality in the case of theodicy. But consigning theodicy to the netherworld of the inscrutable, insolvable, or intractable is not only inconsistent with the thrust of Jewish tradition; it is damaging to the vitality of the religious community.[24]

Many theologians and rabbinic leaders, particularly from the more modern wings of Orthodoxy, have openly taken the position that no previously formulated theodicy is truly fully satisfying. Needless to say, the ramifications of this situation do not end at that point. They include disheartenment, lukewarm religious commitment, and abandonment of faith.[25]

This is a problem for both the believer and the nonbeliever. In the mind of the latter it stands as a major obstacle to a religious commitment, while for the former it sets up an ongoing internal tension to constantly challenge and cast doubt upon the validity of his faith.[26]

> If we were to place the impressive weight of evidence testifying to the existence of God in one scale, it would be outweighed for many by one hydra-headed fact, the existential tragedy of suffering, the burden of human misery, from which none are free. For untold sensitive men and women, the frail bark of faith has crashed on the hard rock of the persistence of evil in a world allegedly created by a good God.
>
> —Gordis[27]

10.05   Cohesiveness

One may choose a secular or perhaps agnostic approach to life, or one may choose a religious approach to life. But if one chooses a religious approach and wishes to distinguish oneself from the unsophisticated, a unified religious philosophy is in order. The philosophy chosen may turn out to be flawed or totally wrong, but at least its formulators and adherents perceive it to be unified.

Formulations of a unified theodicy/theology were wanting even before the Holocaust; the Holocaust merely dealt these formulations a further blow.[28]

Judaism requires both leaps of faith and a leap of the will. A major leap of faith is required to accept the complete *Masorah* as bona fide and correct; the leap of will is the acceptance of the yoke of Jewish law and canon. The problem posed by theodicy is the wrench it throws in the works for religious man of reason, who has previously taken these leaps of faith and will.[29]

In talmudic explication, as in Euclidean geometry, a line of reasoning or theorem which is not defensible from any and all challenges is unacceptable. A line of reasoning which meets ninety-nine challenges but not the one hundredth is a fatally flawed hypothesis.

In similar terms, a theological formulation must and should be able to handle all challenges satisfactorily to be truly viable! Judaism is a comprehensive system demanding internal logic and consistency. Internal contradiction is not brooked. Common and consistent threads link its voluminous texts. What is true on page 4 of Text A must be true on page 4000 of Text B. And, nagging at this elegant and finely tuned system, which has been scrutinzed and refined over the millennia, is the gaping problem of theodicy. Many have stabbed at solutions, but the challenge remains.

20.00 THEODICY IN FOCUS

20.01 Problematics

It would seem that to resolve the dilemma of theodicy, one or more of the traditional attributes of God—all-wisdom, all-power, all-benevolence—needs to be deleted or seriously curtailed. Traditional theologies of all faiths have been aware of the potential danger of reducing God's attributes, and have attempted to protect the status of the deity.

In arguments used by traditional theologians, what man calls evil sometimes turns out to be good in God's eyes; suffering, pain, and death are the consequences of man's erring belief or behavior, and are therefore seen as just punishments, or as part of a grander scheme for the ultimate cosmic good. Invariably and inevitably, the Divine image is sustained, and it is man who is diminished. God's omniscience, omnipotence, and benevolence can seemingly be held inviolate only at the expense of man's impotence, malevolence, or limited intellect. For this reason, traditional justifications of God's ways tend to read like cases of conflicting interests.[30]

Theology and theodicy are about perfection and absolutes:

- Is God perfectly good?
- Is God perfectly powerful?
- Is God perfectly omniscient?
- Is God perfectly benevolent?
- Is God perfect?
- Is God not by definition perfect?
- If yes, why gross evil?[31]

The question then focuses on man's limits. It focuses on the limits of man's abilities of comprehension vis-à-vis the Divine and the Divine interaction with man.[32]

Century after century most theodicies have either limited aspects of God's power, limited man's claim to virtue, or limited man's ability to comprehend God's virtue. None of these options is truly satisfying to religious man of reason—who wishes to maintain God's power, man's virtue, and man's ability to comprehend.[33]

During World War II, the pious men of a makeshift little synagogue in the Lodz Ghetto spent a whole day fasting, praying, reciting psalms, and then, having opened the holy ark, convoked a solemn *Din Torah* (Torah tribunal) and forbade God to punish his people any further.[34]

The pious in the Lodz Ghetto tale refuse to limit concepts of God's power; they refuse to deny man's virtue; and they refuse to deny man's ability to comprehend. Rather, they will stand with their concepts of God and man intact, and they will invoke God to stay God's hand. While at first glance their action seems bizarre, the theological bases of this action are well grounded in Jewish tradition. In essence, in their profound faith and confidence in God and man, they invoke the logic of theodicy back on itself.[35]

20.02   Holocaust

Whether or not the Holocaust represented a new level or intensity of evil, we are challenged, as were previous post-catastrophe Jewish communities, to reexamine our assumptions and perspectives in light of the realities our generation has witnessed.[36] We must ask the quintessential question afresh: Can some semblance of rationality be applied to our religious commitment in light of the horrors we have seen?[37]

We have come to know things so unheard of and so staggering that the question of whether such things are in any way reconcilable with the idea of a good God has become burningly topical. It is no longer a problem for experts in theological seminars, but a universal religious nightmare.

—Jung[38]

Jobian boils have reappeared in our times more massively spread than before. It is now the comforters, not Job, who feel constrained to place their hands upon their mouths in disbelief.

—Schulweis[39]

Buber writes:

How is a life with God still possible in a time in which there is an Auschwitz? The estrangement has become too cruel, the hiddenness too deep. One can still "believe" in a God who allowed those things to happen, but how can one still speak to Him? Can one still hear His word? . . . Dare we recommend to the survivors of Auschwitz, the Job of the gas chambers: "Call on him, for He is kind, for His mercy endureth forever"?[40]

Authentic tales of glorious and heroic Jewish resistance, and saintly, superhuman action and sacrifice in the face of the Nazi monster, do not constitute a theodicy. To posit God's here-and-now presence at Auschwitz simply aggravates the philosophical problem further.[41]

> There were really two Jobs at Auschwitz: the one who belatedly
> accepted the advice of Job's wife and turned his back on God,
> and the other who kept his faith to the end, who affirmed it at
> the very doors of the gas chambers, who was able to walk to his
> death defiantly singing his "Ani Maamin—I Believe." If there
> were those whose faith was broken in the death camp, there were
> others who never wavered. . . . Those who rejected did so in
> authentic rebellion; those who affirmed and testified to the very
> end did so in authentic faith.
>
> —Berkovits[42]

The victims, who were stripped of everything of which they
could possibly be stripped, found themselves in the hammer-
lock of gross evil incarnate, in an environment itself stripped
to its rawest core. In this crucible environment, in numbers
disproportionate to the greater Jewish population, the victims
usually chose definitively to take their stand on one of two sides
of the religious issue—i.e., they turned either to a complete
religious dedication or to religious rejection. Yet experience
teaches us that conclusions reached in such an environment
are to be taken very seriously.

Jewish theology, as developed through that time, was simply
insufficiently powerful, or at the least insufficiently articulated
and communicated, to hold the allegiance of many sincere
devotees. The fault is neither with Judaism nor with the hallowed victims; it probably lies with the development and explication of the theology.

In response to the classic challenges of theodicy regarding
the Holocaust, in particular, a traditionalist might counter by
challenging the validity of the questioner's scale of magnitude,
and by inquiring as to the questioner's suggested remedy. How
many deaths by atrocity is too many? Three million? Three
hundred thousand? Thirty thousand? Three thousand? Three
hundred? Thirty? Three? One? What would the theologically
troubled have prescribed for the Holocaust—ten plagues, a bolt
of lightning, a column of Divine fire?

These responses are only of limited utility and far from an

answer. But we must ourselves consider the question—why indeed even one death by atrocity? Why indeed one tear?

With regard to the specific challenges to his query, the theodicist might counter the counter as follows: Man can emotionally accept a limited level of risk and pain as a price to be paid for freedom, but a point comes where the price in pain outweighs the communal and individual needs of freedom. What price freedom? (Regarding proposed mechanics of Divine intervention, the theodicist might counter that God, working in mysterious ways, had a plethora of mundane options to curtail the horror.)

20.03   Observations: The Sliding Scale

It might very well be the case that if there were no cases of evil perpetrated by man against man ("moral evil"), we would focus on suffering caused by nature ("natural evil"); and if there were no suffering apparently caused by natural forces except for old-age mortality, we might focus on why some persons live longer than others; and if all people lived to exactly the current actuarily expected age, we might ask why man does not live longer or forever; and if man lived forever, we could then focus on the reverse side of the theodicy question; namely, why goodness is distributed unequally and inequitably.

Solzhenitsyn, in his *Gulag Archipelago,* posits that man always seeks the next higher level of freedom. The prisoner in solitary confinement seeks not liberation from prison or a free life of leisure; he seeks and yearns for removal from solitary to non-solitary confinement, the next higher level of freedom.

Psychiatrist and former concentration camp inmate Victor Frankl, in his book *From Death Camp to Existentialism,* notes that the human psyche manages to absorb itself with the greatest problem facing it, irrespective of the objective seriousness of the problem.

Therefore, while we may demand an explanation for gross atrocity as the salient problem in theodicy, the removal of the existence of gross atrocity, while mitigating the problem, would not in itself remove the general, wider problem of evil.

Theodicy is actually a hierarchical problem ranging from a defense of God in the face of gross mass atrocity, through a defense of God in the face of the tear of a single child. Yet the fact that the removal of the existence of the severer forms of evil would only lead us to address lesser forms of evil does not free us philosophically from addressing the question first with regard to the grossest forms of evil apparent to us.[43]

Of all the philosophical challenges to theistic faith, none is more serious than that posed by evil. For theistic faith posits God to be omnipotent and omni-good. If God is omnipotent, God can prevent gratuitous evil. But gratuitous evil exists. Therefore God seemingly cannot be both omnipotent and all-benevolent. The removal of either one of these components, however, would be a fatal blow to traditional Jewish or Christian monotheism.

The challenges can be articulated in one short paragraph. Yet even the preliminaries to an answer require considerable development. This situation, not uncommon in philosophical issues, has the effect of giving the problem higher standing. In the thirteenth century Thomas Aquinas listed evil as one of the two chief intellectual obstacles to Christian faith, the other being man's ability to explain the world without reference to a Creator.[44]

20.04   Formally Stated

More formally, the problem of evil can be reduced to an apparent contradiction within three propositions:

1. God is omnipotent/omniscient.
2. God is all-benevolent.
3. Gratuitous evil exists.

The truth of any two of the propositions renders the third seemingly impossible. To paraphrase Schulweis, when confronted with cool logic and remorseless evil, we are tempted to sacrifice elements of at least one of the first two classic propositions.

> Invariably, the attempted exculpation of God defends a major aspect of perfection at the expense of another. Each type of theodicy is compelled to divest itself of some vital part of monotheistic belief in order to protect what it considers to be the more valued ideal. It is around that excluded aspect that the arguments and counterarguments of theodicy are centered.
>
> —Schulweis[45]

20.05   Defining Parameters

We will devote considerable attention to a particular area of omnipotence—"omniscience in the here-and-now," an area not overly cultivated in theological formulations.

We posit that religious man, approaching the question of suffering, must first ask: *Is omnipotent/omniscient God always watching in the here-and-now?* If the answer is essentially "yes, always," as most theologians affirm, one is tempted either to sacrifice elements of omnipotence or to put an infinite value on man's freedom in a universe reigned over by a very stoic Divine. If not, one can do mental gymnastics from now until doomsday, but will encounter insurmountable logical obstacles that make it impossible to come up with an inclusive, satisfying answer.

If the answer to our initial question is "not always," then there is some room for maneuver. However, the "not always" must be theologically justified and grounded. The "not always" must be reconciled with traditional religious concepts of omnipotence, omniscience, Providence, omnipresence, reward and punishment, and the biblical God clearly watching and interfacing with man in the here-and-now. The whys and wherefores of the "not always" must naturally be fully explicated and buttressed.

In general, those positing "not always" are challenged by folk wisdom, and those positing "always" are challenged by logic and emotion. Those positing "not always" must explain away numerous scriptural citations of an all-powerful (and, consequently, all-watching) God, and those positing "always" must also explain away various scriptural citations of *Hester Panim* ('Hiding of the Divine Face')—elaborated upon below.

20.06   Appropriateness

Is the whole question of a theodicy appropriate? Immanuel Kant pointed out that if it is arrogant to defend God, it is even more arrogant to assail Him.[46] Yet the Jew in particular, and religious man of reason in general, has always grappled with cosmic whys and wherefores. It is in part this grappling for authenticity which distinguishes religious man of reason from religious fanatic man, (moved by intense uncritical devotion) who is untroubled by reason.

30.00   THEODICY IN THE JEWISH TRADITION

30.01   Outline

For purposes of discussion, we divide traditional Jewish responses into seven major groupings. Many of these theodicies appear in related form in non-Jewish traditions.

    I. Finite man cannot comprehend infinite God's ways.
    II. Man is punished for his sins, failings.
   III. *Hester Panim* (God's Hiding of the Face).
   IV. Other mainstream traditional responses
    V. Man is free.
   VI. Kabbalistic responses.
  VII. There currently is no answer.

Group I. **Finite man cannot comprehend infinite God's ways.**

The underlying implicit theme of this group is that the universe is somehow better with apparent evil in it.[47]

Finite man cannot understand infinite God.[48]

God's ways are inscrutable.[49]

God has His ultimate purposes known to Him. Man must have faith in God's justice.[50]

God's ways will be made understandable to us in the next world.[51]

Group II. **Man is punished for his sins, failings.**

The iniquities of the fathers are visited upon the sons ("vertical responsibility").[52]

Man is punished in this world to increase his reward in the world-to-come.

There is no suffering without sin.[53]

All men are imperfect and sin in some way.[54]

Suffering is due to evil deeds or neglect of Torah study.[55]

Group III. **Hester Panim**

Hester Panim—hiding of the Divine face—a temporary abandonment of the world, a suspension of God's active surveillance.[56]

This concept is almost never applied as a general response to theodicy, but rather as a response to a particular catastrophic series of events. Major attention is devoted to this theme later on.

Group IV. **A. Other mainstream traditional responses regarding the suffering of the *tzaddik* ("saintly" individual) in particular.**

When permission is given to the angel of destruction, he makes no difference between righteous and wicked.[57]

The righteous man should have acted more forcefully in promoting righteousness or interceding for his people.

The *tzaddik* is held to a much higher standard.[58]

A *tzaddik*'s suffering is atonement for all the people.

The righteous will get their reward in the world-to-come.[59]

There are some merits for which God rewards in this world, and there are merits for which God bestows reward in the world-to-come.[60]

The *tzaddik* is "gathered in" prior to the appearance of great evil.[61]

Group IV. **B. Other mainstream traditional responses regarding man in general**

In recompense for his suffering, man will receive his reward in the world-to-come; man suffers in this world to purify him and clear his slate for the world to come; sins are forgiven through suffering.[62]

The individual is punished along with the rest of the community for communal sin ("horizontal responsibility").[63]

The sin of Adam brought suffering upon the world.

The concept of *yissurin shel ahavah*—tribulations of love[64]—
to purify man, to ennoble man, to chasten man;[65]
to raise man to a higher level;[66]
to test man;[67]
through suffering comes redemption;[68]
to increase man's reward in the world-to-come.[69]

To provoke man to reflect on his inadequacies and propel man to develop his potentiality.[70]

The process of Divine justice takes time and man must have patience.

Man is responsible for sin and suffering, not God.

Suffering is a discipline, warning men against sin.

Suffering keeps man from committing the sin of "hubris."

Suffering lessens the physical pride and selfish nature of the individual.[71]

Divine Providence is linked to piety and intellectual attainment; the absence of either leaving man vulnerable to evil.

Nature is morally neutral. *Hashgachah* (Providence) does not apply to acts of nature.

Group V. **Freedom of man**

Implied in this group, there are Self-willed constraints on God's intervention to protect man's freedom.

Man's freedom must be protected, even at the expense of suffering.

Suffering is an indispensable spur to human aspiration and achievement. (This is similar to the [Christian] Irenaean theodicy and kabbalistic *nahama dikissufa,* a concept to be discussed below.)

Suffering pushes man over the brink to rise up against oppression, to demand freedom.[72]

Group VI. **Kabbalistic responses**

The complex kabbalistic response to evil incorporates the following concepts in combination: *tsimtsum;* "breaking of the vessels"; "dualities."[73]

Group VII. **There currently is no answer**

There is no answer. However, the lack of an answer is held not to be a fatal flaw in the overall theology.[74]

We have no answer currently, but the answer will be clarified in the Messianic Era.[75]

30.02   Elaboration

The very fact that well over twenty major theodicies appear in various forms throughout Jewish literature reflects great dissatisfaction with any one existing theodicy. Our purpose, however, is not to critique all theodicies that have been previously suggested. We simply state that we personally do not find any given theodicy or combination of theodicies anywhere near fully satisfying—intellectually or emotionally. This is sufficient reason for us to search further.

Given its long history, one is unlikely to unearth the obvious, perfectly satisfying theodicy. Rather, the goal is to find or formulate a more satisfying theodicy. An examination of the seven groups of responses follows.

Group I. **Finite man cannot comprehend infinite God's ways:**[76]
EXPLICATION

The classic biblical support cited by the proponents of this theodicy comes from the final chapter of Job. The Divine voice addresses Job:

> Where wast thou when I laid the foundations of the earth? Declare if thou hast the understanding.
>
> —Job 38:4

One possible interpretation is that "man's suffering represents an infinitesimally small part of the cosmos. When the world is viewed from a perspective broader than man's, the evil in it is not enough to call God's rule into question."[77] The sentiment is echoed by the third-century sage Yannai: "It is not in our power to understand the suffering of the righteous or the well-being of the wicked."[78]

Thus in Job, a book which Maimonides[79] describes as a parable conceived for the purpose of articulating various theodicies,[80] we find, among other theodicies, one attributed to God and seeming to deliver a message of ultimate unfathomability. Job seems to accept this answer only because of its unmediated Divine origin and the implied promise of ultimate good.[81] Were it not for the Divine revelation out of the whirlwind, Job would continue to insist on the justness of his cause.[82]

It is unclear whether it is Job's fate in particular which is unfathomable, or whether it is Job in particular who has no right to question his fate.[83] Our study will later posit that when religious man finds himself in a vortex of suffering, it is not the appropriate time to commence moral protestations. In contrast, when man demands justice for others, as in the case of Abraham vis-à-vis the inhabitants of Sodom, moral protestations are most in order. Our study will also offer an alternative explanation for the Jobian finale—one which falls within the realm of "intelligibility," as opposed to "unfathomability."

Proponents of Group I theodicies, in any event, might cite the Jobian finale in support of their theses, as well as the events (exclusive of the finale) of the *Akedat Yitzchak* (Binding of Isaac) (Genesis 22:1–10). However, the theodicy of "unfathomability" of the Jobian finale has been on the defensive through most of the Book of Job. It is, moreover, a theodicy which remains isolated from any rational structure, and is strongly contradicted by an impressive array of scriptural texts, prophets, and authoritative rabbinic theologians. (see below)

Group I. **Finite man cannot comprehend infinite God's ways: CHALLENGE**

The classic and possibly most commonly accepted theodicy is the finite/infinite defense. Finite man cannot be expected to understand the ways of infinite God. A closely related defense is the "inscrutability of God" formulation, which implies that almost by definition man cannot understand God. Despite their widespread acceptance, both assertions require scrutiny.

These theodicies are open to the charge that the moral character of God's actions is compromised in order to preserve

God's ultimately unfathomable benevolence. "The moral connotation of goodness is supplanted by amoral metaphysical or
amoral personalistic meanings."[84]

> All the ingenuity spent on the solution of the problem of the
> theodicy will not convince us that evil is not real, that undeserved
> suffering is so only in appearance, that life does not abound in
> irrationality and meaningless destruction.[85]

We may grant that in sum total God's ways are infinite,
mysterious, beyond the full scope of the finite mind, or inscrutable. However, that still does not mean that in God's interaction
with man, comprehensibility is not in order, if indeed not
implicit in a convenantal relationship.[86] Serious religious
thought, from Abraham onwards, has never been quite satisfied
with the "inscrutability" defense of any form of worship, be it
idol worship or child sacrificing, in any classic religious doctrine. For those who adopt the "finite/infinite" defense take
legitimate attributes of God—infinitude and inscrutability—
and then take the most dangerous step of extending them into
overriding grand philosophies. One would like to think that
there is a firm distinction between serious religious philosophy
and fanaticism.

Thus, while there is an important place in religious doctrine
for the "finite/infinite" argument, in major areas of Divine-
human relationship the defense is far from sufficient as a basis
for serious religious commitment. For if the doctrine's major
argument is "inscrutability," a point arrives rather early where,
although doctrinal validity may indeed exist, adherence to the
Covenant cannot be mandated except on moral—as opposed to
intellectual—grounds. Certainly, except for areas specifically
delineated as pure ritual, Judaism, of all religions, should very
carefully explore alternative approaches before yielding to the
"inscrutability" defense in any area of religious doctrine, let
alone regarding the fundamental interaction between God and
man.

One may legitimately take the position that finite man cannot comprehend all the ways of infinite God. However, it is difficult for man to enter into a lifetime commitment to a religious system in which the incomprehensibility factor is paramount. The system adopted by one who is committed to *uvahem nehege yomam valayla* ("and thou shalt study them day and night") must have a fairly solid theological underpinning. Religious man had best, to the absolute limits of human possibility, try to discern the comprehensible aspects in man's relation to his deity.

One is advised to accept the existence of evil in God's universe on the basis of a leap of faith, if the existing theodicies are found wanting. Yet leaps of faith are not easily introduced by Judaism. And leaps of faith, by definition, require faith in the leap. Judaism requires leaps of faith when not emotionally or intellectually infeasible. (see discussion below)

Halakhic man—the Jew committed to God's law in this world—is not an emotional acrobat. He is averse to emotional acrobatics. And in a leap of faith emotion is crucial. Thus a leap of faith regarding the seemingly intractable dilemma of God and evil may be appropriate for some religions, but is quite inappropriate for Halakhic man.

Jewish doctrine is more prudent than most in its approach to leaps of faith, miracles, and prophets. It manifests a general wariness towards extending the supernatural into the mundane. The God of Israel is not seeking the fealty of the starry-eyed who are prepared to charge up the hill on a nod from the local guru. While Judaism is permeated by the transcendent, it is still a religion of carefully delineated law, carefully grounded in Divine texts.

It is a theology which seeks system and order wherever appropriate. It is averse to loose ends. Judaism has confidence that all doctrine is ultimately reconcilable; that all doctrine must be reconciled. And, notwithstanding the fact that all challenges are vigorously and meticulously parried, it is tacitly understood that the weak spots in its articulated philosophical structure must ultimately be resolved. If one cannot give an emotionally or intellectually coherent, satisfying answer to an eighteen-year-old, one has either failed somewhere or is erring somewhere.

Hayim Greenberg, in his article "In Dust and Ashes" (1940), stirringly presents the "finite/infinite defense." He asserts that if a "man of faith" cannot accept injustice and suffering, then he simply does not believe. He concludes: ". . . one who cannot praise God even as he sits in dust and ashes and has no explanation for his suffering, nor any sign from above—such a person is in the final analysis, not a believer."

We differ from Greenberg's line of reasoning. The witnessing of tragedy may lead to a questioning of one's commitment. The issue is not necessarily a lack of sincerity, however, but the failure on the part of the religious establishment to reconcile man's suffering with his inner yearning for genuine faith.

Greenberg maintains: "Religious thought must once and for all renounce rationalist interpretation and justification of the ways of God. There exists no science of God and no way of studying His ways. Religious man . . . must learn from Job to believe without understanding, to trust without explanations."[87] Greenberg posits two types of man: (1) rationalist man, and (2) religious man.

Greenberg, however, seems not to differentiate between religious man and fanatic man. He seems to disregard halachic man, whose religious expression and philosophy is couched in the language of reason. Judaism treads very cautiously before demanding blind faith in any area.

Finite man may not be able to comprehend the infinite, but finite man can discern a logical assault on his senses. An internal logical dilemma is constructed by those positing a neo-Stoic Divine presiding over a world plagued by evil. Jewish law sanctifies life and is averse to the termination of the life of the suffering. Yet simultaneously, some mainstream elements in Orthodox theology postulate an omnipotent, all-benevolent God watching a million Jewish infants and five million adults being shot, starved, gassed, or burnt to death.[88]

Nachmanides (Ramban) addresses the adequacy of Group I ("finite/infinite defense") theodicies in his *The Gate of Reward:*

You may ask us the following question: Since there is a hidden
element in [Divine] judgment . . . why then do you trouble us to
learn the previously explained arguments [theodicies] . . . ? Why
can we not thrust everything upon the belief [in the unfathoma-
ble], which we must ultimately rely on . . . ? This [answer of using
the "unfathomability defense" alone and stopping there] is an
argument of fools who despise wisdom.[89]

While Nachmanides does not reject the broader concept of the
unfathomability of the Divine, he argues that *chiyuv talmud
Torah* ("the obligation to study Torah") requires us to seek to
fathom those aspects of God's governance of the world which
are attainable to the intellect.[90]

A theology should be clear as to (1) which of its components
require leaps of faith, (2) which of its components flow from
reason, and (3) which of its components flow from generally
accepted fact.

Regarding those components which require leaps of faith,
theologians must be cautious. For whereas these can be stacked
ever higher and higher, and "true believers" may be asked to
take yet another leap, the theological balancing act appears
increasingly more and more tenuous to the disinterested ob-
server. The more tenuous a theological structure, the greater
reliance a theological system will have to place on an emotional
constituency, and the more likely it is to lose layer after layer of
its more intellectual wing. In extreme cases a theological system
can find itself bereft of "men of reason."

Just as there are thresholds of pain, there are "leap of faith"
thresholds. These are highly personal and individual. Judaism,
in particular, has always been hard on theological systems
requiring great numbers of presuppositions.

Group II. **Man is punished for his sins, failings: EXPLICATION
AND CHALLENGE**

Theodicy Group II receives more emphasis in historical
responses. It is the theodicy espoused by the "friends of Job."
This is the "fundamentalist view" that man's suffering origi-

nates in sin.[91] Job's friends attempt to defend an obvious wrong as justice. By doing so, they unintentionally degrade Job's idea of God. But because of his faith, Job cannot accept a defense of God that implies an insult to the dignity of God.[92] Ultimately, Job's innocence is vindicated, and the friends' "fundamentalist response" repudiated, by the Divine.[93]

We will address directly one Holocaust theodicy. This theodicy, popular in certain circles, proclaims that the Holocaust was a punishment for European Jewry's transgressions, and explains the Holocaust as a modern-day version of the *tochacha* (admonition of punishment) cited in the Torah portions of *Bechukotai* (Leviticus 26) and *Ki Tavo* (Deuteronomy 28).[94]

Theodicies of "punishment" are less prevalent in newer theological writings,[95] in parallel to the amplification of the (Literal) Written Law by the Oral Law. While there is an old tradition within Judaism that suffering man should examine his deeds, the same tradition admonishes man against pointing at another's suffering as Divine punishment.

The Divine harshly reproves the friends of Job, who have explained away Job's suffering as punishment for sin.

> The Lord said to Eliphaz the Temanite: "My wrath is kindled against thee, and against thy two friends; for ye have not spoken of Me the thing that is right, as my servant Job hath."
>
> —Job 42:7

The Divine, in the final chapter of Job, continues his reproach of the "friends," who have defended God by rationalizing Job's suffering as punishment.

> . . . and My servant Job shall pray for you; for it is only by dint of his [Job's] sufferance of you that I have not done terrible things to you; for ye have not spoken of Me the thing that is right.
>
> —Job 42:8

Norman Lamm, in a blistering assault on the "Holocaust as punishment" theodicy, terms it "massively irrelevant, impudent, and insensitive."[96] He notes that whoever advocates this theodicy "risks violating a most heinous sin of his own—that of *tsidduk ha-din*"—attempting to justify Israel's travail as particular punishment.[97]

Fackenheim articulates the fatal flaw in simplistic "suffering is punishment" theodicies:

> [Fundamentalist] Biblical faith originates as a myth which takes good fortune to be sufficient proof of righteousness, and ill fortune to be sufficient proof of sin. Good fortune is proof of God's mercy and love; ill fortune merely proves that His ways are not our ways. For [fundamentalist] Biblical faith, in short, it is "heads-I-win-and-tails-you-lose"; its God has acquired the logical peculiarity that empirical evidence may confirm Him but that it is systematically unable to falsify Him.[98]

It is, of course, not biblical faith *per se* which leads us into this logical conundrum; It is, rather, a misformulation of Jewish theology.

Group III. Hester Panim: EXPLICATION AND CHALLENGE

The third group of theodicies is also that of Job in his complaint and protest. It is the view of a God who contracts His providence by a *Hester Panim* (Hiding of the Face).

In subsequent chapters, starting in Section 900 of our Unified Formulation, we devote considerable attention to this line of approach. The subject will be covered in depth in that section and subsequently.

As indicated, *Hester Panim* is not employed as a response to the general theodicy dilemma. Rather, it is generally applied by its protagonists to specific historical periods, e.g., the Holocaust. At the same time, while some respected thinkers believe that the Divine has been in a state of Hiding since the destruction of the Temple, this concept has not been fully developed into a theodicy.

Group IV. **Other mainstream traditional responses:** EXPLICA-
TION AND CHALLENGE

A common cord running through much of the balance of
theodicies is that suffering "chastens" man or "challenges"
man. In the Book of Job, Elihu stresses the idea that suffering
frequently serves as a source of moral discipline.[99] Elihu maintains that by inflicting suffering, God chastens man.[100]

Variations and permutations of this theme appear throughout Jewish philosophy. However, this approach essentially con-
cedes the major point: there is indeed such a phenomenon as
undeserved suffering. Thus, it denies the correlation of suffering to sin of Theodicy Group II. Some combine the two
concepts. When suffering is not due to sin, it serves the purpose
of chastisement. Thus, they "cover all bases," with man remaining God's unfortunate target in a no-win world.[101]

Another theme is that while God is perfect, the universe as a
whole is not. This argument runs as follows: Religion must have
the courage to face the facts; it must reject the dogmatic
affirmations of religious thinkers through the ages that the
universe is perfect, since only a perfect creation could have
issued from an omnipotent and perfect Creator. It suggests
that it is the worst form of anthropomorphism to assert that an
omnipotent and omniscient God would only be responsible for
an immaculate universe. It merely states what man, imagining
himself almighty and all-wise, would do. God alone should be
assumed to be perfect. Perfection, according to this theme, is
identical with God; it cannot exist outside Him. But creation is
separate from the Creator. The world is apart from God; it is,
therefore, of necessity, imperfect.[102]

Significant support for this approach can be gleaned from
various elements of kabbalistic literature. The motif of the
"breaking of the vessels," with all of its variations and permutations, plays a major role in Lurianic Kabbalah.[103] The universe
did not end up perfect.

The story of the "blasphemous" tailor presents the theme in
Jewish folklore. When the rabbi reproached the tailor for

taking six weeks to make a pair of trousers, while it took God no more than six days to create the entire world, the tailor parried. "Yes Rabbi," he said "but just see what a world created in a hurry looks like."[104]

The question for those subscribing to the theodicy of an imperfect world reigned over by a perfect Divine is: Why does omnipotent God not intervene in this imperfectly crafted world?[105] Did God not show the inclination and power to do so in biblical times?[106]

One response is the Maimonidean theory of evil and Providence.

> If a man frees his thoughts from worldly matters, obtains knowledge of God in the right way, and rejoices in that knowledge, it is impossible that any kind of evil should befall him while he is with God, and God with him. When he does not meditate on God, when he is separated from God, then God is also separated from him; then he is exposed to any evil that might befall him; for it is only that intellectual link with God that secures the presence of Providence and protection from evil accident.[107]

Stitskin elaborates:

> In this light Maimonides interprets the Book of Job. The bible describes Job as a good, virtuous man, fearful of God when tragedy befell him. But the text does not say that he was an intelligent, wise or clever man. It was only after he had attained a measure of enlightenment, wisdom and the realization that man's highest good lies in an intellectual fellowship with God that his affliction came to an end. In the ultimate situation, when man's encounter is rooted in an intellectual fellowship with God-in-Essence, he is finally relieved of all the accidents of time and space.[108]

Maimonides' views in this area are paralleled in Ibn Daud's *Emunah Ramah*.[109]

Another response often encountered is that the need to maintain man's free will precludes the possibility of Divine intervention. We deal with this theme in the following section.

Group V. **Freedom: EXPLICATION AND CHALLENGE**

Man's freedom, in and of itself, is deemed of surpassing importance. The God of Mercy is limited by the God of Freedom.

Questions this approach raise are as follows: Why did God clearly intervene in Biblical times but no longer? How, indeed, can the *rahamim* (mercy) face of God be so totally eclipsed by the freedom face? What is so absolutely crucial about freedom—from even Divine deliverance from harm? Of what value is the Covenant if God withholds His saving hand? Of what value is freedom if the price is a Holocaust? Granted that man must be free (to commit "moral evil," among other things), why could "natural evil" not have been eliminated? Why can't man's freedom assert itself within bounds of lesser evil? Of what worth is freedom if so much evil befalls innocent bystanders who become hostages to the moral choices of others?

Group VI. **Kabbalistic responses**

This group employs the motifs of "dualities," *tsimtsum,* and "breaking of the vessels"[110] as major elements in creation, imperfection, and evil. These extremely complex, image-laden, and elusive concepts fall beyond the bounds of this study, as they do not lend themselves to brief encapsulization. Nevertheless, a few kabbalistic concepts will be employed in our eventual formulation along with elements of *Hester Panim* and the Freedom arguments.

Group VII. **There currently is no answer.**

The group of responses which posits that we currently have no answer to the problem has been one of the most popular responses, albeit not solutions, to date. By its nature it does not exactly lend itself to extensive analysis.

Naturally, we pay a price for this response. Can one adhere to a theology which does not provide a solution to a fundamental problem?

A variation on this theme is the response that posits a "dynamic tension" existing between the Jew's faith in God and the searing problem of evil, the Jew maintaining both simultaneously.[111]

The early Hasidic master Levi Yitzhak of Berdiczev once interrupted the sacred Yom Kippur service in order to protest that, whereas kings of flesh and blood protected their peoples, Israel was not protected by her King in heaven. Having made his protest, he recited the Kaddish, which begins with these words: "Extolled and hallowed be the name of God throughout the world."[112] The Jew has found it possible to simultaneously protest and praise.

*

Often the religious response will take the following form: One or more of the theodicies noted above will be cited, possibly in hybrid form, and the inquirer will be advised that any logical or emotional gaps must be bridged by "faith in God." This response claims to provide an intellectual solution to the problem of theodicy, but in reality is effectively hinged on the "faith in God" defense. A thousand partial intellectual responses still do not equal one complete intellectual response. A panoply of partial solutions do not add up to one satisfying solution. In this case the whole is less than the sum of its parts. And bridging the shortcomings of a rational and reasoned response with "faith in God" is in reality dependent entirely on "faith." And after all, "is not faith what religion is all about?" Yes, and no. Yes, for Western religion must ultimately rest on at least one leap of faith; but no, blind faith is not the end-all of religion, particularly Judaism.

40.00   OTHER THEODICIES

Most theodicies, or variations thereof, are common to more than one system of religious thought, whether contemporary or ancient, Western or Eastern. There are a number of theodicies, however, which are either clearly outside of Jewish tradition, only peripheral to Jewish thought, or generally identified with non-Jewish sources or traditions. We will briefly cover some of the major ones here.

40.01   Overview

"Ancient man tended to regard misfortune as resulting from cultic neglect in his worship of the gods. A Hittite king once searched long and hard through his records in order to uncover the error that might have angered the gods and brought on the plague that was killing his people."[113]

Monism, the philosophical view that the universe forms an ultimately harmonious unity, suggests the theodicy that evil is only apparent and would be recognized as good if we could but see it in its full cosmic context: "All partial evil, universal good." Dualism as a theodicy, on the other hand, rejects the final harmony, insisting that good and evil are utterly and irreconcilably opposed to one another, and that their duality can be overcome only by one destroying the other.

Under Dualism there arose the Zoroastrian conception of a cosmic war between Ahura Mazda and Ahriman, and the concept of the Kingdom of Satan poised against the Kingdom of God.[114] Each of these polar positions has exerted a powerful pull on Christian thought.[115] In classic Gnostic tradition the evil god prevailed over the good god.

Paul Tillich has attempted a more rational version of the classic "finite/infinite defense." This involves a sort of pantheism, in the tradition of Baruch Spinoza[116] and Cordovero.[117]

Tillich posits the unity of all beings: "Only in the unity of all beings in time and eternity can there be a humanly possible answer to the riddle of inequality."[118] Since my suffering, according to Tillich, is ultimately also your suffering, the pain is distributed evenly.

Aquinas posited that if God had created the universe democratically, with equal measures to all, there would be no fullness and stimulation in Creation.[119] (This parallels elements of the

Augustinian theodicy and the Irenaean theodicy, both of which will be described later.) Given the underlying dynamics, this universe, accordingly, is the "best of all worlds."[120]

Aquinas agreed with Augustine that evil (both physical and moral) is the privation of goodness, of perfection. He posits that evil is necessary so that many goods may find expression. "If there were no death of other animals, there would be no life for the lion; if there were no persecution from tyrants, there would be no occasion for the heroic suffering of martyrs."[121]

It is said that the problem of evil, although insoluble, is counterbalanced and, so to speak, canceled out by the mystery of good. In the words of the old Latin tag, "If God exists, wherefore evil? If God does not exist, wherefore good?"[122] But turning the question on its head does not solve the problem.[123]

Proposed solutions to the problem of evil, some of which overlap theodicies in the Jewish tradition, include the following: evil is an illusion; evil is merely the privation of good; evil has to exist as a counterpart to the good;[124] evil is the by-product of the operations of the laws of nature; the presence of evil brings out the good in people. Inadequacies in these theodicies are pointed out by the contemporary philosophers Mackie[125] and McCloskey.[126]

Other theodicies range from theodicies of an indifferent God—e.g., Camus et al.[127] and Epicurus[128]; a mischievous God—e.g., Russell[129]; a bad God—e.g., Jung[130]; an incomprehensible God—e.g., Kafka et al.[131]; a finitely powerful God—e.g., Kushner et al.[132]; and a God capable of creating only an imperfect world—e.g., the Indian mystic Tagore et al.[133]

The mainstream Christian theodicy is that developed by Augustine (354–430 C.E.),[134] which posits that the original sin of Adam and Eve haunts us to this day.[135]

40.02   Irenaean Theodicy

Alongside the mainstream of Augustinian theodicy is the "minority report" of the Irenaean tradition. It dates to Irenaeus and others of the early Hellenistic fathers of the church in the second and third centuries—prior to Augustine—and it has flourished again in more complex forms during the last hundred years.

In contrast to Augustine, who regarded man as having been created by God in a finished state, and as then falling disastrously away from this, Irenaeus saw man as still in process of creation.[136] The "minority report" "sees moral evil as an inevitable result of God's creation of man as an incomplete creature, at the beginning of a long process of moral and spiritual development."[137] Labeled the "soul-making" theodicy, it is based on the assumption that there are certain very valuable human qualities which could not be fully developed without subjecting man to suffering and challenge.[138]

The Irenaean theodicy is paralleled by a rabbinic interpretation/insight on Genesis 2:3: *me-kol melachto asher bara Elokim la-asot* ("from all His work, which God created to make"). What is the meaning of the words "to make"? It is man who completes unfinished creation and achieves a closer state of perfection. Man, as a partner with the Divine, helps complete creation.[139] (See also below in section 100.)

The kabbalists developed this general concept in their formulation of the *nahama di-kissufa* ("bread of shame") theodicy: If the good bestowed by God is not deserved (as in a world with no challenge), the recipient's pleasure will be lessened, or even negated, by the feelings of shame which always accompany undeserved favors.

Hick encapsulates the Irenaean position:

> The main features of the Irenaean theodicy stress the creation of man, through the processes of natural evolution, at an epistemic distance from God, giving him a basic freedom in relation to his Creator; and man's consequent self-centredness as an animal organism seeking survival within a harsh and challenging world which is however an environment in which he can develop, as a morally and spiritually immature creature, towards his ultimate perfection; this development beginning in the present life and continuing far beyond it. Such a theodicy sees moral

and natural evil as necessary features of the present stage of
God's creating of perfected finite persons, although the precise
forms which they have taken are of course contingent. Thus the
ultimate responsibility for the existence of evil belongs to the
Creator; and Christianity also believes that, in His total awareness
of the history of His creation, God bears with us the pains of the
creative process.[140]

A tangential attack would apply the Schlesinger line.

If it is claimed that God has greatly improved the world by
providing opportunities for virtuous responses to suffering to
exist, then it would also have to be admitted that he has impaired
the world to no less degree by also providing opportunities for
vicious responses. Surely the world could have been no worse off
by having opportunities for neither.[141]

The central problem, acknowledged by Hick, is whether "the
end justifies the means," whether all the "growth" in the world
can justify the suffering of one child. Moreover, if Irenaeus is
correct, pain and suffering should be distributed in more equal
measure, to allow for equal personal growth potential, and not
overly victimize some. Again, if the end purpose is "growth
through challenge," an omnipotent Deity should *a priori* have
created man with the desired characteristics.[142] Finally, does
not the idea that God placed obstacles before man contradict
our conception of God?[143] Does it not position God as the
primary source of the problem?

In the words of its chief contemporary elucidator, Hick, the
ultimate question regarding the Irenaean theodicy remains:
"Can there be a future so good, so great as to render acceptable, in retrospect, the whole human experience, with all its
wickedness and suffering as well as all its sanctity and happiness?"[144]

Our survey may lead the reader to ask the following questions:

Are we making too much of the theodicy dilemma?

Perhaps religious thought is not necessarily so intellectually rigorous?

Perhaps we must simply take a "leap of faith" that all is ultimately for the best?

Perhaps God's concept of morality is different from ours?

The next three sections (50.00, 60.00, and 70.00), which conclude Part I of this book, directly address these questions.

50.00   GENERAL INTELLECTUAL THRUST OF JUDAISM

50.01   Intellectuality

Judaism's intellectuality is, along with its monotheistic orientation, one of its essential characteristics. According to a midrash, Abraham's break with idol worship was both an intellectual and a religious revolution. Judaism is rightfully proud and rightfully protective of the intellectual rigor of Talmudic exegesis and of post-Talmudic scholarship. The "people of the book" must carefully protect the intellectual strength, authenticity, and vigor of the book as well.

Judaism has survived in large measure because of its intellectual rigor. It is puzzling that a religion whose concern with intellect, as a rule, borders on the extreme, does not currently demand more from its theology in general, and its theodicy in particular. Areas are either left unexplored or are consigned to the netherworlds of the "inscrutability of God" or "finite man's inability to grasp the infinite."

Theologians sometimes ignore the fact that the finite/infinite defense can equally well apply to systems of belief which are anathema to Judaism. Idol worshippers, devil worshippers, and child-sacrificers can all give the finite/infinite defense a good workout. The finite/infinite defense has its place, but we question its appropriateness as a central element of Jewish theodicy.

Most Western religious philosophies correctly proclaim that

the Divine essence is inscrutable and unfathomable. However, the relationship between the Divine and man is not relegated to those unfathomable domains. The distinction is crucial.

Certainly, Judaism is quite averse to the idea of an arbitrary God. According to the pagan *Atrahasis* epic (of the Great Deluge), the god Enlil engineered the flood for a somewhat arbitrary reason, namely, because the noise of humanity was disturbing his sleep. But in the biblical version human vice was the catalyst.[145]

The philosophy of medieval Spanish Jewry, generally considered the "Golden Age" of Jewry, placed reason quite high on the pantheon of Jewish values. It treated reason as the very mode in which and by which man and God relate to each other.

According to Saadia, we will reject any prophet if he calls upon us

> to follow that which is contrary to our reason. . . . I state it as a rule, that all which may be found in the books and words authored by one of us, who believe in One God, speaking of Our Creator and His deeds in language which true speculation contradicts, we may be absolutely certain that the expressions are used figuratively. Those who search for their true meaning will find it.
>
> —Saadia[146]

But for Judaism, intellectualism, while crucial, is still only a base. It is a necessary, but not sufficient component. Ultimately, it is a means toward an end. From this finely crafted intellectual base the Jew constructs a spiritual ladder heavenward, paralleling Jacob's dream.[147]

It is this dual approach which distinguishes the Jew, and which has been the key to his survival through the millennia. But the intellectual base still remains crucial.[148]

The crucial nature of the intellect is a central theme of Abraham Ibn Ezra,[149] who goes beyond our position in extolling the primacy of the intellect.

The highest virtue in life is reason. . . . The soul must further take pains to know its own origin and comprehend its own nature, with the help of Wisdom whose "eyes" are undimmed, bringing the far-off, remote places near to us and making night appear like day.[150]

It is not a visual image but an intellectual perception, which provides a true vision of God.[151]

The theme is paralleled by his more famous fellow medieval Maimonides, who considers intellectuality as the route towards "cleaving to God."

For the intellect that God made overflow unto man and that is the latter's ultimate perfection, was that which Adam had been provided with before he disobeyed. It was because of this that it was said of him that he was created in the image of God and His likeness.[152]

Moses Ibn Ezra follows through on the theme. "The Active Intellect is the first of God's creations."[153]

In contemporary times, Rav Joseph B. Soloveitchik makes rationality a central concept in his conception of "Halakhic Man," whom he differentiates from "homo religiosus."

. . . his most characteristic feature is strength of mind. He does battle for every jot and title of the Halakhah, not only motivated by a deep piety but also by a passionate love of the truth. He recognizes no authority other than the authority of the intellect (obviously, in accordance with the principles of tradition). He hates intellectual compromises or fence straddling, intellectual flabbiness, and any type of wavering in matters of law and judgment.[154]

A religion which is intellectually elitist in its basic dogma cannot afford weak links in its philosophical underpinnings;[155] nor can it afford a philosophy not convincing to its educated adherents, which in Judaism's case involves practically all its adherents. A religion confronted by challenges on all sides,

and indeed often from within as well, has very little margin for
laxity. On the other hand, a religion which convincingly articulates and grounds its dogma can survive anything and everything.

A religious man of reason (including the man of Halachah),
bridles at religious fervor which lacks firm intellectual supports.
While cognizant of the authentic possibilities of rapture and
bliss, he is wary of them. To him the world of reason and of the
intellect is not the enemy. The religious man of reason, and
particularly the man of Halachah, yields to no man intellectually. He is sometimes dismissed as a blasphemer by those who
stress fervor over reason. Yet religious man of reason need not
waver in response to the vacuous sloganism of fanatic elements
of the right, just as he need not cow under overrated assaults
from the left. It is thus incumbent on him to seriously examine
and reexamine, and if necessary refine, his intellectual and
religious understanding of basic issues.[156]

On the one hand, it is crucial that he guard that his religious
practices are not added to or subtracted from gratuitously by
zealots of the religious left or right. On the other hand, the
intellectual components of his theological formulation must be
clear, intelligible, and well-developed. That which is emotionally grounded must be demarcated from that which is intellectual.[157] And that which is alleged to be in the realm of the
intellectual must be defensible on those grounds.[158]

50.02   Inquiry

The importance of philosophical inquiry is pressed home
through the centuries.[159]

> . . . whenever the Torah, according to what appears from the
> external meaning of its words, disagrees with some things which
> are clear from the point of view of Philosophic Thought, it is
> proper that we should interpret them in a manner which is in
> agreement with Philosophic Thought. In this (way) none of the
> tenets of (our) revealed religion will be destroyed. . . . How much

more proper is it that we should not disagree with Philosophic Thought when we do not find the Torah disagreeing with it.

—Gersonides[160]

The Lord informed us that complete clarification will come to us if we search and reason in every phase of the revelation.

—Saadia[161]

Support comes as well from an heir to the kabbalistic tradition, the late Chief Rabbi of Palestine, Abraham Isaac Kook.

As a result of this moral and intellectual refinement, a preliminary conditioning for the actions of the higher spiritual influence, there developed in the Jewish people the inclination to pursue the study and cultivation of nature, the desire for free inquiry, for a clear and rational ethic. This became the heritage of Israel, which is to be found always among Jewish groups and individuals in each generation.

—A. I. Kook[162]

50.03   Geometry

Judaism and Halachah have their own inner logic and cohesive structure. In some sense this can be thought of as an inner theological geometry.

. . . there is practical value, as well as theoretical validity, in the display of an inner logic within Judaism, which dispels anarchy and sets limits.

—Fackenheim[163]

The statement of Galileo that "the great book which ever lies before our eyes—I mean the Universe—is written in mathematical language and the characters are triangles, circles, and other geometrical figures" applies as well to the Halakhah. And not for naught did the Gaon of Vilna tell the translator of Euclid's geometry into Hebrew [R. Barukh of Shklov], that "To the degree that a man is lacking in the wisdom of mathematics he will lack one hundredfold in the wisdom of the Torah."

—Soloveitchik[164]

Rabbinic thought must have coherence.

—M. Kadushin[165]

Indeed Judaism congratulates itself on its internal cohesiveness. This claim is valid primarily in the realm of talmudic exegesis and Halachic development. In the realm of Jewish philosophy the same claim cannot truly be made. There are more than a few loose ends. While we may presume that embedded in Jewish canon and tradition lies a cohesive, integrated, and powerful philosophical structure, if it has been articulated we have not seen it. Thus, while over the millennia there has been a near-obsessive touching up of the minutiae of Halachah on the frescos of the cathedral dome, the underlying philosophical foundation has been allowed to remain less than convincingly completely developed.[166]

60.00   LEAPS OF FAITH

Man of Halachah is prepared to take leaps of faith, but, notwithstanding his acceptance of his own finitude, he is averse to the emotionally absurd. Thus, Judaism generally shies away from leaps of faith that are either intellectually flawed or emotionally grating.[167] Judaism has historically distinguished and differentiated itself by carefully circumscribing the "blind faith" aspect of religion and carefully appealing to reasoned theological development. While Judaism embraces selected "leaps of faith" as well as the concept of purely ritual law (*chok*), the general thrust of Jewish theology, given the choice, is the line of reasoned analysis.

Judaism already requires several serious "leaps of faith" from its adherents.[168] One can argue that these include the (interrelated) leaps that—

there is a Divine, as Judaism perceives God;
the Torah and its text are genuine, correct, and accurate;

the *Masorah* is correct;
the Divine will cares about my adherence to Judaism today;
there is a moral imperative for the Jew to be a man of
    Halachah.

Thus several crucial leaps of faith are embraced by Judaism.
And while by definition monotheistic religion requires at least
one "leap of faith," the greater any religion's reliance on "leaps
of faith," the more fragile its foundations.[169] Religious viability
can be endangered by right-wing theological enthusiasm, just
as it can be sapped by left-wing rationalism.

Surely religious man takes as a premise that finite man
cannot fully comprehend infinite God. Nevertheless, within
that context, it is surely a plausible exercise to construct a
palatable theological edifice.

Judaism, on the whole, is receptive to *chukim,* which are, by
definition, without any apparent reason other than their Divine
origin. Judaism, as a religion, is receptive to emotionally palatable "leaps of faith" and, according to most, to Divine "miracles";[170] but as a religious system it is emotionally honest and
intellectually rigorous.

The fact that Judaism contains strong intellectual components should not be confused with Hermann Cohen's "religion
of reason." For, contrary to Cohen's formulation, Judaism does
indeed validly contain not only a high level of reason, but also
major leaps of faith along with a very strong ritual component.
The ritual component is often not grounded in any rationale
other than that it is Divinely ordained, which is its necessary
and sufficient grounding. However, even the ritual component
is somewhat subject to intellectual analysis.

Judaism has historically been what Marshall McLuhan would
call a "cool" religion, as opposed to a "hot" religion. It is not
frenzied, starry-eyed, or frantic.

It does invoke and require "leaps of faith," yet it is well-
considered, thoughtful, and even occasionally somewhat cynical
in its religious approach. It will sift through the evidence
endlessly before deciding a particularly intractable issue. Juda-

ism tries to "cool off" overzealous would-be converts. While its ultimate aim is a spiritual upliftment, it is still wary of extremes and of overemotionalism in any direction. It is wary of the self-denying ascetic and is wary of the man of frenzy.

The development of *Masorah* through the present day is a continuum of reasoned analysis, debate carefully circumscribed by accepted doctrine, rules of explication, and prior halachic guidelines.

Indeed, one of the elements which has sustained the Jew through the fearsome millennia has been the careful grounding of Jewish law and doctrine. This has inculcated an internal confidence which has withstood the manifold severe tests of time.

From our theological perspective, we would maintain that Judaism can embrace limited "leaps of faith," provided the leaps are not counter-intuitive. A "leap of faith" may be positive-intuitive or neutral but should not be counter-intuitive. In order to incorporate a "leap of faith," Jewish man must have faith in the leap. Eliezer Berkovits notes as follows:

> Yehuda Halevi, who was not a rationalist, found it necessary to exclaim: "God forbid that there should be anything in the Torah that is contrary to reason!" The Torah is not absurd and the authentic Jew does not engage in religious acrobatics. To believe in the absurd is absurd.[171]

Bleich drives home the point:

> Jewish philosophers have repeatedly stressed that God cannot command man to accept the illogical or the irrational. The human intellect, no matter how much it may desire to do so, cannot affirm the absurd. Man may, if prompted by a sufficiently compelling reason, postulate the existence of unicorns or mermaids, but he cannot affirm the existence of a geometric object which is at one and the same time endowed with the properties of both a square and a circle. He cannot fathom the concept of a square circle, much less affirm the ontological existence of such an object.

Propositions which constitute objects of belief must, then, first, and foremost do no violence to human credulity. They must be readily apprehended and accepted by human thought.[172]

Judaism does not teach that God requires of man a "leap of faith" in the Kierkegaardian sense, i.e., blind faith to the extent of acceptance of the absurd. It teaches, rather, that God's beneficience assures man that his diligence and perseverance will ultimately lead to understanding and intellectual satisfaction.[173]

Aquinas notes:[174] "Faith signifies the assent of the intellect to that which is believed."[175]

Theology can parry almost any philosophical challenge by responding that God's ways are mysterious. No one challenges the assertion. The crucial point is whether Judaism wishes to embrace this proposition as a substitute for an integrated philosophical structure. Judaism prides itself on a religious intellectual rigor, if not an intellectual elitism, as well. But Judaism cannot have it both ways. If Judaism claims to be intellectually rigorous, the philosophical underpinnings of God's interaction with man need philosophical structure—and a philosophical structure which is integrated with the balance of Jewish philosophy. If the philosophical underpinnings of the interaction between God and man are essentially allowed to rest on the proposition that the ways of God are mysterious, then Judaism is not fatally flawed, but the claim to intellectual defensibility becomes most vulnerable to challenge.

70.00   RATIONAL MORALITY BETWEEN MAN AND GOD

70.01   The Moral Divine

The moral core of the Divine permeates Scripture and Jewish writings.

The Rock, His work is perfect, for all His ways are justice.
—Deuteronomy 32:4

The Lord is righteous. He loves righteousness.

—Psalms 11:7

Righteousness and justice are the foundations of his throne.

—Psalms 97:2

The king's strength loveth justice . . .

—Psalms 99:4

That I am the Lord who exercises mercy, justice, and righteousness in the earth; for in these things I delight, saith the Lord.

—Jeremiah 9:23

But let justice well up as waters and righteousness as a mighty stream.

—Amos 5:24

The Eternal who is righteous, He will not do unrighteousness.

—Zephaniah 3:5

Indeed, the moral core of the Divine is not challenged by any but peripheral elements in Jewish and Christian tradition. The interrelated general philosophical question is whether the Divine morality roughly parallels mortal conceptions of morality.[176]

70.02   Moral Intelligibility and Absoluteness

A pivotal issue in theodicy is whether the interaction between the Divine and man is morally intelligible. Those who posit that it is not leave themselves wide latitude in addressing the classic theodicy dilemma, but detract from the internal elegance and power of Judaism.[177] Those who posit in the affirmative,[178] in the tradition of Abraham, Isaiah, and Maimonides, set a higher standard for Judaism but a tougher task regarding theodicy.[179]

We would assert as follows: Exclusive only of one's personal situation, man does have the right to seek the moral underpinnings of the interaction between man and the Divine. (On our exclusion of "one's personal situation," see the discussion of "bifurcation" in the appendix.) Schulweis notes:

> God wishes man to understand Him morally so that he can emulate Him morally. God informs Abraham of His plans for Sodom and Gomorrah, "for I have known him to the end that he may command his children and his household after him, and they may keep the way of the Lord, to do righteousness and justice" (Genesis 18:19). Nothing vitiates the moral purpose of the covenant as much as the envelopment of God in a mist of supramoral inscrutability. It is the measure of the greatness of His personality that He is morally intelligible.
>
> "For the Lord will do nothing, but He revealeth His counsel unto His servants the prophets" (Amos 3:7). For Jeremiah, God wishes to be known. To know God is no metaphysical exercise. It means to imitate God's moral concern for the weaker vessels of society. "Did not thy father eat and drink, and do justice and righteousness? Then it was well with him. He judged the cause of the poor and needy; then it was well. Is not this to know me? saith the Lord" (Jeremiah 22:15).[180]

Once we differentiate qualitatively between human morality and Divine morality, we enter a netherworld of theological and moral chaos.

"Thus I have explained to you that the stream of reason which flows toward us from the Lord, may He be exalted, is the bond which unites us with Him" (Maimonides).[181] If reason is the "very bond which unites us," it would follow that the moral interaction should be within reason, as well.

> Woe unto them who say of evil, it is good, and of good, it is evil; that change darkness into light and light into darkness; that change bitter into sweet and sweet into bitter.
>
> —Isaiah 5:20

> It is not in heaven, that thou shouldest say, "Who shall go up for us to heaven, and bring it down to us, that we may hear it and do it?" Neither is it beyond the sea, that thou shouldest say, "Who

shall go over the sea for us, and bring it unto us, that we may
hear it and do it?" But the word is very nigh unto thee, in thy
mouth and in thy heart, that thou mayest do it.

—Deuteronomy 30:12–14

This strain of thought, however important it may be in Jewish
writings, is of course not unique to Judaism. John Hick notes:

A theology cannot go unchallenged when it is repugnant to the
moral sense that has been formed by the religious realities upon
which their theology itself professes to be based.[182]

To take the liberty of inverting the thrust of Saint Ignatius'
dictum: We should never fail to believe that white is white, even
if our hierarchic church defines it as black.[183]

Shubert Spero concludes that the values which God has
commanded man to follow are actually God's ways.[184] He notes
that the rabbinic teaching of *imitatio dei* is found in several
statements:

What does the text mean, "Ye shall walk after the Lord your
God"? . . . to follow the attributes of the Holy One, blessed be
He . . .

—T. B. Tractate Sotah[185]

As the All-Present is called compassionate and gracious, so be
you also compassionate and gracious.

—Sifrei[186]

As He is compassionate and gracious, be also compassionate and
gracious.

—Mekhilta, Shabbat[187]

Fackenheim, following the Midrash, notes that morality for
Judaism is "nothing less than a threefold relationship involving
man, his neighbor, and God Himself."[188] Consequently, if morality is to serve as the basis for the relationship, it must be
intelligible.

70.03   "Protest Literature"

From its beginning, Israel has never yielded its right to call for a rational Divine justice, to ask that God's justice be morally justifiable and answerable, as well, to the standard He has set for man.[189]

Scriptural writings, commencing with Abraham, give standing to the doctrine that God's inscrutability is nevertheless held to the moral standards expostulated for man.[190] The Divine, as well, in the cases of Sodom and Nineveh, for instance, is portrayed as yielding to the universally perceived moral standard at the expense of elements of Divine prestige.

> And Abraham drew near, and said:
> "Wilt Thou indeed sweep away the righteous with the wicked?
> Peradventure there are fifty righteous within the city;
> wilt Thou indeed sweep away and not forgive the place
> for the fifty righteous that are therein?
> That be far from Thee to do after this manner,
> to slay the righteous with the wicked,
> that so the righteous should be as the wicked;
> that be far from Thee;
> shall not the Judge of all the earth do justly?"
>
> —Genesis 18:23–25

> Right wouldest Thou be, O Lord,
> Were I to contend with Thee,
> Yet will I reason with Thee:
> Wherefore doth the way of the wicked prosper?
> Wherefore are all they secure that deal very treacherously?
> Thou has planted them, yea, they have taken root;
> They grow, yea, they bring forth fruit;
> Thou art near in their mouth,
> And far from their reins.
>
> —Jeremiah 12:1–2

> Awake, why sleepest Thou, O Lord?
> Arouse Thyself, cast not off forever.

Wherefore hidest Thou Thy face,
And forgettest our affliction and our oppression?
For our soul is bowed down to the dust;
Our belly cleaveth unto the earth.
Arise for our help.
And redeem us for Thy mercy's sake.

—Psalms 44:24–27

How long, O Lord, shall I cry,
And Thou wilt not hear?
I cry out unto Thee of violence,
And Thou wilt not save.
Why doth Thou show me iniquity,
And beholdest mischief?
And why are spoiling and violence before me?
So that there is strife, and contention ariseth.

—Habakkuk 1:2–3

Thou that art of eyes too pure to behold evil,
And that canst not look onto mischief,
Wherefore lookest Thou, when they deal treacherously,
And holdest Thy peace, when the wicked swalloweth up
The man that is more righteous than he?

—Habakkuk 1:13

As God liveth, who hath taken away my right;
And the Almighty, who hath dealt bitterly with me;
All the while my breath is in me,
And the spirit of God is in my nostrils,
Surely my lips shall not speak unrighteousness,
Neither shall my tongue utter deceit;
Far be it from me that I should justify you.

—Job 27:2–6

God, where art Thou? Where is the God of justice?

—Malachi 2:17

In theological development, what appears to be a non-ra-
tional Divine morality is oft blamed on man's finite capability

of understanding, or on man's sinfulness. God is thus defended at the expense of man. Man, however, resists being maneuvered into this defensive position. The "partner of God in creation" doggedly insists, as does Job, on a rational morality of the Divine.[191]

*

Granted, there are many who need no answer to various challenging philosophical questions in order to be secure in their faith. Granted, their approach is viable. Granted, Judaism may be approached on different levels. Yet those who quest for an integrated underlying philosophical structure may legitimately claim the right to a palatable response. And Judaism is sufficiently internally cohesive to provide one. Do we not have the self-confidence that the philosophical structure is ultimately cogent? Five hundred years after Golden Age of Judaism, is there to be "no room at the inn" for the intellectually demanding?

PART II
The "Quest for Potential" Unified Formulation

80.10   APPROACH TO CORE THEODICY RESOLUTION

Most theodicies, in formulating their particular schemas, first focus on the maximum limits of God's capabilities in various areas. They begin by asking: What are the limits of God's power, knowledge, mercifulness, etc.? However, this may not be the optimal line of approach.

The challenge of theodicy is closely linked with the question of the purpose of man.[192] Consequently, approaching our problem by analyzing the extent of Divine power, without first focusing on the "purpose of man" question, may be approaching the question from the wrong direction. It may be that God limits Himself in responding to man's needs or to God's ultimate purpose(s). These factors will prove pivotal in pointing a way to a solution.

The God of Scripture is multifaceted and more subtle and complex than the God of the philosophers. God is singular, but not necessarily the monolithic super-unity posited by many distinguished Jewish and non-Jewish philosophers.

In their sincere attempt to understand the attributes of God in the abstract, as opposed to understanding His interaction with man, many highly rationalistic philosophers, in the end, only shift the problem of theodicy onto a different plane. The result often makes God's actions less comprehensible or defendable. Articulating the incomprehensible can be a dangerous business.

If, however, we address the following questions, we may discern a more optimal line of approach:

What is the purpose of man?
Under the dominion of which of God's possible manifestations—
can man come closest to God?
can man come closest to reaching his own potential?

A God who created the world and the universe for man may conceivably limit His own powers for the ultimate benefit of man. God's use of His powers may be affected by man's cosmic requirements, and in particular, by man's quest for his potentiality. This is our crucial pivot. Without it, we are doomed to come up against the same insurmountable dilemmas in our solution as earlier formulations faced.

80.20 "QUEST FOR POTENTIAL" CORE THEODICY

80.21 Outline

The core of our theodicy runs as follows:

"Quest for Potential" Core Theodicy

1. The purpose of man is to quest for his potential—spiritual and other.
2. The greater man's freedom, the greater his ability to attain his potential.
3. Freedom requires privacy, responsibility, and selfhood.
4. In order to yield man greater freedom (along with greater privacy, responsibility, and selfhood), God has contracted His here-and-now consciousness, in correlation to mankind's ascent in knowledge.
5. With the Divine consciousness increasingly contracted from the here-and-now, and evil existent in the here-and-now, man is increasingly forced to confront evil on his own.

80.22 Discussion

I contend that this formulation essentially resolves the key issues and provides a theodicy option more satisfying than the preexisting ones. This five-point formulation handles the classic theodicy dilemma. God is indeed omniscient, omnipotent, and all-benevolent. At the same time this formulation reconciles the existence of God with the existence of gross evil. It addresses, as well, the "purpose of man" question; it addresses manifest Divine intervention in Pharaoh's Egypt and the absence of manifest intervention in Hitler's Europe; in addition it begins to address the question of how man's freedom can be reconciled with an omniscient God.

80.23   Need for Unified Formulation

Having come this far, one is impelled by the prior inquiry and by the implications of the core theodicy to further develop the overarching philosophical structure. The Quest for Potential core theodicy will be clarified and elaborated as part of the nine-section (100–900) Unified Formulation.

The Unified Formulation also handles several other crucial theological and philosophical questions, in an attempt to provide a comprehensive and cohesive framework.

How does this quest for potential relate to the origins of man, God, and the universe? From whence (infinite) God?

Why can there not be a world of bliss and full freedom simultaneously?

Why are potential and freedom so crucial?

Why is there evil at all if God is omnipotent?

To address these questions and other, related ones, we must begin at the dawn of the universe.[193] We must go beyond a mere theodicy, however relatively safe and elegant, towards a unified and comprehensive theodicy/theology. Therefore, instead of starting with the goal and working backwards, we must commence at "the beginnings of the beginning" and proceed onwards.[194] Thus while we are entering a far riskier arena, we are certainly playing for far larger stakes.

One may view the theological problem of evil, not as a weak link in Jewish theology, but rather as a major direction-finder for Jewish theology/philosophy. The process of conceptualizing a satisfying theodicy leads to the correct formulation of the broader theological framework.[195]

By definition, a postmodern Jewish theodicy must not operate in a vacuum. It should, furthermore, not begin in 1939 or with Abraham in 1900 B.C.E. It should attempt to start in the beginning of the beginning—as far as we can comprehend "beginning."[196] It must, moreover, be alert to the consistency level of its doctrinal flow, from creation through the highs and lows of Jewish experience, through the ultimate goals of man.

Halachic man is entitled to a comprehensive, palatable, unified philosophy of Judaism. The purpose of Jewish philosophy is not to pinpoint the exact parameters of God's attributes, but rather to develop a cogent, unified philosophy. A palatable solution to the basic problems we address, that pushes Jewish doctrine to its outer limits, is preferable to a philosophy of Judaism that is safely tucked within the boundaries of common-wisdom Jewish doctrine, but which cannot adequately deal with major issues.

*

For purposes of the following discussion, the physical aspect of the cosmos will be called the *universe*. The term *cosmos* refers to all aspects, including the state of out-of-time preexistence "preceding" creation.

90.00   ETERNAL ORIGINS

90.01   Mainstream

Most mainstream theistic philosophies posit God's eternity. One example from the Jewish tradition is the oft-cited phrase from the Adon Olam prayer (author unknown), "He [always] was, He [always] is, He [always] will be."[197] Inasmuch as these matters are beyond our comprehension, it is argued, further attempts at explication are not deemed necessary or possible, however desirable.

The Pentateuch commences with the creation of the world as we know it. The question of God's origins is not addressed.

90.02   Fault-Line: Gap in Western Philosophical and Scientific Formulations

One may argue that the development of complex philosophical structures predicated on this unfathomable premise is severely flawed by its failure to explicate—in even the broadest of strokes—the existence, or emanation, of a "Somethingness" out of "nothingness," or the wherefore of "eternalness." Whether this entity is finite or infinite, existing in-time or out-of-time, holy or Holy, where is the bridge from "nothingness" to "Somethingness"? In particular, how does one begin to explain, in even the broadest of strokes, the existence of an infinite Somethingness?

This severe philosophical "fault-line" runs from Plato through Philo through Spinoza. The gap is not bridged. The situation is somewhat analogous to erecting a magnificent skyscraper with no idea of the parameters of the foundation—theoretically possible, but somewhat inelegant and risky.

Those who postulate a creation at the hands of an inexplicably eternal God merely shift the origin question to another plane. Whereas before the origins of the universe were unfathomable, now the origins of the Creator of the universe, the Divine, are unfathomable.[198] This situation, in turn, is somewhat analogous to that faced by those who "solve" the problem of the origin of evil by postulating Satan as the source of evil. But wherefore Satan?

It is interesting to note that the problem faced by science regarding the initial origins of the universe, and the problem faced by religion regarding the initial origins of the universe, are strikingly parallel.

The "Big Bang" theory postulates the origin of the universe in a tiny point of incredible mass. However, science does not go beyond this point. It does not address what existed before the "Big Bang." Current research in physics leads scientists into searches for smaller and smaller subatomic particles. Refiners of the Big Bang theory postulate that at one point the total matter and energy in the universe fit into one very small point, the ultimate atomic explosive. But where did this point come from? Where/why did the smallest subatomic building block originate? Where/why did the first pulse of energy originate?[199]

Why should quantum physics exist at all? As the contemporary physicist Stephen Hawking asks: What "breathed fire" into the equations?

Mainstream religious doctrine posits the universe as having its origin from an infinite God.[200] Gersonides maintains that God created the world out of "body which does not preserve its shape."[201] But where did this "body" come from? Many religious philosophers, including the early Kalam,[202] John Philoponus,[203] Maimonides,[204] and the mainstream view of the sages of the Torah[205] maintain *creatio ex nihilo*—creation by God out of nothingness. However, wherefore the Divine?

Thus, when stripped to their essentials, both science and religion face the same formidable hurdle. What actualized that which you posit as having always existed? What/where was the essence of the initial actualization?[206] How can any "entity" be posited as having always existed?

Classic philosophy is caught in a similar trap. Some philosophers maintain that the world has been generated and has passed away an infinite number of times.[207] But where did the first world originate from? How was the first world actualized? The Neoplatonists maintain that the world was generated by God from something.[208] This "something" is often referred to as primal matter. But where did this primal matter originate? What are the origins of the God who fashioned this primal matter? Some philosophers, most prominently Aristotle,[209] maintain that the universe existed eternally. But wherefore the universe? Whyfor this universe? Whyfor any universe? Indeed, whyfor anything at all?[210]

The "eternal origins" question is in our view the twin intractable problem in religious philosophy to the theodicy question. In our view it is inextricably linked to the theodicy question; the correct solution to either question should yield the solution to the other.

90.03   Partial Exception

There is one great exception to the approach of mainstream Jewish philosophy to the "eternal origins" question. Whereas questions of eternal origins and the dynamics of creation are not addressed by classic Jewish philosophy, the kabbalists concentrated their creative energies and their mental, emotional, and perhaps mystical powers, on these very areas. Specifically, they focused on the stages of Divine emanation and the stages of creation.[211] Indeed, the kabbalists knew that they ultimately had to work their way back to the dynamics of creation—in order to reconcile the existence of evil in the Middle Ages. However, the kabbalists by and large leapfrogged the field of classic philosophy into the field of mysticism and imagery. And it would seem that they attempted too much.

90.04   Philosophical *Terra Incognita*

A significant step would seem to be missing in Jewish philosophy, one which takes on the challenging but viable goal of investigating the schematics of a solution without entering the world of mysticism. This approach would seek cohesiveness without trying to fill in all the unfathomable detail. This approach would put the discussion, however daring, more in the realm of philosophy and less in the realm of mysticism.

Until this middle terrain is fleshed out, however difficult the task, the truly complete solution to theodicy will always remain just out of reach. Thus, in a sense the theodicy dilemma forces us onto this most difficult and nonstructured of terrains.

In the Jobian finale, the Divine response to Job's remonstrations challenges Job's comprehension of cosmic origins, and cites his lack of understanding as the reason for his inability to become reconciled with God. The Divine response, a *sui generis* response of poetic splendor, maintains the precise theme throughout two complete chapters, commencing as follows:

Then the Lord answered Job out of the whirlwind,
and said:

Who is this that darkeneth counsel
By words without knowledge?
Gird up now thy loins like a man
For I will demand of thee, and declare thou unto Me:
Where wast thou
when I laid the foundations of the earth?
Declare if thou hast the understanding . . .
Whereupon were the foundations thereof fastened?

—Job 38:1–6[212]

99.00   THE UNIFIED FORMULATION: OUTLINE SUMMARY

THE UNIFIED FORMULATION

100

100.00   Holy potential is at the epicenter of the Divine.

200

200.00   Holy quest for potential is the underlying core dynamic of the cosmic order.

300

300.10   Two possible but mutually exclusive sets of dynamics were open to man (at Eden).

300.20   The two dynamics are:

"Tree of Life/Bliss"	*"Tree of Knowledge/Potential"*
1. A "gilded cage" existence	A life of challenge, freedom, privacy, and responsibility
2. Intellectual satedness	Pursuit of knowledge
3. Limited growth potential	Infinite growth potential
4. Dependence	Independence
5. Eternal life	Mortality
6. "Leashed" "natural evil"	"Unleashed" "natural evil"
7. Bliss	Pain and joy
8. Limited potential for "moral good," "moral evil"	Higher potential for "moral good," "moral evil"
9. Lesser dignity	Higher dignity

300.30   In a world predicated on potential, man inexorably took the route of "Tree of Knowledge/Potential."

300.40   "Natural evil" and "moral evil" would consequently forevermore plague and challenge man.

400

400.10   Evil is the implicit flip-side, or converse, of good. Evil is anti-polar to good.

400.20   With the creation of potential for good, which is required for man to be able to reach his spiritual potential, potential for evil indirectly, but nevertheless, inexorably, came into existence as a consequence.

400.30   To destroy evil would, at the least, destroy good.

400.40   While an omnipotent Deity may have an impact on nature, even an omnipotent Deity does not violate universal laws and dynamics implicit in the universal Deity's essence, as violating them could unravel the cosmos.

500

500.10   Man is finite + seeking to approach Infinity

500.20   The purpose of man is to quest for his potentialities—spiritual, intellectual, and all other.

500.30   The closer man approaches the achievement of his spiritual and other potentialities, the closer he comes to fulfilling the primal quests of creation.

500.40   Man, (infinite) God, and the universe are all questing for their potentialities.

600

600.00   Man is innately free and striving for fuller freedom.

700

700.10   In order for man to reach his full potential, he must operate from a base of freedom. (This is a law of the universe in concert with balance of dynamics of Tree of Knowledge chosen at Eden.)

700.20   The greater the freedom component of man's base, the greater his ultimate potential (inherent in Tree of Knowledge chosen at Eden).

800

800.10   Man is ascendant—at least in knowledge.

800.20   As mankind and Judaism ascend in knowledge (and possibly in consciousness) on the road to fulfilling a primal drive of creation, there is an implicit demand for fuller freedom. (This is implicit in our paradigm of the Tree of Knowledge.)

800.30   A demand for fuller freedom (as a consequence of an ascent in knowledge) has embodied within it a demand for greater privacy, responsibility, and self-hood—so that man can more ably quest for his potential.

900

900.10   As mankind ascends in knowledge, implicitly demanding more freedom, there is a proportional contraction *(tsimtsum)* of Divine here-and-now consciousness. This is a primary form of *Hester Panim* which yields man ever greater freedom, privacy, responsibility, and selfhood with concomitant potential.

900.20   As the contraction of real-time Divine consciousness continues, (as mankind ascends in knowledge and freedom) there is a commensurate lower incidence and level of direct particular Providence—for the sake of the general Providence of allowing mankind to quest for its full potentialities.

900.30 Quest for potential is an overarching and inviolate holy cosmic dynamic. A violation of quest for potential would be a violation of a core Divine dynamic—which was integral to creation itself, integral to the Divine essence, and integral to the potential of the cosmic order.

end/beginning

An in-depth treatment of the component elements of the Unified Formulation follows.

100

100.00 THE EPICENTER OF THE DIVINE

Holy potential is at the epicenter of the Divine.

100.01 The Divine Name

And Moses said unto God:
"Behold, when I come unto the Children of Israel, and shall say unto them:
The God of your fathers hath sent me unto you: and they shall say to me: What is his name? what shall I say unto them?"
And God said unto Moses:
I-WILL-BE-THAT-WHICH-I-WILL-BE; and He said: "Thus shalt thou say unto the Children of Israel:
I-WILL-BE hath sent me unto you."
—Exodus 3:13–14[213]

The name of the God of Israel first proclaimed to Israel—*Eheyeh Asher Eheyeh*, "I-Will-Be-That-Which-I-Will-Be"—is in effect a declaration that the holiest state of the holy is God of Potential. God is the actualization of potential in its conscious holy form. All that we know of God's universal name is that which it stands for: holy potential within potential within potential *ad infinitum*. For the infinite God of Israel is a God of willed potential.

Holy potential is more than human potential writ large. "To whom will you liken Me that I shall equal?" (Isaiah 40:25, cf. 46:5). Holy potential transcends time, space, and the cosmos. Holy potential tracks to the forward wave of the cosmos, to the forward wave of time. Embedded within it are thus potentialities rippling infinitely forward, embedded within infinite concentric circles cycling outward to infinity.

> Has it not been told you from the beginning? Have you not understood the foundations of the earth? It is He that sits above the circle of the earth . . . That stretcheth out the heavens as a curtain, And spreadeth them out as a tent to dwell in.
>   —Isaiah 40:21–26 (cf. 44:24, 45:12)

100.02   The Primordial Divine

The infinite potentials/Potentials of the Divine, including the potentials to create the universe, within which God would create man to strive for his own munificent potentialities,[214] are inherent in the eternal Divine.[215]

> Who calls the generations from the beginning,
> I, the Lord, First,
> And the Last, I am He.
>   —Isaiah 41:4 (cf.44:6, 45:11)

> the Holy seed
> shall be the stock thereof.
>   —Isaiah 6:13

> . . . who shut up the sea with doors,
> When it broke forth,
> and issued out of the womb?
>   —Job 38:8

Out of whose womb came the ice?
And the hoar—frost of heaven,
who hath gendered it?

—Job 38:29

*

Independent of time, matter, and energy, and indeed, independent of a universe, existed Holy Divine Potential—the primordial Divine.[216] At the eternal origins of out-of-time: Holy
Potential within potential within potential . . . *ad infinitum*—
tracking to the forward edges of time.[217]

At the embryonic stage of holiness, deep in the womb of
nothingness, deep at the core of out-of-time, hinged on an
indefinable and infinite circularity, there was an ascending holy
metaphysical fire: Yearning, imploring, calling forth into the
void.[218]

[The concept of a primordial Divine has clear and direct
precedent in the concept of the *En Sof* of Kabbalah.[219] See
section 100.03 below.]

Traversing the Bridge

And as nature abhors a vacuum, Holy Potential abhors nothingness. This is a cosmic axiom.

Simultaneous with the eternal origins of out-of-time, an
equilibrium of nothingness was thrown into disequilibrium by
its own Holy Potential. Exploding and imploding. Echoing
through this day and racing towards infinite time, Holy Potential screamed forth.

Genesis

Flowing from the Essence of the Divine, the infinite holy
potential of the Divine demanded more expression.[220] Among
these elements were the potentials for creation of the universe,
and within the latter the potentials for man to quest for his

spiritual potential,[221] as well as others, including mercy, love, truth, justice, beauty, and harmony.[222] The holy potential core of the Divine demanded more than just potential.[223] For the potentialities of Divine creation are inherent in the eternal Divine origins and in the Divine Essence itself.[224]

At the eye of the primal cosmic storm, warping from out-of-time towards time, unzipping the cosmic void into positives and negatives, the infinite Divine blaze leapt forth. A creative supra-conscious dynamic, transcending time, space, and eternity. Focusing its holy metaphysical force. Genesis.[225]

> and God divided the light from the darkness.
>
> —Genesis 1:4

A holy dynamic flows forth through this day, tracing its origins to the inner core of the Divine. Beneath the eddies and swirls at the surface of the cosmic stream, beneath the deep and powerful major cosmic currents, from out of the epicenter of the holy, flows the deepest primal current—questing, beseeching, and indeed, screaming—for ultimate potentiality.[226]

*

100.03   Kabbalistic Parallel

Lurianic Kabbalah can be refocused in the light of this formulation. Indeed, if one takes the liberty of stripping Kabbalah of its majestic imagery down to its very core, it would seem that major elements of kabbalistic doctrine were groping or heading in this very direction.

We would draw the following parallel and relationship:

Infinite Holy Potential   *En Sof*
cosmic quests for potential   *Sefirot*

A neo-kabbalistic variation of "infinite holy potential" would posit that the *En Sof*—the infinite, the root of the Ten *Sefirot,* "the Root of all Roots"[227]—demanded greater expression. Within the obscurity of mystical doctrine, one factor is clear: the *En Sof*—the Primal/Infinite Divine—had "neither qualities nor attributes."[228]

Our neo-kabbalistic development would posit that the kabbalist's Ten *Sefirot,* the next level of Divine emanation, demanded more tangible expression.[229] The Ten *Sefirot* are variously described as the Ten Spheres, Regions, Faces, Manifestations, Crowns, Stages, Garments, Modes, Branches, Powers, Emanations—of God.[230] The Ten *Sefirot* are "the ten spheres of Divine manifestation in which God emerges from His hidden abode."[231] They are most commonly enumerated as follows:

KETER ELYON	"Supreme Crown"
HOKHMAH	"Wisdom"
BINAH	"Intelligence"
HESED	"Love/Mercy"
GEVURAH	"Power"
RAHAMIM	"Compassion"
NETSAH	"Everlasting endurance"
HOD	"Majesty"
YESOD	"Foundation"
MALKHUTH	"Kingdom of God"[232]

One interpretation, which converges with our study, is that they are "the ten stages of the inner world, through which God descends from the inmost recesses down to His revelation in the *Shekinah.*"[233] We would recast the *Sefirot* as primal quests for potentiality which enable Infinite Holy Potential to "traverse the bridge" from "emptiness" to "Somethingness" and mandating Creation. They are the "transition from *En Sof* to creation."[234]

There is, indeed, a significant current in kabbalistic doctrine which links the *Sefirot* with the concept of potentiality.[235]

Every *Sefirah* is transformed from a general attribute of God into what the Kabbalists call a *Partsuf,* a "countenance" of God, which means that all the potentialities implied in every *Sefirah* are now brought under the influence of a formative principle.

—Vital[236]

100.04   Buttress and Elaboration

God's life-giving powers flow from the very highest degree of Holiness—from His Own Presence—down to the flesh-and-blood, cause-and-effect world in which we human beings live.

—Scherman[237]

Leviticus 12:1–4 presents the rule that when a woman gives birth she descends in purity.[238] Moreover, when a woman gives birth to a daughter she descends twice the level of purity that she descends when she gives birth to a boy. The Or HaChaim explains that this perplexing formulation teaches us that during pregnancy a woman achieves a higher level of holiness, since she is carrying another life.[239] The conception of a daughter who will maintain within herself a greater creative potential, raises her to a higher level of holiness. After the potential leaves her womb, her level of purity descends. Inasmuch as a female fetus represents a higher level of potentiality, upon the birth of a girl the mother's level of purity descends doubly. For potential creation is indeed holy. And the level of creation potential is directly related to the level of holiness.

The cosmic fate is interlinked with the fate of God, the universe, and man.

Remember the former things of old:
That I am God, and there is none else;
I am God, and there is none like Me;
Declaring the end from the beginning,
And from ancient times things
that are not yet done.

—Isaiah 46:9–10

Soloveitchik notes:

> . . . the Jewish people see their own fate as bound up with the
> fate of existence as a whole. . . . When the historical process of
> the Jewish people reaches its consummation and attains the
> heights of perfection, then (in an allegorical sense) the flaws of
> creation as a whole will also be repaired. "He bade the moon
> renew itself for those who were burdened from birth, who like
> her will be renewed and will extol their Creator on account of
> the name of His glorious kingdom" [from the blessing over the
> new moon].[240]

God is represented in *Tanach* as a many-faceted deity. It is for
this reason that He is known by many Names.[241] We postulate
that the primal essence of God is potentiality, i.e., a supradi-
mensional metaphysical intangible. Potential is implicit through
God, and through God, the universe and man.[242]

The essence of God is eternal, timeless and infinite.[243] The
Primal Essence inexorably quests after its own infinite potentiality.[244]

> Creation finds its expression in man's fulfilling all of his tasks,
> causing all of the potentiality implanted in him to emerge into
> actuality, utilizing all of his manifold possibilities, and fully
> bringing to fruition his own noble personality. The power stored
> up within man is exceedingly great, is all-encompassing, but all
> too often it slumbers within and does not bestir itself from its
> deep sleep. The command of creation, beating deep within the
> consciousness of Judaism, proclaims: Awake ye slumberers from
> your sleep. Realize, actualize yourselves, your own potentialities
> and possibilities, and go forth to meet your God. The unfolding
> of man's spirit that soars to the very heavens, that is the meaning
> of creation.
>
> —Soloveitchik[245]

If man's future potentialities are so crucial, with his existence
and striving for spiritual and intellectual achievement energizing the universe, it would seem that the cosmic order itself

might be jeopardized if man annihilated himself. Thus the imperatives of potential do not exceed the limits necessary for survival.[246] On the other hand, if potential is at the essence of the Divine, we indeed have grounds for optimism. For only an awesomely positive potential down the road could dynamize all.

> Radiant is the world soul,
> Full of splendor and beauty,
> Full of life,
> Of souls hidden,
> Of treasures of the holy spirit,
> Of fountains of strength,
> Of greatness and beauty.
> Proudly I ascend
> Toward the heights of the world soul
> That gives life to the universe.
>
> —Kook[247]

* * *

> He hangs the world upon nothingness.
>
> —Job 26:7[248]

Our conception adheres to classic Jewish doctrine of a spiritual and conscious God of infinity.[249]

The question then arises: Is spirituality at the beginning of the process or at its culmination? We are comfortable with the notion that it is at both the beginning and the end, a continuum. This is congruent with traditional religious thought. We add, however, that elements of circularity in time, God, or time/God can be theorized to buttress the concept of a cosmos dynamized by potentiality.[250] In the primordial realms of the infinite, potentialities and circularities reign supreme.

Somewhat in parallel to the construction of a geodesic dome, where all parts support one another, so too in creation, the potentialities of all creation support each other as well as the holy actualization spark. Thus, where the overwhelming thrust of classic Western philosophy is linear (i.e., A caused B caused C), our formulation is circular, with embedded potentialities providing the crucial supports and linkages.

100.05   Man—and the Quest for Potential

Man's ultimate quest for potentiality is a primary imperative of the universe.
Soloveitchik notes:

> Man initially is receptive, is pure potentiality. But creation, by definition, means spontaneity, actuality, action, renewal, aspiration, and daring.[251]

> With respect to the very first reference to man in Genesis (1:26) "let us make man in our image," Ibn Ezra comments: "Now I shall explain something you should know, namely, that the entire act of creation was for the purpose of man in accordance with the commandment of God. . . . Accordingly, since man's rational soul never dies it is comparable in its eternity to God. . . . And, therefore, the prophet states that 'he saw the Glory of God as the appearance of a man.' "[252]

The portions of the Torah (Pentateuch) and Prophets read on the first day of Rosh Hashanah, the Jewish New Year, focus on the belated conception of a child by Sarah and Hannah. The focus is not on the creation of the world, which would seem the natural selection. The focus is, rather, on the problem of conception faced by two important personages in Jewish history. Why this focus on Rosh Hashanah? Thus we might reinforce our notion that biological conception parallels the creation of the universe. For the potential of Sarah to conceive Isaac and the potential of Hannah to conceive Samuel are implicit in creation, which is itself predicated on holy potential. Thus the conception of Isaac and Samuel, each of whom would bring cosmic potential a significant step closer to fruition, are indeed events quite relevant to the anniversary of creation. The pain of the childless mother reflects the pain of the ultimate Creator who yearns for ultimate fulfillment of the goals of creation.

Thus, while creator potential is not the only potential, it is essential for the achievement of manifold other potentialities. (*Peru urevu,* "Be fruitful and multiply," is the first *mitzvah* [Divine precept] and is categorized by some as *mitzvah rabbah,* a great *mitzvah.*) Other potentialities, including spiritual and intellectual attainment, are dependent on it. Consequently, creator potential receives a sanctity distinct to itself.

100.06   Linkage: Linkage of God's Potential to Man's Potential

I, even I, am He
that blots out your transgressions
for My own sake.

—Isaiah 43:25

And by Israel [the Lord] will be glorified/beautified.

—Isaiah 44:23

I will place salvation in Zion,
For Israel, my glorifier/beautifier.

—Isaiah 46:13

I was wroth with My people,
I profaned Mine inheritance [Israel].

—Isaiah 47:6

An already infinite God inexorably seeks His own potentialities, as difficult as this concept may be for the finite to comprehend. To any "infinity" one can add. This does not detract from the infinitude aspect of the original infinity. Divine perfection is Divinely enhanceable. This does not detract from the original perfection.

It is for this reason that the potential of the Deity is linked to, and influenced by, man's striving for potential[253] and by man's ascent. The greater man's freedom and consequent ascent, the greater the cosmic potential.[254]

Inasmuch as the cosmic Divine potential is intertwined with that of man, one must come to the conclusion that while man is totally dependent on the Divine, God is also somewhat dependent on man, to whatever small degree.[255] That elements of a dependency exist, is recognized in Jewish tradition.[256]

The Midrash makes this point:
When the Israelites do God's will, they add to the power of God on high. When the Israelites do not do God's will, they, as it were, weaken the great power of God.[257]

"Ye are My witnesses, saith the Lord, and I am God" (Isaiah 43:12). That is, when you are my witnesses, I am God, and when you are not My witnesses, I am, as it were, not God.
                              —Midrash Rabbah, Psalms 123:1[258]

Genesis 1:26 states: "And God said: 'Let us make man in Our image . . .'" The Zohar responds to the question of why the plural "us" by explaining that man is a partner (*shutaf*) with the Divine in the creation of man.[259] The rabbinic/kabbalistic concept of *tikkun olam* ("perfecting/completing the world") further complements the theme of man's partnership with the Divine.

Were it not for My covenant, day and night, the laws of heaven and earth I should not have ordained.
                              —Jeremiah 33:25

God is in need of man for the attainment of His ends.
                              —Heschel[260]

When Israel performs the will of the Omnipresent, they add strength to the heavenly power; as it is said: "To God we render strength" (Psalms 60:14). When, however, Israel does not perform the will of the Omnipresent, they weaken—if it is possible to say so—the great power of Him who is above; as it is written, "Thou didst weaken the Rock that begot Thee."
                              —Pesikta[261]

100.07   Focus: Potential and the *Mitzvot*

The first directive to man in the Torah is not what one might expect in a Divine text. It does not focus on interaction between God and man, nor on fraternal interaction between man and man. Rather, the first directive to man is *peru urevu*, "Be fruitful and multiply" (Genesis 1:26). The first directive to Noah after the flood is the same (Genesis 9:12). Fulfillment of creator potential is a holy thrust of the cosmos, flowing directly from the core of the Divine essence.

*

We can now also begin to unravel the perplexing aspect of the two *mitzvot*, each noted twice, whose affirmative perform-ance, according to Scripture, is rewarded with long life: (1) "Honor thy father and mother" (Exodus 20:12, Deuteronomy 26:17), and (2) *shiluach ha-kan*, the requirement to send the mother bird away prior to taking her young (Deuteronomy 22:6–7). For the link between creator and potential is sanctified and protected. Honoring the link is obligatory.[262] Destruction of the link in the mother's presence is profane. Divine potential flowing through life potential was the original source of life; and thus, symmetrically, sanctification of potential is rewarded by long life.

Nachmanides, in his commentary on the *mitzvah* of *shiluach ha-kan* declares: "Scripture will not permit a destructive act that will bring about the destruction of a species, even though it has permitted the ritual slaughtering of that species for food."[263]

We are directed not to boil a kid (goat) in its mother's milk (Exodus 23:19, 34:26; Deuteronomy 14:21).[264] This thrice-stated directive becomes the basis of the demanding kashruth laws of separating milk and meat. We are also directed not to sacrifice or kill an ox or ewe and their respective young on the same day(Leviticus 22:28).

*

Perhaps the psychic ground of the vast body of law permeat-ing from these directives is the Divine sanctification of the link

between creator and potential which in no way must be profaned. While the partaking of the goat's meat, its kid's, or its
milk individually is certainly permitted, the use of one of a
creator's (life-sustaining) potentialities to complete the termination of another of its (life-giving) potentialities is thrice-
forbidden. While the killing of an ox or its offspring is certainly
permitted individually, the killing of both on the same day,
whether for mundane or holy purposes, is forbidden. The
sanctity of the creator link is clearly established and protected.
Jewish law expands the kid/milk directive into the voluminous
laws requiring the separation of meat and milk products. The
link of potential is thereby sanctified every day at every meal.

*

The *mitzvah* of bringing first fruits (*bikkurim*) as an offering
to the Divine is cited three major times in the Pentateuch
(Exodus 23:19, 26; Deuteronomy 26: 1–11; also see Numbers
18:13). Even at face value the *mitzvah* may be interpreted as a
celebration/sanctification of holy potential[265]. As the Divine is
the cause behind all new fruit, we are instructed to bring a holy
offering of the first of the new fruit.

The particulars of this directive are amplified by the last
tractate of the Mishnah order of *Zeraim*. The Mishnah clarifies
that if the vine from which the first fruits have been plucked
has withered prior to the actual offering in Jerusalem, the
offering is still brought, but no invocation[266] is made—*niktzatz
ha-ilan, mevi vi-eino korei*. The potential of the mother vine has
an effect on the holiness of the first fruits.[267] Inasmuch as
mitzvat bikkurim is a celebration/sanctification of holy potential,
the "de-potentializing" of the mother vine lowers the holiness
of the fruit sufficiently to disqualify it from the invocation of
bikkurim.

*

Potential becomes a salient element elsewhere as well. The
proscription of *neveilah* (Deuteronomy 14:21), i.e., the prohibition of eating of a carcass which has died, as opposed to having

been properly slaughtered, may be related, as well. Having entered a state of "nonpotentiality" by nonritual means, its purity level has been lowered to unacceptable levels.

*

An examination of the textual placement of these directives provides fascinating juxtapositions. The directive of kid/milk is stated three times. In its first two (Exodus 23:19, 34:26) it appears in the same verse as, and exclusively with, the directive of *bikkurim*. The third occurrence (Deuteronomy 14:21) appears in the same verse as, and exclusively with, the proscription of *neveilah*. The verse immediately following contains the directive of tithing. The underlying motif is not so obscure, after all.

*

Newtol Press, professor of biology at the University of Wisconsin, observes that the laws of kashruth, with regard to permitted and prohibited animals, have the clear effect of conserving the earth's energy and the survivability potential of vulnerable species.[268] In particular, the most vulnerable of the vertebrates, carnivorous animals, are protected by forbidding them as a source of food. Of the mammals, only herbivores that are also ruminants (e.g., cows) i.e., which can digest even plentiful grass, are permitted. This subset of vertebrates has the greatest chance of finding sufficient food, and it is this subset alone which is permissible as food. Aside from any other reasons for it, kashruth has the effect of preserving the ecological potential of planet earth.

Ideally, the Torah would have preferred vegetarianism, and indeed, this was the Torah position before the Flood. As a concession to mankind, the Torah permitted the slaughtering and consumption of animals. Within this context, the Torah then maximizes potential, as noted above.

*

While man is clearly given dominion over earth (Genesis 1:26, 9:2–3), he is also given the responsibility for preserving the earth. He must protect life-giving potential even in military contexts. Deuteronomy (20:19–20) directs that only non-fruit-bearing trees may be cut down for siege works. The rabbis further extended this prohibition to proscribe shifting the course of a stream for the military purpose of drying up trees,[269] condemned the stopping up of wells,[270] and proscribed the killing of animals unnecessarily.[271]

The laws of kashruth, the rabbinic injunctions against *bal tashchit* (unnecessary destruction), the laws of *shmitah* (fallow fields during the seventh year) and land redemption upon Jubilee (Leviticus 25:23–24), have, aside from their more obscure metaphysical rationales, the ecological effect of first preserving, and then increasing, the world's physical potential.

*

Life and death have I placed before thee, the blessing and the curse. Mayest thou choose life, that thou mayest live, thou and thy descendants.

—Deuteronomy 30:19 (cf. 30:15, 11:26)

200

200.00   THE UNDERLYING DYNAMIC

Holy quest for potential is the underlying core dynamic of the cosmic order.

Holy quest for potential—our parallel to the kabbalistic *En Sof*—is the "primal scream" of the cosmos. Holy Potential, emanating through and from the Divine essence, radiates through the universe—questing, pulsating, exploding, reaching, energizing, expanding, in time and out-of-time.[272]

It is at the core of the holy/natural drive of the cosmos. It is the primal engine of cosmic existence.[273]

200.01   General Quest for Potential

200.01a   Natural Order

And all the goodliness of God is as the flower of the field.

—Isaiah 40:6

God, as the cosmic ruler, is beheld in His boundless majesty reigning supreme over creation, His will crystallized in the natural law, His word determining the behavioral patterns of nature.

—Soloveitchik[274]

The Spirit of God hovered over the face of the waters and over the void. And God said, Let there be light.

—Genesis 1:2–3

From there on through this day the majesty of creation seeks its maximal potential.[275] Life is daring.[276] The cosmos strives not just for survival; it quests for its maximal potential:[277] Long before Prometheus stole fire from the gods to give to man, God grasped life from out of the void and created fire and man.[278]

200.01b   Mortal[279]

Man inevitably seeks out the highest mountain, literally and allegorically. He girds himself and summons the guts, energy, and means to challenge it. Sometimes quixotically, sometimes daringly. Sometimes a fine line.[280]

Man will construct gossamer cathedrals with spires reaching heavenward, and project space probes to the far ends of the cosmos.[281] Man stands questing, hands lifted heavenward.[282]

Soloveitchik describes "Adam the first"[283] as "aggressive, bold, and victory-minded. His motto is success, triumph over cosmic forces. He engages in creative work, trying to imitate his Maker (*imitatio Dei*)."[284]

200.01c   Universal

The universe seeks its maximum and optimal potential—inexorably.[285] For this, we postulate, is its *raison d'être*. We can only speculate on the precise hierarchic standing of various potentialities, but we suspect that spirituality is near the apex.[286]

For those philosophers who are of the opinion that God

fashioned the world out of primeval matter, or that random combinations of primeval matter evolved into the universe, ultimately the question narrows down to: Where did the smallest subatomic particle come from? Ultimately they must bridge the gap from "nothingness" to "somethingness."

For all those who postulate eternal God or gods, the question remains: In what sense is eternity to be understood?

In Jewish philosophical tradition only the kabbalists face the issue. And their solution is the obscure *En Sof*. We propose a parallel solution: that the infinitely holy quest for potential— the core of the Divine—bridged the gap.

> The perception that dawns on a person to see the world not as finished, but as in the process of continued becoming, ascending, developing—this changes him from being "under the sun" to being "above the sun."
>
> —Kook[287]

> The universe is not static, it is on the march to the future.
>
> —Gordis[288]

> Now things desire their perfections.
>
> —Aquinas[289]

> History, therefore, is moving toward a final perfection.
>
> —I. Greenberg[290]

> . . . the full worth of reality is found not in its actual, but in its potential value.
>
> —Berkovits[291]

> The creative act is an escape from the power of time and ascent to the divine.
>
> —Berdyaev[292]

In contrast, classic Aristotelianism does not focus on potentiality in general in any significant way. According to the classic position, a potential is actualized only by some actually existing thing as its cause. It is the "Prime Mover" who actualizes potentialities.[293]

In our system, however, "Holy Potentiality" is a thoroughly overarching dynamic, emanating from the infinitely holy through creation to the far reaches of the cosmic order. Soloveitchik notes: "He is the Lord of the hosts, who resides in every infinitesimal particle of creation and the whole universe is replete with His glory."[294]

The infinitely holy potentialities themselves, embedded within eternity, are inherent in the eternal origins of the Divine. This is one of our crucial divergences from the Aristotelian line of approach.[295]

200.02   Spiritual Quests for Potential

200.02a   Cosmic

At the Genesis Point, a Divine spark leapt forth. The spark initiates a cycle of becoming, creation, and rebirth. It is the core of this spiritual blaze of potentiality whose ultimate perfect achievement is a primal cosmic end. It is this transcendental flame which directly continues the spark of Life which the Divine infused through Primal Man.

200.02b   Mortal

Man is a creature with the ability to undertake a search for the Tree of Knowledge. He is a creature with the ability to undertake a long-term spiritual quest. With dominion over the earth, man as a species is not burdened with a battle for survival with nonhuman creation.

Man's restless spirit seeks to transcend its limits.[296] Man must dare to reach down into the depths of his own spirit and find his essence;[297] this is his spiritual quest.[298]

By prayer, study, piety, contemplation, solitude, abstinence, penance, sacrifice, charity, purity, and love, man approaches his goal. This is a resolute and continuous assault, day after day, century after century. Man seeks to draw the Divine near. Man seeks to grasp the Divine.

200.03   Ultimate Quests for Potential

200.03a   Cosmic

The cosmic thrust for potential is man-centered. Within this constraint, the cosmos seeks its own perfection. The quests for spirituality and perfection, and the attendant quests for freedom, harmony, and beauty find their source in the metaphysical spark which actualized the cosmos. It was the origin of this quest of quests which bridged the gap from "nothingness" to "Somethingness."

200.03b   Mortal

Man always seeks to raise himself to a higher level.[299] This quest is in effect an extension of a primal cosmic thrust. Judaism attempts to channel and consecrate this imperative. Quests for fame, fortune, power, and security, to whatever extent their extensions are employed to the ultimate ends of the universe, fulfill this overriding cosmic thrust.[300]

Mankind is probing, alert to potential advance. While a significant segment of humanity idealizes the past and/or the status quo, a dynamic segment is always tugging it forward, from the day on which a first voice rang out, crying to mankind slumbering on the raft of Earth, "We are moving! We are going forward!"[301]

Mankind sanctifies its explorers, especially its successful ones. For mankind is also an explorer expedition—with its own scouts way up in their cold, wet, and lonely crow's nests. Sweeping the skyline end to end with their lucky eyepieces. Scanning for new land mass. Ah, there! peeking over the horizon! There it is!— or was it only a midshipman's mirage?

300

300.10   DUALITY OF TWO MAJOR DYNAMICS

Two possible but mutually exclusive sets of dynamics were open to man (at Eden).

300.11   Inverse and Dualities

The concepts of "inverse" and "mutual exclusivity" are crucial to our Unified Formulation. Under our formulation, the Tree of Knowledge is in both an "inverse" and a "mutually exclusive" relationship with the Tree of Life.[302]

The more general theme of opposites and inverses—or what Nicholas of Cusa, in the fifteenth century, would have called "the coincidence of opposites,"[303] pointing to paradoxes in the heart of reality—finds significant expression in Jewish thought.[304]

God has made one thing opposite the other.
                                        —Ecclesiastes 7:14

. . . all that I have created, I created in pairs.
                                        —Midrash Rabbah[305]

300.12   Inverses and Polarities

As scientific thought develops, new relationships between component elements of the universe are perceived. Increasingly the concept of inverse/polarity, or negative relationships, emerges. Obverses and inverses have been found to exist where only unitary entities were previously suspected.[306]
Positive particles imply the existence of negative particles.

   protons and anti-protons
   electrons and positrons
   quarks and anti-quarks
   leptons and anti-leptons
   T-rishons and anti-rishons
   mesons and anti-mesons

North polarity comes with south polarity; dark with light; life with death.

Anti-matter has been proven to exist.
Does anti-time exist?
Does anti-light exist?
Does anti-energy exist?

None of these can be totally rejected out of hand.

The concept of balanced opposites is not new. Oriental philosophy posits a formulation of the *yin* and the *yang* balancing out the universe.[307]

300.20   TREE OF LIFE / TREE OF KNOWLEDGE

300.21   Components of:

The two dynamics are:[308]

Tree of Life/Bliss	*Tree of Knowledge/Potential*
1. A "gilded cage" existence	A life of challenge, freedom, privacy, and responsibility
2. Intellectual satedness	Pursuit of knowledge
3. Limited growth potential	Infinite growth potential
4. Dependence	Independence
5. Eternal life	Mortality
6. "Leashed" "natural evil"	"Unleashed" "natural evil"
7. Bliss	Pain and joy

8. Limited potential for "moral good," "moral evil"	**Higher potential for "moral good," "moral evil"**
9. Lesser dignity	**Higher dignity**

300.22   Elaboration on Structure of "Trees"

There are two major types of existence possible for man in a universe created by God. The two sets of dynamics are mutually exclusive.[309] The dynamics within each set are interrelated and interdependent.

The first type of existence is one of aggressive providence, a gilded-cage existence. Man's needs and nature's travails are handled by God on behalf of man. Under the dynamics of a Tree of Life existence, man in general is treated as an infant in a comfortable home. All is lush and relatively problem-free. High growth and dignity are sacrificed on the altar of bliss and eternal life. All is taken care of.

But there is also the Tree of Knowledge set of dynamics: A life of challenge, freedom, privacy, and responsibility; aggressive pursuit of knowledge; pain and joy in greater extremes; a life of independence and risk; mortality by virtue of natural and moral evil; diminished Divine Providence to "leash" natural evil; infinite growth potential; a higher potential for "moral good" and "moral evil"; a higher level of dignity for man by virtue of his freedom and responsibility. Man's individualism, creativity, and capacities for good and growth will have a greater arena for expression, along with man's cruelty and nature's calamities. In seeking to control his environment and to prevail over it, man comes closer to a true image of God.[310] The biblical narative regarding Eden indeed touches on the dynamics of knowledge, temptation, free choice, evil, privacy, and pain juxtaposed against eternal life in a garden of bliss.

Berkovits notes: "The area of imperfection also seems to be the source of freedom in the world. The absolutely faultless is unfree."[311]

The dynamics of the Tree of Life form a complete set, as do

the dynamics of the Tree of Knowledge. These sets are mutually exclusive. One may not simultaneously operate under the full dynamics of the Tree of Life set and the full dynamics of the Tree of Knowledge set.

The sets are in inverse proportion. The more one increases the influence and magnitude of elements inherent in one complete set, the more one decreases the influence and magnitude of the dynamics inherent in the other complete set.[312]

One cannot simultaneously possess full freedom and eternal life, because each is an inherent dynamic of mutually exclusive sets. The operation of one set in full force would imply the relative quiescence of elements of the other set.

As full and aggressive Divine Providence, along with all the other elements of our Tree of Life paradigm, decreases, all elements of the Tree of Knowledge paradigm—including the elements of challenge, freedom, privacy, and responsibility— increase. The expansion of one set implies the contraction of the other set.

Man cannot have the "best" elements of each set simultaneously, as, for example, both pursuit of knowledge and eternal life, not as a Divine punishment, but rather due to the implicit nature of the dynamics. God will not unravel the relationships, as they are inherent in the cosmic essence, which is inherent in God's nature, as well.[313] For God to unravel the relationships would be to unravel the fabric of the cosmos. Universal truths are extensions of the Divine, and vice versa, and consequently, immutable by definition.

300.23   Shorthand: Symbolism of Eden Parable

The Garden of Eden saga, properly interpreted, symbolizes the overriding cosmic inverse,[314] whose workings may not be impeded.[315]

The Midrash portrays Abraham as expostulating with God: "If you want a world, you will not have justice; if it is justice you want, there will be no world. You are taking hold of the rope by both ends—you desire both a world and justice—but if you do not concede a little, the world cannot stand."[316]

Thus, when man chose to eat from the Tree of Knowledge, he chose to accept the entire set of dynamics of the Tree of Knowledge, and he turned his back on the entire set of dynamics of the Tree of Life. It was actually man who determined his own "expulsion" from the Garden of Eden's bliss. It was man seeking the destiny of Tree of Knowledge with all that the choice implies.[317]

To proceed one step further, it may be proposed that at Eden man gave his *imprimatur* to creation itself. For, creation is inexorably interwined with the dynamic of the Tree of Knowledge. In choosing the Tree of Knowledge, man retroactively ignited a crucial link in creation.

The Garden of Eden tale, which is fittingly placed at the commencement of the biblical narrative, is a philosophically exquisite theodicy/philosophy wrapped in an image-laden, but ultimately sophisticated, parable.

The Eden theodicy must be placed at "front and center" of the Torah, for theodicy is central to any monotheistic theology. The major thrust of our Unified Formulation stares us in the face, cloaked in a parable.

300.30   INEXORABILITY

In a world predicated upon potential, man inexorably took the route of "Tree of Knowledge/Potential."

As a parent is reluctant to set his beloved children out on their own in a harsh world, God was reluctant to set mankind out on their own too early.

Children you are, to the Lord, your God.
—Deuteronomy 14:1[318]

The Divine cautioned man to wait, to remain longer in the protective Divine cocoon of Eden. But man would wait no longer.

The path of the Tree of Knowledge presented a choice to live as a free, independent individual, to commence a quest to fully realize potentialities, to break the umbilical cord tying man to the bliss-font of the innocence of Eden.[319] Man risks death in order to fully live life.[320]

Man is indeed free. Even prior to eating from the Tree of Knowledge, man had free will. He could act contrary to a Divine admonition.[321]

One cannot easily conclude that Adam and Eve "sinned," and were consequently "punished" *per se*, as sin is somewhat problematical pre-Tree of Knowledge.[322] That which on the surface seems to be recorded as "punishment" for "original sin" is in actuality man, in concert with the primordial cosmic thrust, choosing the set of dynamics noted in biblical shorthand as the Tree of Knowledge.[323]

In fact, the relationship between freedom, privacy, Providence, and suffering is crucial to the events of the Garden of Eden. Once man asserts his freedom and tastes of knowledge, the immediate and direct result is an end to the eternal life of bliss and the expulsion from the care of the Garden of Eden, the essence of providential care.

Man's choice was not only between knowledge and eternal life; it was between knowledge/freedom/potential and a "gilded cage" existence. In fact, even the infinitely powerful and wise Deity, who tried to direct man away from the Tree of Knowledge, was unwilling, if indeed able, to forcefully foreclose the option.[324]

In many ways the Nazi plague was a direct attack on these very eternal values of liberty, individualism, and the value of the creative human spirit. But the Nazi would replace the gilded cage of eternal bliss of the Garden of Eden with the concentration camp of debasement and death of Auschwitz. Evil incarnate would pervert/invert the essence of creation, and its primal target would also inexorably be the primal carrier of the Divine word.

The psychic force of the event of mankind's grand choice exerts its pull on us through the millennia, notwithstanding the inadequacies of the particular interpretation and subsequent doctrine. It is interesting to note the centrality in Christian theodicy of the Garden of Eden drama. The mainstream Augustinian philosophy of original sin and the fall of man traces evil in the world directly to the original "sin" at Eden. In the Augustinian formulation, all mankind is punished for man's original sin at Eden. There are many theological and philosophical problems with this formulation, yet it remains the mainstream Christian doctrine on evil.

Common Jewish and Christian exegesis holds that Eve and Adam sinned in partaking of the Tree of Knowledge. In the Jewish philosophical tradition there is a spectrum of viewpoints on the Garden of Eden and its manifold symbolisms.

Our interpretation is that while Eve acted in contradiction to Divine *tziviteecha* (caution), the category of classic "sin" is simply inapplicable to the pre-Tree of Knowledge state. Rather, Eve, the symbolic mother of mankind, and Adam, the symbolic father of mankind, exercised their divinely granted measure of freedom to decline the warning of the Divine, and to choose the path of dynamics known by the title "Tree of Knowledge."[325] Man forsook the low-risk approach to life favored by the Divinity at that point for a bolder and riskier approach to life,[326] which, while not favored by the Divinity then, was nevertheless definitely permitted.[327] Man took the route advanced by John Stuart Mill: "Better Socrates dissatisfied than the fool satisfied; better the fool dissatisfied than the pig satisfied."[328]

Berkovits notes:

Since man, without the challenge and the freedom of meeting it in responsible action, would not be human, we might as well say that, to the extent to which we are unable to attach sense and dignity to human existence, man is of necessity linked to imperfection. He who desires man in all his nothingness and potential glory must also desire the imperfections of man's cosmic condition.[329]

Accordingly, the Spanish philosopher Miguel de Unamuno concluded *The Tragic Sense of Life*, with the words: ". . . and may God deny you peace but give you glory!"[330]

According to the common reading, *ve-etz ha-da-at tov ve-ra* is to be understood as "and the tree of knowledge of good and evil." According to our reading, this phrase is to be read, "and the Tree of Knowledge; consequently both good and evil." According to the common reading, Eve and Adam "sinned" when they ate from the Tree of Knowledge. According to our reading, Eve and Adam did not sin; they "contravened a caution," which is a crucial step below "sin."

The common reading of the Garden of Eden saga is actually predicated on an internal contradiction. If Adam and Eve only gained knowledge of good and evil as a consequence of eating from the fruit, how can they have "sinned"—an act which presumes some understanding of good and evil—in the prior partaking of the fruit?[331] Furthermore, the Hebrew phrase describing the tree should then be *ve-etz da-at tov ve-ra*, "the tree of knowledge of good and evil," not *ve-etz ha-da-at tov ve-ra*, "the Tree of Knowledge; good and evil." There is a "superfluous" *heh* in the text if we employ the common reading.

On what level is the Garden of Eden tale to be understood? Did the first man and woman determine the course of untold billions? Was my destiny charted by one or two primitives?

We would posit that First Adam was not simply the literal "first man." One must rather posit that he was a *shaliach*,[332] a representative on behalf of mankind to come. In a cosmos predicated on potential and containing elements of circularity, First Adam, in concert with inexorable thrusts of the cosmos, chose the Tree of Knowledge/Potential.

The essential choice in the Eden saga was made by Eve, the mother of mankind, and not by its father. The one who bears the child and suffers the pain in childbirth, chose to set her children along the more arduous, but hopefully more rewarding, path of Tree of Knowledge/Potential.[333] The one who carries and gives life chose the path which also ultimately abrogates life[334] because this same treacherous path also yields a fuller life.[335]

300.40   UNLEASHED EVIL

"Natural evil" and "moral evil" would consequently forever-more plague and challenge man.[336]

Increased potential for good implies increased potential for evil.[337] As mankind exercised the option of Tree of Knowledge, the component of "unleashed natural evil" came into play, along with the component of "higher potential for moral good, moral evil." Along with the extensions of other potentialities, the potential exercise of evil is far greater. As mankind can no longer count on the Divine to shield him from evil, by virtue of the freedom aspect of Tree of Knowledge/Potential, man had best be strong, because the forces of evil can be quite strong.[338]

The Garden of Eden saga is shortly followed by Cain's killing of Abel. Fratricide. Not only is man one of the very few species in which members kill one other; man will literally kill his own blood brother. The species with the highest potential for knowledge is internally, and apparently morally, the most dangerous. Man has the audacity to ask, "Am I my brother's keeper?" (Genesis 4:9).[339]

400

400.10   EVIL AND POLARITY

Evil is the implicit flip-side, or converse, of good. Evil is anti-polar to good.[340]

All evils are negations.

—Maimonides[341]

Evil is the base of the good.

—Baal Shem Tov[342]

Good is set against evil, and life against death: so is the sinner against the godly. So look upon all the works of the Most High, and these are two and two, one against another.

—Ecclesiastes 33:15

Light is steadily pitted against the dark, and light will increasingly overcome the dark.

—Kook[343]

Good and evil we know in the field of this world grow up together almost inseparably. . . . It was out of the rinde of one apple tasted that the knowledge of good and evil as two twins cleaving together leapt forever into the world.

—John Milton[344]

400.11 Introductory

We reject the concept that evil and good are part of one continuum.[345] We decline to put torture on the same continuum as mercy, preferring rather to treat them as components of distinct but interlocked opposites.[346]

In a sense, then, the world is an arena between the good and evil, with man holding the balance.[347]

When God engraved and carved out the world, He did not entirely eradicate the chaos and the void, the deep, the darkness, from the domain of His creation. . . . However, the forces of relative nothingness at times exceed their bounds. They wish to burst forth out of the chains of obedience that the Almighty imposed upon them and seek to plunge the earth back into chaos and the void.

—Soloveitchik[348]

The most extreme form of dualism, and that which would, if it could be accepted, possibly solve the problem of evil, postulates two deities, one good and the other malevolent.[349] Such a dualism was embodied in the ancient and now essentially defunct Zoroastrian religion. Zoroaster taught that two rival gods existed, Ahura Mazda (or Ormuzd), the source of good, and Angra Mainyu (or Ahriman), the source of evil. In the early Christian centuries a similarly dramatic dualism was taught by Mani (born about 215 C.E.) and became the basis of the Manichaean religion, which so strongly attracted St. Augustine prior to his conversion to Christianity. In the twelfth and early thirteenth centuries the Albigenses in the south of France revived a Manichaean-like dualism until the sect was stamped out of existence by the Catholic Church.[350]

400.12   Evil and the Jews

In Jewish thought Amalek symbolizes absolute evil, and the Jewish people are commanded to (1) remember the evil of Amalek, and (2) wipe out all traces of Amalek.

If evil is the polar antithesis of good, and the polarity of good, one may reason that evil is attracted to good just as magnetic opposites are attracted. And if, as we maintain, the Jew is God's witness and the primal carrier of God's law, we may argue that evil is attracted to the Jew, the primal crucible of the Divine good.[351]

The historic vicissitudes of the Jews, in the context of our system, thus become an unsought "Purple Cross" for a people of the light. Evil inexorably shadows the Jew.[352]

One may argue that when evil does emerge, the Jew, the primal keeper of the holy will, is a natural target, again implicitly and by definition. At that point, when the Jew is weak on any front, he is a vulnerable target.

400.13   Source and Existence of Evil

The classic philosophical dilemma runs as follows:

If God is omnipotent, why is there evil at all?
If God is all-benevolent, why did He create evil?

If God did not create evil, then do we conclude that God is not the source of all?

Philosophical discussion then turns on the question of whether evil actually exists, or is just the absence of good. The debate involves the questions of (1) whether evil only appears so from a mortal perspective, and (2) whether man subjectively divides his experience into positive and negative sides of a neutral center, as opposed to one continuum.

With regard to the major questions, the Platonic view, also adopted by Philo of Alexandria, maintains that since God is all-good, evil is nothing but the absence of good. God produces the positive, good forms and determines them to last a period of time. When this time period has elapsed, evil forms take their place.[353]

Joseph ibn Zaddik and Abraham ibn Ezra are in basic sympathy with the notion that God is the source only of good. Ibn Ezra maintains further that evil is due to defects in the object receiving impressions. Abraham bar Hiyya and Hasdai ben Abraham Crescas assert that God is the source of both good and evil.[354]

Building upon our previous postulations of a cosmos predicated upon dualities, including the notion of evil as the flip-side, or converse, of good, we assert the following proposition:

400.20   EVIL AND NECESSITY

With the creation of potential for good, which is required for man to be able to reach his spiritual potential, potential for evil indirectly, but nevertheless, inexorably, came into existence as a consequence.[355]

He [God] creates evil only in so far as he produces the corporeal element [good and existence] such as it actually is; it is always connected with negatives, and is on that account the source of all destruction and all evil.

—Maimonides[356]

I form the light, and create darkness;
I make peace, and create evil;
I am the Lord,
Who has made all these things.

—Isaiah 45:5

There is no possible source of evil except good.

—Aquinas[357]

Evil has its source in the good.

—Augustine[358]

Without evil goodness would not be possible either.

—Berkovits[359]

Man cannot quest for spiritual heights unless there is intense good to use as a "spiritual ladder." The creation of good, however, mandates the existence of its polarity, evil.[360]

Good and evil form a duality. Creating potential for good, by definition, creates the inverse potential for evil along with it.[361] Good only exists with its duality, evil. In order to create potential for good, potential for evil was, by definition, created.[362] God's omnipotence or non-omnipotence is not the issue. It is rather a question of definition. By definition, good comes packaged with concomitant evil.[363]

Existence of potential for good → Existence of potential for evil.
God created potential for good.
Therefore: God created potential for evil.

Evil exists not (à la the Irenaean and Augustinian theodicies) because God necessarily had a productive need for evil to exist. Rather, it was in the Divine/cosmic interest for good to exist, and evil is the inevitable duality of good.[364] Evil exists because dualities are inherent in the universe. In a world of active Divine intervention, gross evil is held at bay by the omnipotent intervening Divinity. In a world of lesser intervention, as in a world where the Divine is in a state of greater contraction of here-and-now omniscience, evil gains power.

In a world where mortals lower their "moral guard," evil has a chance to achieve "critical mass" and emerge with increased destructiveness.

400.30   THE REMOVAL OF EVIL

To destroy evil would, at the least, destroy good.

In Jewish tradition, omnipotent God is constrained from destroying evil, for by doing so He might well destroy good. He cannot imprison evil, for by doing so He might well imprison good. God can, however, in some respects and through mortal proxies, attempt to outmaneuver evil, to trap evil into acting towards the neutral or even towards the good. Optimally, evil is outmaneuvered or bested by man.

The relationship of good and evil is illustrated in the Talmud.

A powerfully suggestive myth on the nature and forms of evil is recorded in the Talmud, which tells of the capture of the Evil Tempter. The captors sought to kill it but were warned that with its destruction, the entire world would fall apart. They imprisoned it nonetheless. Three days later they looked throughout the land for a fresh egg and could not find one, for when the sexual drive is extirpated, no eggs are available; where the libido is destroyed, civilization is ended. Those who held the Evil Tempter captive were themselves held fast in the vise of a dilemma. If they killed the Tempter, the world would be unable to endure; if they let it loose, evil would be free to roam the land. The captors begged for half-mercy, asking that the Tempter should live but not tempt. To this request the divine echo responded, "They do not grant halves in heaven." The myth reminds man that evil is often mixed with good.[365]

400.40   UNIVERSAL LAWS

While an omnipotent Deity may have an impact on nature, even an omnipotent Deity does not violate universal laws, as they are implicit in the universal Deity's essence, and violating them could unravel the cosmos.

God indeed is bound by His own universal laws,[366] for they are intertwined with God's essence.[367] Just where the physical laws and imperatives of the universe end, and God begins, is an open question under our formulation and under many other formulations.

The removal of all potential—both good and evil—from the universe would have dire consequences. It would be both effective cosmocide—the destruction of a cosmos which was/is energized by holy potential—and, as well, akin to Divine suicide, since holy quest for potential is at the epicenter of the Divine. Thus potentials for evil are not so easily truncated by the Divine.

> . . . we do not ascribe to God the power of doing what is impossible.
>
> —Maimonides[368]

> God is no capricious potentate, violating the laws that He himself has promulgated. In Einstein's words, "God does not play dice with the universe."
>
> —Gordis[369]

While in some quarters variations on the proposition that the existence of potential for good necessitates the existence of potential for evil are employed as a self-contained theodicy, there is no such intent here, for the classic question remains: Why does an omnimerciful, omnipotent God not intervene and counter specific evil? Thus, proposition 400—that good and evil form a duality—addresses the important but more abstract question of why evil exists at all in a cosmos reigned over by a good and omnipotent Divine. It does not answer the question of intervention.

500

500.10   FINITE +

Man is finite + seeking to approach Infinity.

Man should be categorized not as "finite being," but more accurately as "finite + being."[370] Man's potential approaches the infinite.[371]

Inversely, God, in order to allow the possibility of the finite/infinite potential of man to reach fruition, must contract elements of His infinitude.[372] This concept would parallel the kabbalistic concept of *tsimtsum* regarding creation.

> When I look at Your heavens,
> The work of Your fingers,
> The moon and stars
> That You have established—
> What is man that You think of him?
> Mortal man that You remember him?
> Yet You have made him little less than God,
> You have crowned him with glory and splendor.
>
> —Psalm 8:4–6[373]

> . . . there is no limit to the possibility of ascending toward the heights.
>
> —Kook[374]

> . . . it is possible for everyone to achieve ever higher states of inspiration up to the very highest level, and every man can rise to become the equal of Moses our teacher, if he should but will to do so.
>
> —*Sefer Hagilgulim*[375]

> Because man is the sole living creature known to us in whom the category of possibility is so to speak embodied, and whose reality is incessantly enveloped by possibilities, he alone amongst them all needs confirmation.
>
> —Buber[376]

They bear convincing witness to the tragic truth that humanity is still only a potentiality and far from being a reality.

—Berkovits[377]

In the endless development of the human race towards its ideal spirit of holiness alone may the individual soul achieve its immortality. It [the soul] is always only the upswing, always only the totality of the upswings that are gathered together in the endless development.

—Hermann Cohen[378]

The metaphysics of Leon Stitskin's philosophy of "personalism"[379] "delineates man as potential, a self-identifying activity of consciousness to be actualized by constant involvement with life's experiences, and a process of conceptualization when ideas are transformed from being mere copies of phenomena to becoming ultimate purposes."[380]

And so man, created as a personal being in the image of God, is only the raw material for a further and more difficult stage of God's creative work.

—Hick[381]

Man surpasses himself infinitely.

—Pascal[382]

To be a man means to try to be God.
    Human reality is a pure effort to become God, to become *ens causa sui.*

—Jean-Paul Sartre[383]

. . . the spirituality of our nature makes us potentially God-like. The potentiality must be actualized.

—Merton[384]

500.20   PURPOSE

The purpose of man is to quest for his potentialities—spiritual, intellectual, and all other.[385]

> My heart rages
> Like a boiling pot,
> Like a stormy sea.
> I aspire for the heights,
> For lofty visions
> Fed by divine lights,
> By souls hidden in the realms above.
> I will not be bound in chains,
> But I will bear a yoke;
> I am a servant of God
> But not a slave of slaves.
>
> —Kook[386]

The purpose of each individual human is to seek his own particular potential, spiritual,[387] intellectual, etc. (within moral parameters). Each person presumably has his own potentialities different from anyone else's.[388] To some extent man is thus not measured against an absolute, but rather against his own particular potentiality.[389]

> The task of man has been defined by Luria . . . as the restoration of his primordial spiritual structure or Gestalt. That is the task of every one of us, for every soul contains the potentialities of this spiritual appearance outraged and degraded by the fall of Adam, whose soul contained all souls.
>
> —Scholem[390]

As Scholem indicates in the preceding passage, Lurianic Kabbalah sees man as trying to regain what he once lost, whereas our formulation views man as trying to reach fresh heights of spirituality. However, under either formulation man's quest for spiritual potential remains a central task. Luria views this as the primary/preeminent task of man, and we see it as the foremost primal quest of man.

And God blessed them, and God said to them: "Be fruitful and
multiply and replenish the earth, and conquer it."

—Genesis 1:28

Populate the earth and conquer it. But there was no one to
conquer it from—Adam and Eve were the sole human inhabitants of the earth. And further, why the positioning of the two
important directives in one sentence?

Rather, the sentence should be understood as: "Populate the
earth and master it! Conquer its potential—you and (through)
your offspring."

The commentaries note that there is a letter (*vav*) missing
from the word *ve-kiv-shu-ha*, "and conquer/master it." The key
word is incomplete, deficient. We suggest that the key word is
left "open" because the quest itself is not finitely demarcated.
It is boundless. For potential brushes up against infinity. The
quest is not one attainable by a single person or generation. It
is a goal to be quested after by the elevation of generation after
generation, onward through time.

When gratuitous hate (*sin'at chinam*) is ascendant, man's
spiritual development is stymied. All is for naught. When the
Jew focuses his awesome potential energies invalidly instead of
positively and outwardly, his forward ascent comes to a halt. A
Beit Hamikdash (Holy Temple) or synagogue becomes simply an
affectation, inasmuch as its primary goal, the spiritual elevation
of man, is blocked.

Once one has established the bounds between what a religion
claims and what it can prove, one may then seek to elevate
oneself spiritually. Judaism provides a route. It gives direction,
while Jewish law circumscribes the path which may be taken.
Well-established direction provides plentiful room for spiritual
construct and elevation.

Halakhic man is also a homo religiosus in all his loftiness and
splendor. His soul, too, thirsts for the living God, and these
streams of yearning surge and flow to the sea of transcendence
to "God who conceals Himself in His dazzling hiddenness" [the

first line of a kabbalistic *piyyut* recited at the conclusion of the
third Sabbath meal].

—Soloveitchik[391]

Thus, attainment of a share in the world-to-come is more in the
nature of development of potential than of reward and punishment.

—Bleich[392]

[In] Judaism the idea of the good is penultimate. It cannot exist
without the holy. The good is the base, the holy is the summit.
Man cannot be good unless he strives to be holy.

—Heschel[393]

. . . within Judaism the sacred, as far as it may be a human
concern at all, is not found in the realm of Being, but in that of
Becoming. Man is called upon to sanctify himself; to sanctify this
earthly Adam in this world. *K'dusha,* holiness, is sanctification.
And sanctification is a process in time and not a miracle outside
of time.

—Berkovits[394]

To be human, in the personalistic sense, is to be potentially
divine. As such he is driven to live in consciousness of responsibility and challenge to realize his potential.

—Stitskin[395]

As a person rises in knowledge and understanding, in the study
of Torah and in the cultivation of good attributes, in his intellectual and moral propensities, he marches forward toward the
future. . . . By perfecting his ways and actions, personal and
social, there is open to him a great light that directs him to
endless progress.

—Kook[396]

. . . man—dwelling as he does in two different worlds and
undergoing profound inner struggles—is given the chance to
rise far beyond the level of our existence and the place in which

he spiritually finds himself, and to act on higher worlds without
end.

—Steinsaltz[397]

500.30   MAN'S ASCENT/CREATION

**The closer man approaches the achievement of his spiritual
and other potentialities, the closer man comes to fulfilling a
primal quest of creation.[398]**

Theoretically, attainment of spiritual potentiality would obviate the need for Divine contraction. For Divine self-contrac-
tion is solely for the purpose of granting man the necessary
freedom to achieve his potential.[399] The broad concept of
mankind's ultimate redemption (and salvation) transcends most
major religious lines; it is common in Western religions and
Eastern religions, "archaic religions" and "modern religions."
Seemingly this concept is rooted in man's religious instinct.
Hope springs not just eternal, but almost universal.

When mankind has reached its spiritual potential, a primal
purpose of creation will, hopefully, have been fulfilled, and a
redemptive age, hopefully, achieved. Jewish philosophy is
therefore on the right track when it is reluctant to deny a role
for other religions in the ultimate Divine scheme.[400] For the
spiritual ascendency of mankind in general is intertwined with
the Jewish role, and of course plays a most important role in
the general development for potential.

... the quest for perfection, which is the most idealistic striving
of our nature, directs us to seek the higher unity that must
finally come in the world. In that day—God will be one and His
name one.

—Kook[401]

... the divine remains committed to, and yearning for, the
attainment of the final perfection.

—Greenberg[402]

However, "perfection" and "infinity," while possibly approachable, are not necessarily attainable. Nor is the possible impossibility of their attainment necessarily a cause for despair. The approach should prove wondrous enough.

500.40   COMMON QUESTS

Man, (infinite) God, and the universe are all questing for their potentialities.[403]

> . . . the Jewish religion may truly be considered as the ideal of religion, the religion of the future, the "I shall be what I shall be."
>
> —Kook[404]

> It is logical that every spark of life has a soul, that it yearns to ascend, and that it ascends by divine grace, which is active at all times. . . . A chaotic world stands before us as long as we have not attained to that degree of higher perfection of uniting all life-forces and all their diverse tendencies.
>
> —Kook[405]

> . . . the world is best conceived of as . . . a living organism with boundless potentialities for growth.
>
> —Gordis[406]

Quest for potential courses from the Divine to man and through the cosmic order.[407] All strive towards ultimate perfection. All sail parallel cosmic oceans.

Man is the keystone of the cosmic quest for perfection. However, man is not alone in his quest. For the entire cosmic order is interlocked with man's potentialities.

600

600.00   MAN'S FREEDOM

Man is innately free and striving for fuller freedom.[408]

600.01   Centrality of Concept in Judaism

Man's freedom is an important element in Judaism[409] and Judaism carefully defends the sanctity of the self. Man cannot achieve true spiritual heights from a state of nonfreedom. The concept of man's freedom is an overarching one in Judaism.[410]

Man has freedom of choice.

—Nachmanides[411]

In Judaism, the pure and free man stands next to the focal point of the one free God.

—Hirsch[412]

Man's spirit is free and independent. It is not subject to the lawful structure of the universal, to the necessity of the species. The "universal" in the existence of the man of God is free from the chains of scientific lawfulness, for it was created in accordance with the principle of freedom and is wholly grounded in that principle.

Choice is granted to every human being. If a man wants to follow the good path and be good, the choice is his; if he wants to follow the evil path and be wicked, the choice is his. . . . Indeed, man's entire spiritual existence is enhanced by his unique privilege to create himself and make himself into a free man.

—Soloveitchik[413]

As the medieval intellectual elite well understood, an emphasis on human freedom does not inevitably lead to a dilution of commitment of faith. The contrary is possible. The Karaite sect, for instance, which preceded and overlapped the rise of classic Jewish philosophy in the Middle Ages, and which produced some of the most restrictive regulations known within a Jewish context, contained a strong emphasis on rationality and the inviolability of the individual conscience and freedom.[414]

Although our sages may not always have been emotionally

comfortable with the thought, most of them have conceded man's innate freedom to choose his own path. Man is created *betzelem Elohim* ("in the image of God") and not as an obsequious bond servant. So insistent is Halachah on man's innate freedom that the *eved ivri*—the Jew who sells himself into slavery—is required to undergo an ignominious procedure if he wishes to extend his indenture.

God wishes priests as worshippers, not slaves, either of the body or the mind. Only the service of free man is truly meaningful to God.[415] Thus the deliverance from Egypt was necessary for God's purposes. The dying out of the slave generation in the Sinai desert, and thus of the slave mentality, was also necessary for His ultimate purposes. Man is a partner (*shutaf*) with God in governing the world; therefore man by definition has inherent freedom, as he is a partner in the cosmic creation/development.

600.02   Definition of Man's Freedom

Judge Irving Younger builds upon the thoughts of John Stuart Mill in defining freedom:

> Exclusive only of such conduct which infringes (in a non-remote manner) on the legitimate interests of other members of society, man is sovereign over his own body and soul.[416]

Judaism carefully delineates the basic proscriptions on man's innate freedom in the form of the *sheva mitzvoth b'nei Noach* (the Seven Commandments of Man, also known as the Noachide Laws).

1. The establishment of courts of justice.
2. The prohibition of blasphemy.
3. The prohibition of idolatry.
4. The prohibition of incest.
5. The prohibition of bloodshed.
6. The prohibition of robbery.
7. The prohibition of eating flesh cut from a living animal.

Man is called to respond, and he responds with his deed. . . . He alone must choose and do in complete freedom of commitment.

—Berkovits[417]

The covenant then rests upon the juridic-Halakhic principle of "free negotiation, mutual assumption of duties and full recognition of the equal rights of both parties concerned with the covenant."

—Soloveitchik[418]

Man is created *betzelem Elohim* ("in the image of God"), and, as God is free,[419] Israel is free.[420] Any denigration of Israel's freedom is by definition a debasement of God.[421] Freedom is an enemy of God's enemies.[422]

For God had made man free and unfettered, to employ his powers of action with voluntary and deliberate choice for this purpose.

—Philo[423]

Another of the rights granted man under the Jewish theocracy, perhaps a more basic right, is the right of personal liberty and freedom. For our Sages this right was a fundamental human right. Not only did they recognize it in their general social outlook, as might perhaps be expected, but their very penal code is so drawn as to preserve this right even for the lawbreaker.

—Belkin[424]

[Religion] will continue to hold aloft the banner of man's inalienable freedom.

—Gordis[425]

. . . it is life itself, and not merely religion, that insists that man is free.

—Gordis[426]

600.03   Qualifications and Limitations—Within Freedom

Freedom, though, is not the ultimate aim. Freedom as the necessary base for ultimate growth is the point.[427]

> . . . freedom enhances when it is marked and contained by reason, but when reason fails to find language, freedom is destructively cut loose or bends toward untruth or succumbs to sheer willfulness. . . . freedom without the containment of reason returns to caprice, and reason without the imagination of freedom is supineness and passivity.
>
> —A. Cohen[428]

Mainstream Jewish theology posits that man is free,[429] although the Jew who strays from the Halachic path does so at his own peril. The principle of reward and punishment is positioned as not being a limitation on man's freedom, since the individual is ultimately free to pursue his own path.

The "freedom maximalists," who are in the minority, posit that man is absolutely free.[430] Either man is free or he is not free. Ultimately the theologian must make a choice. Man cannot be free in one context and a slave in another context, all under a sacred umbrella.[431]

One of the central questions in covenant theology is: Why should man today be bound by the covenants of Abraham and Sinai? The inherent covenantal obligations of the individual form the subject of a complex and rich debate, closely interlinked with the question of the absoluteness of individual man's freedom. But the broader concept of man's freedom, while seemingly at least somewhat delimited by mainstream Jewish theology, is indisputably and insistently upheld.

Torah enhances man's freedom by placing a high value on man's intellect, which in turn fosters increased freedom and spiritual growth. Judaism attempts to be expansive vis-à-vis man's spiritual growth. At the same time, Halachah, considered in isolation from its intellectual and spiritual aspects, is in most respects a restrictive element on man's actions. On the whole

Judaism glorifies freedom,[432] while at the same time Halachah charts man's mundane freedom for ultimate purpose.

Some rabbinic authorities have expressed a fear of broad freedoms, a fear that too many adherents would be lost. Classically the fear was that "even one rejecting generation could terminate the holy tradition of forty generations." However, the cure is worse than the threat of the disease. The Jew pays a price for his freedom, but on the whole will be stronger for it. The Jew emerges from the crucible of freedom physically battered and sometimes almost annihilated. But the Jew is not unaware of the imperatives and cruciality of freedom. Both major covenants were entered into from bases of freedom. Man is attracted to, and cherishes, a freedom-based religion.[433]

700

700.10   NECESSITY AND FREEDOM

In order for man to reach his full potential, he must operate from a base of freedom. (This is a law of the universe in concert with balance of dynamics of Tree of Knowledge chosen at Eden.)[434]

The God of the Ten Commandments is the God of Freedom.

I am the Lord thy God who brought thee out of the land of Egypt, out of the house of bondage.
—First Commandment (Exodus 20:2, Deuteronomy 5:6)

The Divine introduction is clear: Not the God of Creation;[435] not the God of Power; but the God of Freedom. Freedom as a base for the commandments, and as a base for the ultimate attainment of spiritual redemption.

700.20   FULLER FREEDOM

The greater the freedom component of man's base, the greater his ultimate potential (inherent in Tree of Knowledge chosen at Eden.)[436]

Man is most alive when he is keenly conscious of the reality and inviolability of his own freedom, when he is aware of his power over his own destiny. He is possibly only fully alive when he is sensitized to his capacity to consecrate that freedom for ultimate ends.[437] Indeed, man can truly be considered fully alive only when he has actualized the freedom inherent in the self.[438]

One cannot achieve one's potential from a base of dependency.[439] Greatness is not achieved while leaning on someone's shoulder. So too, man, in his ultimate quest for potential, must finally stand completely on his own.[440] Only from a state of freedom and independence can the true test of man take place.[441]

Freedom, for all its dangers and dark aspects, may ultimately serve a sacred purpose.[442] For it is through freedom, and not in shackles, that man bursts through to the transcendent.[443] The Divine created man free in order that man might develop this freedom and ultimately consecrate it.[444]

> The inner essence of the soul . . . must have absolute inner freedom.
>
> —Kook[445]

> And Halakhic man, whose voluntaristic nature we have established earlier, is, indeed, a free man. He . . . looks forward to the kingdom of God "contracting" itself and appearing in the midst of concrete and empirical reality.
>
> —Soloveitchik[446]

> Freedom is an act of self-engagement of the spirit, a spiritual event.
>
> —Heschel[447]

One cannot frighten people into goodness. In order to be good, man has to choose the good; but there is choice only where there is freedom.

—Berkovits[448]

The Ideal Man is still only an ideal. Before he becomes reality, freedom will have to find its place in the context of the Law.

—Berkovits[449]

800

800.10   MAN'S ASCENT/KNOWLEDGE

Man is ascendant[450]—at least in knowledge.[451]

Mankind has come a long way in the acquisition of knowledge since Eden. Buddhism, Christianity, and Islam have all sprung up and flowered in the meanwhile. Yehudah Hanassi, Rashi, Hillel, Ibn Ezra, Aquinas, Euclid, Galileo, Plato, Tennyson, the Vilna Gaon, Jefferson, Einstein—all of them have raised mankind up further rungs on the ladder of knowledge. Man has extended *Masorah*. Man has probed the atom, the mind, the body, time, and the cosmos—inexorably, continuously, successfully.

One can presumably argue that overall—morally, spiritually, on some levels intellectually—man has not ascended. However, it is inarguable that in the realm of the acquisition of knowledge there has been an ascent of man.[452] And it is on this crucial ascent of knowledge[453]—in direct continuum to the partaking of the Tree of Knowledge—that we pivot a crucial part of our formulation.[454]

Has man's "level of consciousness"[455] ascended, as well, over the millennia? Is there an element in the accumulated wisdom which is part of a species knowledge passed down from generation to generation? The philosopher Pierre Teilhard de Chardin registers in the affirmative on both of these points.[456]

Notwithstanding the accuracy of this view, man's general ascent in knowledge remains indisputable.[457]

From Aristotle's assumption that "man by nature desires to know," Aquinas derives a Divine purpose for such a universal desire. Man's innate sense of wonder, according to Aquinas, is divinely implanted. The ultimate uniqueness of man is in the operation of his intellect, which will not rest until it reaches the source of its being.[458]

800.20   KNOWLEDGE AND FREEDOM

As mankind and Judaism ascend in knowledge (and possibly in consciousness) on the road to fulfilling a primal drive of creation,[459] there is an implicit demand for fuller freedom. (This is implicit in our paradigm of the Tree of Knowledge.)[460]

> There is no free man except he who is immersed in Torah.
> —rabbinic dictum

When man acquires knowledge, he acquires a greater desire for freedom.[461] This is true of individual man and of groups of man.[462] We contend that this can be applied to civilization as well, and that as a civilization ascends in knowledge, it demands ever increasing levels of freedom on all fronts.[463]

We will later on formulate that, in turn, this freedom further opens the gates for man to achieve his ultimate goals.[464] For ultimate spiritual goals[465] can be best quested for from a base of the fullest possible freedom.[466]

↑ *knowledge* → ↑ *freedom (privacy, responsibility, selfhood)* → ↑ *potential:*

> The only thing of value is the fear of God. But no one can reach this stage of the fear of the Lord until he ascends the ladder of wisdom and has acquired understanding.
> —Abraham Ibn Ezra[467]

God endowed man with a rational faculty, which is also referred to as *lev* (literally: heart) in order to actualize every soul's potential in due time.

—Abraham Ibn Ezra[468]

In the final chapter of Maimonides' *Guide to the Perplexed,* four levels of human perfection are listed in ascending order, with the acquisition of metaphysical knowledge regarded as the true end, the highest perfection, the mark of man, and the path to immortality.[469]

. . . the possession of notions which lead to true metaphysical opinions as regards God. With this man has obtained . . . the highest human perfection . . . which gives him immortality, and on its account he is called man.

—Maimonides[470]

↑ *knowledge* → ↑ *freedom:*

One can make a case for a correlation between the intellect and active Providence, but we would make it in precisely the opposite manner as Maimonides seems to do, and we would make the case on a collective level, as opposed to the individual level. That is, Maimonides correlates Providence directly with the individual's intellectual and spiritual attainment; we correlate a contraction of Divine here-and-now consciousness with civilization's intellectual attainment.

We posit that as the cumulative knowledge of Israel and civilization rises, the cumulative psyche of man demands greater freedom (in accordance with the dynamics of Eden).[471] This in turn demands a corresponding contraction of here-and-now consciousness on the part of the Deity to yield man greater freedom and concomitant privacy, responsibility, and selfhood.[472]

The kabbalists posit that the initial creation of the universe could only be brought about by a Divine contraction. We posit that man's achievement of his potential necessitates elements of Divine contraction.

The receiving of the Torah at Sinai, the compilation of Scripture under Ezra in Babylon, the advent of the Mishnah, the emergence of medieval Jewish scholarship, the advent of great centers of learning in Europe—each of these would represent a quantum step-up in the disseminated knowledge for the people of Israel, in particular.

However, even on a less grandiose level, the ascent of an individual in any area affects the whole. The individual thus has an impact on the whole, and the whole has an impact on the individual.[473]

Whenever a person raises himself through good deeds, through a higher stirring of his yearning for godliness, for wisdom, justice, beauty and equity, he perfects thereby the spiritual disposition of all existence. All people become better in their inwardness through the ascendency of the good to any one of them. . . . Such virtue in any one person is due to spread among the general populace, to stir each one, according to his capacity, toward merit, and thus all existence thereby becomes ennobled and more exalted.

—Kook[474]

. . . every thought, every tremor of anticipation and desire on the part of man work their way until they reach the Holy One Himself, the Infinite, Blessed be He.

—Steinsaltz[475]

The dynamics of Tree of Knowledge/Potential mandate that the cumulative growth of knowledge necessitates an expansion of man's freedom.

800.30   PRIVACY, RESPONSIBILITY, AND SELFHOOD

A demand for fuller freedom (as a consequence of an ascent in knowledge) has embodied within it a demand for greater

privacy, responsibility, and selfhood—so that man can more ably quest for his potential.

↑ *freedom* → ↑ *privacy*
              ↑ *selfhood*
              ↑ *responsibility*

800.31   Freedom and Privacy

↑ *freedom* → ↑ *privacy:*

Let us take it as a "given" that "His ways are not our ways," "His knowledge is not our knowledge," "His wisdom is not our wisdom." Yet our freedom is our freedom. Our privacy is our privacy. And, regardless of the attributes of God, an invasion of our freedom/privacy by another or Other or holy Other is still an infringement of our freedom/privacy. The probability that we do not comprehend the parameters of the possible intrusion only aggravates the intrusion. It does not ameliorate the intrusion.

One can make a case that privacy is an important component of liberty; that intrusions into privacy are intrusions into liberty; that intrusions into liberty ultimately lead to intrusions into privacy.

Man cannot demand both complete personal freedom with concomitant privacy, and, at the same time, a God who intervenes when peril threatens. With freedom comes risk. For the Jew this risk is doled out generously.

Thus, God's omniscience inherently conflicts with man's privacy needs. Man's need for privacy is symbolized by the need of Adam and Eve for clothing subsequent to eating from the Tree of Knowledge. The concept of the Deity as all-knowing and all-watching in the here-and-now is thus somewhat anomalous to the privacy needs of post-Edenic man. The fact that

God's knowledge is different from man's does not obviate the problem. It may be presumed that a significant portion of mankind desire privacy vis-à-vis all intellects equal to or greater than man's.[476]

Norman Lamm writes:

> The *Halakhah*'s legal and moral doctrines of privacy can be shown to be based upon certain fundamental theological considerations. The Bible teaches that man was created in the image of God, (Gen. 1:26, 27) by which is meant that the creature in some measure resembles the Creator. . . . "Dignity" (*kavod*) is thus a correlative of privacy. . . . As concealment is an aspect of divine privacy, so is it the expression of human privacy. . . . So sacred is this center of privacy in man that even God does not permit Himself to tamper with it; that is the meaning of the freedom of the will, the moral autonomy of man.[477]

> The Talmud records an opinion that once a man has confessed his sins to God on the Day of Atonement, he should not confess them again on the following Yom Kippur—and applies to one who does so the verse, "as a dog that returneth to his vomit" (Prov. 26:11). These are strong words, and they reveal to us the contempt of the Rabbis of the Talmud for the indignity inherent in the loss of privacy—even one's own privacy, and even before his Maker only.[478]

800.32   Privacy and Potential

Privacy would assume a more important place in man's hierarchy of values in the post-Edenic era, and would maintain a distinct relationship with potential.

> And the eyes of them both were opened, and they knew that they were naked.
>
> —Genesis 3:7

> And He [God] said: "Who told thee that thou wast naked? Hast thou eaten of the tree [of knowledge] whereof I admonished thee not to eat?"
>
> —Genesis 3:11

Privacy had become an issue for man of knowledge. For example, sexual relations in private for the purpose of procreation assume dimensions of holiness; sexual relations in public are an abomination.

Achievement of potential requires freedom, and freedom requires privacy. Thus, privacy is linked with potential on several levels.

800.33   Freedom and Responsibility/Selfhood

↑ *freedom* → ↑ *responsibility and* ↑ *self-hood:*[479]

Eliezer Berkovits writes:

> The God who calls man to responsibility is the guarantor of his freedom to act responsibly. As man accepts responsibility, he enters upon his God-given heritage of freedom. Or as the rabbis read it: "Freedom—on the Tablets." Granting him freedom and calling him to responsibility, God has expressed his confidence in his creature, man. This, notwithstanding man's disappointing performance in history, freedom remains for the Jew the foundation of his optimism.[480]

> Man finds the meaning of his human existence in his capacity for decision, in his freedom of choice. It is a dreadful freedom, for it also means responsibility, but without it man would be as nothing.
>
> —Herberg[481]

Thus, man's freedom is linked to man's needs for privacy, responsibility, and selfhood. This multifaceted correlation may be traced back to the dynamic of knowledge/potential chosen by man at Eden.[482]

900

900.10   CONTRACTION OF DIVINE CONSCIOUSNESS

As mankind ascends in knowledge,[483] implicitly demanding more freedom, there is proportional contraction (*tsimtsum*)[484]

of Divine here-and-now consciousness.[485] **This is a primary
form of *Hester Panim* which yields man ever greater freedom,
privacy, responsibility and selfhood—with concomitant potential.[486]**

900.11   Building Blocks

900.11a   Freedom and Divine Consciousness

In order for man to be free, and in order for man to be in a
position to attain his true spiritual heights, man cannot remain
in a position in which God's consciousness protects him from
all threats.[487]

Man cannot enjoy total freedom in an environment of a fully
watching God.

900.11b   Conceptualization

What is here-and-now consciousness? What is contraction of
here-and-now consciousness?

We use the term *here-and-now* synonymously with the term
real-time. Real-time consciousness is knowledge of events in the
here-and-now. Contraction of real-time consciousness would be
the removal of one's knowledge of events in the here-and-now
to a knowledge of events out-of-real-time.

Can man at all conceptualize these concepts, or are they total
abstractions? Man has indeed been given some inkling into the
concepts of real-time and non-real-time knowledge, although
one should not hasten to equate man's range of knowledge
with the Deity's. Rather, one can attempt to draw some rough
parallels in order to grasp the basic concepts.

The specific concept of real-time consciousness as juxtaposed
to non-real-time consciousness has attained a concreteness in
modern times. As a result of twentieth-century physics and an
increased understanding of the speed of light's impact on

perception, man has accepted the idea that human perception of time functions simultaneously on several different levels.

For instance, when we gaze at the stars, what we see is that which existed X light years ago. What we see may no longer exist when we see it. What we do not see may indeed now exist. Man views the heavens in a state of non-real-time consciousness.

Thus, even mortals have practical experience with concepts of real-time and non-real-time observation. This is not meant to imply that the Deity's knowledge levels are the same as man's. In fact we presume both a qualitative and a quantitative difference. The illustration of man's perception of the stars is merely to give one possible example of non-real-time knowledge experienced on a mortal level on a daily basis.

900.11c   Multiple Levels of the Divine

Thus man must seek his potential; potential demands freedom; intellectual attainment demands greater freedom; freedom demands greater privacy and independence; greater privacy and independence demand Divine contraction. Potentially God's consciousness is present throughout real-time and out-of-time. However, in the greater cosmic interest, the potentially infinite real-time consciousness of the Deity is contracted.

Over time, God manifests and contracts His various potentialities to different degrees, to different ends, in different dimensions—all beyond mortal comprehension or perception, in spite of the fact that the general principle is within our comprehension.

"And [if] they say to me, 'What is His name?' what shall I say to them?" and the reply came to him, *EHEYEH–ASHER–EHEYEH* [I–WILL–BE–THAT–WHICH–I–WILL–BE].

—Exodus 3:14

The words "YHVH is His name" are added, then, to teach that . . . a God manifest in history manifests Himself differently according to the exigencies of the historical moment.

—Fackenheim[488]

As an infinite entity, God has infinite levels and possible permutations of manifesting His consciousness—and consequently of intervening with man. In turn, for man to be truly free and to be in a position to fulfill his great potential, there comes a point where a full manifestation of Divine consciousness in the here-and-now cannot be maintained on a steady basis.

The acceptance of *El Moleh Rachamim* and Divine omnipotence as tenets of Jewish theology forces us to address the here-and-now aspect of God's omniscience. For, notwithstanding the need for man's freedom, God's mercifulness should force His hand.

It is indeed emotionally abhorrent to imagine a nonintervening God of Israel watching His children being used for medical experiments sans anesthesia in the factories of death. In the wake of Auschwitz it is difficult enough to maintain a belief in a nonintervening Deity à la Aristotle's Unmoved Mover. It is pressing beyond credible limits to posit an active intervening God during the period.[489] We reject, as a basis for a Jewish theological structure, a God who operates in a Kafkaesque moral theater. We are forced almost inexorably to address at least the here-and-now aspect of God's omniscience.

Thus, an omnipotent Deity can indeed have foreknowledge, and here-and-now omniscience. It is, however, due to the Divine exigencies of the cosmos and the Divine plan for it that God contracts God's consciousness.

Our explication of contraction of here-and-now Divine consciousness as a form of *Hester* should not be viewed as simply an on/off state. Rather it should be viewed as a range or spectrum, ranging from a high level of real-time conscious state to a totally non-real-time conscious state, with infinite multidimensional variations in between.

Norman Lamm points out that in between the two extremes in the relationship between God and Israel—on the one hand, complete severance of the dialogue between God and Israel (classic *Hester Panim*), and on the other hand, resumption of the dialogue *(Nesiat Panim)*—there are intermediate levels indicated by the Talmud.[490] Thus, depending on the level of *Hester,* human prayer or entreaty has commensurate possibilities of penetrating the veils of Divine consciousness (elaborated on below).

The connection between ascent in knowledge and the dynamics of freedom/potential is embedded in the Garden of Eden tale and is not a twentieth-century invention. The concept of every action having a reaction also has applicability on a cosmic level. Ascents in one realm lead to descents in other realms. Thus, when viewed from the above perspectives, one can develop a fair case for positing that ascents in knowledge, on the part of man, lead to an effective quasi-descent, or contraction, in an aspect of knowledge (here-and-now) on the part of the infinite Divine. Man is, after all, a partner with the Divine in creation.

900.11d   Uniqueness of Divine Knowledge

It has been posited by many distinguished philosophers that the Divine exists beyond time or out-of-time.[491] It is also within the bounds of both Jewish and Christian theology that God's knowledge is different from man's knowledge and that it is above time.[492]

Maimonides, for example, removed God from all relation to time. God, according to Maimonides, stands above time. His knowledge, therefore, is unique.

> His [God's] knowledge is not the same kind as ours, but totally different from it.
>
> —Maimonides[493]

> Things reduced to actuality in time are known by us successively in time, but by God they are known in eternity, which is above time.
>
> —Aquinas[494]

Yet religious tradition clearly teaches that the Deity has interacted with man in the here-and-now, e.g., at Sinai. Thus a Deity which exists out-of-time also, at least sometimes, interfaces with man in-time.

Thus it is not a quantum leap to proceed from that point and posit that there are also different levels of Divine consciousness. These might range from here-and-now consciousness through various levels of out-of-time consciousness.[495]

900.11e   Pivot of Our Formulation

Our formulation attempts to reconcile (1) an omnipotent, omniscient, all-benevolent, morally comprehensible Deity with the existence of gross evil; (2) a Deity who clearly interacted with man in the here-and-now in biblical times, yet does not visibly do so in post-Temple times; (3) Man's freedom with God's omnipotence and omniscience; and (4) Maimonides' postulation, with which we agree, that God's knowledge is completely unlike human knowledge, with the concept that man was created *be-tzelem Elokim* ("in the image of God"); (5) the concept of Divine omniscience with concepts of *Hester Panim* ("Hiding of the Divine Face"); and (6) concepts of *Hester Panim* with concepts of *sachar va-onesh* (reward and punishment).

This element of our formulation will pivot on a stratification of Divine omniscience into various modes of omniscience. We will distinguish between (1) here-and-now (real-time) omniscience and (2) a spectrum of non-here-and-now omniscience.

Gersonides hits the crux of the dilemma and grasps at the solution in a way that comes very close to our formulation.

> . . . there remains no alternative but (to posit) that in one way He knows them [particulars concerning man] and in another way He does not know them. Would that I knew what these two ways are![496]

> [Lord] Incline Thy ear to us.
>
> —Isaiah 37:15

When He shall hear, He will answer thee.

—Isaiah 30:23

Ye fast not this day
So as to make your voice to be heard on high.

—Isaiah 58:2

Hear my words, O Lord;
penetrate my thoughtful meditations;
Hearken unto the voice of my cry . . .

—Psalms 5:2–3

Rouse Thyself!
Why sleepest Thou, O Lord?

—Psalms 44:18

For the cause of all is not in the thick darkness, nor locally in any
place at all, but high above both place and time.

—Philo[497]

Thus, our general assertion that Divine omniscience is not
always here-and-now omniscience is not a total innovation on
our part.

900.11f   Parallel of God: Israel to Father: Child

Children, you are, to the Lord, your God.

—Deuteronomy 14:1

And He said: "I will hide My face from them,
I will see what their end shall be;
For they are a very froward generation,
Children in whom is no faithfulness."

—Deuteronomy 32:20

The fact that I have the power to watch over my child when
he is away from home, even without his knowing that I am
watching, does not motivate me to watch him, or to arrange to

have him watched, irrespective of my resources. If I have confidence in him, he may rise to my confidence. If I do not have confidence, he will be less likely to attain his potential level of responsibility.

Conversely, as a young man is not truly free and cannot truly reach his potential while under his father's roof, so too, in parallel, Israel cannot reach its full potential while under the full conscious gaze of the Divine. Thus we posit that civilization, like a child, has various levels of development, and appropriate relationships with the Divine at each level.[498]

> As a father disciplines his child, so God disciplines you.
> —Deuteronomy 8:5

> This is fact that humanity as a whole can exist in four basic states. In this respect, the history of man is very much like the life of an individual. Like a single person, the entire human race is born and reaches maturity.
> —Luzzatto[499]

As far as man is concerned, the state of God at Sinai and the state of God during the Holocaust are but two discrete possibilities of multiple, if not infinite, possibilities of Divine states.

900.12   Grounding

900.12a   *Hester Panim*

Classic *Hester Panim* has been defined as a "temporary suspension of God's active surveillance" (Soloveitchik).[500] We will define "contraction of real-time consciousness" as a form of *Hester Panim*. This "Hiding of the Face" concept has ample citation throughout *Masorah*.

> And I will forsake them, and I will hide my face from them, and they shall be devoured.
> —Deuteronomy 31:17[501]

And I will hide within hiddenness My face in that day.

—Deuteronomy 31:18

And when ye spread forth your hands,
I will hide Mine eyes from you;
Yea, when ye make many prayers,
I will not hear.

—Isaiah 1:12

And I will wait for the Lord,
that hideth His face from the house of Jacob,
and I will look for Him.

—Isaiah 8:15

Verily Thou art a God that hidest Thyself.

—Isaiah 45:14

In a little wrath I hid My face from thee for a moment.

—Isaiah 54:8

I hid Me and was wroth.

—Isaiah 57:15

And your sins have hid His face from you.

—Isaiah 59:1

For Thou hast hid Thy face from us.

—Isaiah 64:10

When He hides His face, who can behold Him?

—Job 34:29

Oh that I knew where I might find Him!

—Job 23:3[502]

Where is there an allusion to Esther in the Torah?
"And I will hide My face" [Deuteronomy 31:18].

—Chullin 139b

. . . in the days of Esther there will be a concealment of the divine countenance.

—Rashi on Chullin 139b

For thus says the Lord, that after seventy years of Babylon are completed, I will remember you and perform My good word concerning you to make you return to this place.

—Jeremiah 29:10

900.12b   Divine Self-limitation

The broader concept of Divine Self-limitation and subsequent emergence also has ample evidence in *Masorah*.

For behold,
the Lord cometh forth out of His place.

—Isaiah 27:2

The Lord is exalted,
for He dwelleth on high.

—Isaiah 33:4

I will hold me still,
and I will look on in My dwelling-place.

—Isaiah 18:5

Seek ye the Lord while He may be found,
Call ye upon Him while He is near.

—Isaiah 55:6

He is God in His holy place.

—Psalms 68:5–6

Oh that I knew where I might find Him!
That I might come even to His seat!

—Job 23:3

He dwells in the highest mystery,
He rests in the shadow of Shadai.

—Psalms 91:1

God's involvement with the realm of finite reality is imaginable
only as an act of divine "self-limitation." . . . He "reduces"
Himself so that He may enter into the narrow straits of a
relationship with finite existence.

—Berkovits[503]

900.12c   Divine Contraction and *Tsimtsum*

Mankind's growth requires elements of Divine contraction.
This is an extension of the important kabbalistic motif that
Divine contraction was/is necessary for the very existence of the
world.

The concept of contraction appears in both the Midrash and
the Kabbalah. In the voluminous kabbalistic literature it often
recurs in many forms. Its principal form is that of *tsimtsum*.

> *Tsimtsum* originally means "concentration" or "contraction," but
> if used in the Kabbalistic parlance it is best translated by "with-
> drawal" or "retreat." . . . The Midrash—in sayings originating
> from third century teachers—occasionally refers to God as hav-
> ing concentrated His *Shekhinah,* His divine presence, in the
> holiest of holies, at the place of the *Cherubim,* as though His
> whole power were concentrated and contracted in a single point.
> Here we have the origin of the term *Tsimtsum,* while the thing
> itself is the precise opposite of this idea: to the Kabbalist of
> Luria's school *Tsimtsum* does not mean the concentration of God
> at a point, but his retreat away from a point.
>
> —Scholem[504]

> How did He produce and create the world? Like a man who
> gathers in and contracts *(metsamtsem)* his breath, so that the
> smaller might contain the larger, so He contracted His light into
> a hand's breadth.
>
> —*Sefer ha-Iyyun*[505]

> The world becomes possible only through the special act of
> Divine withdrawal or contraction [*tsimtsum*]. Such Divine non-
> Being or concealment, is thus the elementary condition for the
> existence of that which is finite.
>
> —Steinsaltz[506]

Thus our formulation is predicated on a parallel Divine *tsimtsum* to carry forward the potential of creation. Metaphorically, the All-Potential Face and the All-Mercy Face of the Divine force a contraction of the All-Power (*Gevurah*) Face and the All-Knowledge Face of the Divine.

Kabbalistic doctrine is far from limited to one version of *tsimtsum*, particularly with regard to creation. There is considerable discussion, including whether or not *tsimtsum* is to be taken literally and whether or not *tsimtsum* is even unitary. (For instance, Aaron ha-Levi of Staroselye bases his system in his work *Avodat ha-Levi* on the premise of a "double *tsimtsum*."[507])

The Midrash applies the concept of Divine contraction/decontraction to the postcreation world, as well.

> Originally God's home manifested in earth's nether sphere; when Adam sinned, it ascended to the first *rakia'* [firmament]; when Cain sinned, it ascended to the second *rakia'*; when the generation of Enosh sinned, it ascended to the third; when the generation of the Flood sinned, to the fourth; with the generation of the separation [of tongues], to the fifth; with the Sodomites, to the sixth, with the Egyptians in the days of Abraham, to the seventh. But as against these there arose seven righteous men: Abraham, Isaac, Jacob, Levi, Kohath, Amram, and Moses, and they brought it down again to earth. Abraham brought it down to the sixth, Isaac to the fifth, Jacob to the fourth, Levi to the third, Kohath to the second, Amram to the first, while Moses brought God's presence down below to earth.
>
> —Bereshit Rabbah[508]

A present-day allusion to another of the many kabbalistic modes of contraction can be found in the writings of Joseph B. Soloveitchik (and Eliezer Berkovits), among others.

> Judaism explains the concept of holiness from the perspective of the secret of "contraction." Holiness is the descent of divinity into the midst of our concrete world—"For the Lord thy God

walketh in the midst of thy camp . . . therefore shall thy camp be holy" (Deut. 23:15)—it is the "contraction" of infinity within a finitude bound by laws, measures, and standards, the appearance of transcendence within empirical reality.

—Soloveitchik[509]

900.12d   Integration of Divine *Hester;* Self-limitation; Contraction

Jewish theologians carry forward the interrelated themes of *Hester,* Self-limitation, and contraction of the Divine.[510]

. . . in a sense, God restricts Himself from seeing evil, as the Prophet exclaims, "Your eyes are too pure to look upon evil, You cannot gaze upon wrongdoing" [Habakkuk 1:13].

—Aryeh Kaplan[511]

. . . one of the basic concepts of man's predicament was that God should hold back His Light and hide His presence.

—Luzzatto[512]

God hides Himself, putting aside His essential infiniteness and withholding His endless light to the extent necessary in order that the world may exist.

—Steinsaltz[513]

The Bible knows of God's hiding His face, of times when the contact between Heaven and earth seems to be interrupted. God seems to withdraw Himself utterly from the earth and no longer to participate in its existence. The space of history is then full of noise, but as it were, empty of divine breath. For one who believes in the living God, who knows about Him, and is fated to spend his life in a time of His hiddenness, it is very difficult to live.

—Buber[514]

. . . the distinction between two types of Divine punishment, *Hester Panim* and *Middat Hadin.* . . . In Deut. 31:17, the Torah describes the ultimate punishment of *Hester Panim:*
    Then My anger will flare up against them in that day and I

will abandon them and hide My face from them, and they
shall be devoured and many evils and distress shall befall
them; so that they will say in that day, "Are not these evils
come upon us, because our God is not in our midst?"
Hester Panim involves a temporary abandonment of the world, a
suspension of His active surveillance, as Rashi clearly explains,
"as though I do not see their distress."

—Soloveitchik[515]

The Holocaust, in Rav Soloveitchik's view, is a case of *Hester
Panim*.[516]

In the context of post-World War II Jewish philosophical
thought, the *Hester Panim* of Rav Soloveitchik is not radical.
However, in the context of the flow of Jewish rabbinic theological doctrine, the attribution of *Hester Panim* to any discrete event
is a major statement, if not challenge, and a courageous attempt
to grapple with the theological conundrum posed by the Holocaust. Indeed, most Jewish philosophers seem unwilling to
grapple with the whole subject, and when doing so, tread very
carefully. The introduction of the concept of *Hester* to the
Holocaust, however, opens a Pandora's box of theological questions, as was probably not unforeseen by Soloveitchik.

By employing *Hester Panim*, one is indeed opening the entire
matter of Providence to examination, elaboration, and extension. For the concept is too highly charged when not carefully
and satisfactorily delimited. Our own Unified Formulation,
which is quite broader in its delimiting of Providence, will
indeed cite the attribution of Soloveitchik and others of *Hester
Panim* to the Holocaust in support of our formulation.

Ascribing the Holocaust to periodic *Hester Panim*, as Soloveitchik seems to do, or, along similar lines, to an "eclipse of God"
à la Fackenheim or Buber, opens a further gamut of extremely
problematic questions: What was the demarcation line, before
and after, and why? If the *Hester* was punishment, for what
sin(s)? Were six million people, including a million children, so
guilty? Was a warning given, and, if not, why not? Even if the
forebears were the sinners, was the denouement commensurate? Under what possible moral schema should innocents born

during the Holocaust period be forced to pay so horribly for others' sins? Does not humankind deserve some Divine protection in spite of its failings? Why did the Divine (suddenly) effectuate *Hester Panim* in the mid-twentieth century? Did the *Hester* neatly end just in time for the establishment of the State of Israel, and if so, why?[517] Does Jewish philosophy neatly turn the Divine on a dime to reconcile the historic turnaround in Israel's fortunes? Or does the *Hester* continue? Is there *din v'mishpat* (judgment and sentence) for those living during a time of *Hester*? Was there *hashgachah* (Providence) outside of Europe, while there was *Hester* in Europe? If the *Hester* was not punishment, why indeed was there *Hester*?

If, during the tragedy, *Hester Panim* is the prevailing state, would not prayer then seem to be efficacious only when it is least needed, and not efficacious when it is most needed? Or is the concept of prayer itself not indeed much more complex and much more difficult than previously accepted by mainstream Jewish theology?

Can one simply declare *Hester Panim* for a discrete, horrific, inexplicable sequence of events without fully addressing the accompanying theological issues?

Thus, providing *Hester Panim* as the neat solution to the problem of the Holocaust, or of evil in general, without providing a complete and synchronous theology to house it, would seem to leave untenable philosophical and theological chasms. When a cataclysmic tragedy befalls the Jewish people, do we conveniently pull out the *Hester Panim* rabbit, only to about-face when dire tragedy is not transpiring and then admonish the masses that their every thought, let alone deed, is currently being monitored by the Deity?

900.12e   Two Overlapping Paths to *Hester*.

Hester Panim is generally pictured by the Bible as punishment. Indeed, this parallels the "establishment" biblical perspective on man's newfound lot of knowledge/freedom/mortality/potential/post-Eden as being a form of punishment.

But this is only a partial truth, for *Hester* has embedded within it potentialities as well.

> In a little wrath I hid My face from thee for a moment;
> But with everlasting kindness will I have compassion on thee,
> Saith the Lord, thy Redeemer.
> —Isaiah 54:8–9

The realm of freedom involves a severe degree of pain, and a paternalistic Deity may be presumed to be wary of subjecting man to the severe possibilities of pain and evil in a world of lessened Providence. A paternalistic Deity has more patience than man regarding man's ultimate quest for potential and growth. However, in an environment where man ignores Divine admonition, in effect asserting an immature form of rebellion, the response of God is truly to give man more of the freedom he is asserting. God will give man further levels of freedom, i.e., *Hester Panim*, commensurate with the magnitude of his rebellion. Man will thus reap the vicissitudes of freedom, along with its worldly pleasures and along with its potentialities.[518]

900.12f   Clarification of Biblical *Hester*

Our formulation integrates the concepts of *Hester Panim*, Divine Self-limitation, Divine contraction, and *tsimtsum*.

The contraction of real-time consciousness clarifies biblical *Hester*. We formally define contraction (*tsimtsum*) of Divine here-and-now (real-time) consciousness as a primary form of *Hester Panim*.

We reinvoke Gersonides' "there remains no alternative but (to posit) that in one way He knows them and in another way He does not know them. Would that I knew what these two ways are." We reject ("minimalist") definitions of *Hester* which do not yield whatsoever on God's surveillance; we reject ("maximalist") definitions of *Hester* which posit a complete suspension of Divine surveillance—in time and out-of-time.[519]

The "minimalists" face a greater challenge reconciling their definition with the clear thrust of Scripture. The "maximalists" face a greater challenge reconciling their definition with the Jewish concepts of Divine omniscience, *din ve-mishpat* (judgment and justice), and *sachar va-onesh* (reward and punishment) for those living within a period of *Hester*.

We choose to define *Hester Panim* as a contraction of real-time consciousness, as opposed to a total severance of consciousness, in order that we may preserve other Jewish concepts of omniscience, omnimercifulness, and *sachar va-onesh*.

We posit that the Divine essentially does not exercise individual *a priori* omniscience for the same general purpose, i.e., to yield man bona fide freedom. If *Hester* were then a total blockage of Divine consciousness—in-time and out-of-time—for a specific period, how does one truly reconcile the other two concepts?

We view both "sin" and "quest for knowledge" as having embedded within them assertions of freedom. Consequently, the result of either or both is an increased contraction of the Divine.

Thus man demands or asserts his freedom in two major ways:

1. by ascent in knowledge, and
2. by sin.[520]

Both result in a lowering of Divine providential care. Both result in higher freedom. Both cause-and-effect relationships appear in the Torah.

At Eden man is admonished that knowledge will yield man the travails of freedom; we postulate that the freedom comes by way of a Divine contraction. Later on man is admonished that extreme sin will yield a complete *Hester*; we postulate that *Hester* means a Divine contraction.

In *I and Thou*, Buber taught that God speaks constantly to man. Many years later he was moved to fall back on the traditional Jewish doctrine of the "Hiding of the Face" and asserted that an eclipse of God is possible at any time.[521]

"Eclipse of the light of heaven, eclipse of God—such indeed is the character of the historic hour through which the world is passing. But it is not a process which can be adequately accounted for by instancing the changes that have taken place in man's spirit. An eclipse of the sun is something that occurs between the sun and our eyes, not in the sun itself. Nor does philosophy consider us blind to God. Philosophy holds that we lack to-day only the spiritual orientation which can make possible a reappearance "of God and the gods," a new procession of sublime images.[522]

900.13   Dynamics of Conflict Resolution

900.13a   Conflict: Divine Presence/Man's Freedom

Specifically, there is a contradiction between the Divine presence and man's freedom.[523] There is a proportionality between the level of God's presence and the level of man's nonfreedom.

> In the presence of God, there is no freedom. No one who stands in God's presence can deny him.
> —Berkovits (on Buber)[524]

> . . . the original religious experience of the encounter [at Sinai] had to be momentary in order to be endured by man; and even while it lasted, the Divine Presence could reveal itself only from behind some protective barrier, or else man could not have survived the "terror" of the Almighty.
> —Berkovits (on Buber)[525]

Consequently, for the very existence of man, let alone for the freedom of man, various dimensions of contraction of the infinite Divine are necessary.

> Every new act of emanation and manifestation is preceded by one of concentration and retraction. In other words, the cosmic process becomes two-fold. Every stage involves a double strain, i.e., the light which streams back into God and that which flows

out from Him, and but for this perpetual tension, this ever
repeated effort with which God holds Himself back, nothing in
the world would exist.

—Scholem[526]

. . . the world becomes possible only through the special act of
Divine withdrawal or contraction. Such Divine non-being or
concealment, is thus the elementary condition for the existence
of that which is finite.

—Steinsaltz[527]

The greatness of God's personality is revealed in the self-limitation of His absolute power so that He may enter into a proper
moral relationship with man.

—Schulweis[528]

900.13b   Conflict: Divine Knowledge/Man's Freedom

One problem with positing a steady-state Divine real-time
omniscience is that it involves a violation of privacy—a privacy
which was mandated at the denouement of the Eden narrative.[529] It also would compel intercession by a merciful Deity to
counter evil at a certain threshold. This second factor would
again limit man's freedom by virtue of the fact that it limits
man's freedom to perform evil or that which might ultimately
lead to evil. Again, freedom to act only in morally prescribed
ways, while in many respects desirable, limits man's freedom
and potential. Since gross evil does exist, we conclude that real-
time omniscience is not a steady-state situation.

For we are disinclined to the notion of a super-stoic Deity
who sits on the sidelines observing great evil and abomination,
and does not intercede in order to achieve "higher" purposes.
For then to what avail is the concept of *El Moleh Rachamim*—a
God full of mercy? To the extent that we anthropomorphize
God's moral interaction with man, following well-established
Jewish traditional doctrine, we plead guilty.

900.13c   Divine Foreknowledge

Divine knowledge has been viewed as being in conflict with human freedom.[530] Most Jewish medieval philosophers, including Saadia, Maimonides, Ibn Daud, and Gersonides, specifically sought to delimit God's foreknowledge in one way or another to safeguard man's freedom. Aristotle had maintained that in general God does not know particulars. Ibn Daud and Gersonides as well as Thomas Aquinas were specifically concerned with Divine foreknowledge, which all three severely circumscribed with regard to "contingent particulars" (particular events which are contingent on other events/decisions/actions) to protect man's freedom.

Ibn Daud wrote:

That it [would be] vanity for a man to plough and to build buildings and to plant plants and to subjugate beasts and to increase acts of mercy and to choose weapons with which to fight, since what will happen already is decreed. Similarly it [would be] vanity to worship God, may He be exalted, since prosperity or its opposite is already decreed. The matter is clear that the truth is the opposite of this.[531]

Ibn Daud perceives a contradiction between absolute freedom of the will and God's foreknowledge. It is inconceivable that a just God would punish man if he were not master of his own actions. Therefore, man must be free. Ibn Daud maintains, however, that this entails a significant modification of the notion of divine omniscience. If a man is free, and if freedom and foreknowledge are incompatible, it must follow that God does not have prior knowledge of man's choices. Nevertheless, argues Ibn Daud, this in no way constitutes an imperfection in the nature of God. If a contingent action is truly contingent, he contends, it cannot be known in advance.

—Bleich[532]

Anthony Kenny critiques Aquinas's philosophy which simultaneously attempts to maintain man's freedom, Divine foreknowledge and Providence:

Accordingly, just as there is a problem how God's foreknowledge may be reconciled with human freedom, so also there is a problem how human freedom may be reconciled with God's providence.[533]

Therefore, either God cannot know what I shall do tomorrow, or else whatever I shall do tomorrow will not be done freely.

—Kenny on Aquinas[534]

The prophet said of Him: "He will be silent in His love" (Zephaniah 3:17). The very silence of God in history is due to His concern with man.

—Berkovits[535]

However, the problem with total *a priori* Divine omniscience is not, as is widely posited, that it *a priori* proscribes human free choice by virtue of the fact that the knowledge of God is immutable. For one can posit that it is theoretically possible, given complete data, including knowledge of thought patterns, for a Deity to know a contingent future. The fact that the Deity knows I will choose to jump off a cliff does not force me to jump off the cliff. If I do not jump off the cliff, the Deity's foreknowledge would simply be different.

The problem with foreknowledge is rather that a merciful and omnipotent Deity would be compelled to tamper with history to ameliorate evil at a given threshold. The possibility of intercession by the Deity thus (1) throws off the initial calculation of foreknowledge—since it is conditional on God's nonintervention; (2) limits man's freedom to commit evil; (3) increases man's dependence; and (4) lowers man's potential. Freedom to act only within the framework of non-gross evil limits man's freedom. Yet gross evil does exist, implying significantly delimited Divine foreknowledge of particulars, if we are to simultaneously preserve the concepts of man's freedom and God's omnipotence.

Thus, while we might concede foreknowledge of a general ultimate denouement, somewhat in parallel to Saadia Gaon,[536] we are certainly averse to the concept of a willed foreknowledge of anything more particular.

Our basic thrust with regard to foreknowledge would find parallels in Abraham ibn Daud's *Emunah Ramah*[537] and in Gersonides' *Milchamoth Hashem*.[538]

The concept of Divine foreknowledge of particulars would seem in direct contradiction to numerous scriptural narratives. In numerous places Israel is told that if it hearkens to God's word it will be blessed, and if it strays from God's word it will suffer.[539] What is the point of this conditional phraseology if there is Divine foreknowledge of the particulars of Israel's future actions? One must go through logical somersaults, not only to reconcile human freedom with Divine foreknowledge, but in the attempt to reconcile the clear intent of scriptural text itself.

The "*Hester* minimalists" (who retain essentially complete Divine surveillance even during *Hester*) can more easily posit Divine foreknowledge, as foreknowledge does not directly contradict the implications of their minimalist definition of *Hester*, but face formidable and hitherto unassailable barriers to erecting a satisfactory theodicy. The "*Hester* maximalists" (who posit a complete blockage of Divine surveillance during *Hester*) are in an opposite situation, and face the manifold additional problems regarding Divine omniscience, judgment, and reward and punishment noted previously.

900.14   Summation (of Section 900.10)

900.14a   Divine Attributes

Jewish philosophy is on the wrong track when it first attempts to provide a detailed delineation of the attributes of the Divine,[540] and then tries to provide a construct explaining man's relationship with the Divine. Rather, Jewish philosophy should first try to outline the parameters of man's relationship with the Divine, being bound only by core concepts regarding Divine attributes. Only then should it even consider trying to provide a more detailed delineation of Divine attributes, and then only insofar as attributes are mandated by the Divine-mortal interaction.[541]

In general, when attempting to delineate the Divine, one is on much safer footing positing what the Divine is not, rather than positing what the Divine is.[542] To take Maimonides a step further,[543] we would add that one is on surer footing positing what God does not always do, rather than positing what God always does. Therefore we posit that the Divine does not always exercise here-and-now omniscience.

Who is like the Lord our God
    Who is enthroned on high?

—Psalms 113:5–6

For My thoughts are not your thoughts,
    Neither are your ways My ways,
        saith the Lord.
For as the heavens are higher
        than the earth,
So are My ways higher than your ways,
    And My thoughts than your thoughts.

—Isaiah 55:8

"To whom then will ye liken Me,
    that I should be equal?"
        Saith the Holy One.

—Isaiah 40:26

Can we conceptualize a Divine of various levels of contracted consciousness? Can we live with a post-*churban* II God of severely contracted consciousness? While we posit a rational morality of God, should we not posit a more conventional Divine omniscience?

900.14b   Proportionality

According to many Jewish theologians *Hester Panim* is generally viewed as punishment and as historically exceptional. Under our formulation, where *Hester Panim* is increasing as man's knowledge is increasing, a high level of *Hester Panim* is treated as an exception only in pre-*churban* II (destruction of the Second Temple) times.[544] In the post-*churban* II era, we would treat it as increasingly the rule.[545] This approach parallels the views of Soloveitchik and Lamm, among others.

> In the Second Temple siege, God did not show up, like the cavalry in the last scene of a Western movie, to save the day. God had, as it were, withdrawn, become more hidden, so as to give humans more freedom.
>
> —Greenberg[546]

> The Second Destruction means the end of prophecy; direct revelation is inappropriate in a world where God is not manifest.
>
> —Greenberg[547]

> Historical existence has been stripped of sacral implication for more than two centuries.
>
> —Cohen[548]

> Rabbi Eleazar lamented that, ever since the destruction of the Temple, the gates of prayer were closed, and only those of tears were still open. In earlier Jewish experiences the divine self-concealment had only been partial and temporary. Now it seemed otherwise. Now Rabbi Eleazar was forced to say: "Since the day of the destruction of the Temple, a wall of iron separates Israel from her Father in heaven."
>
> —T. B. Berachot[549]

> The period of openly revealed miracles ended with Esther and Mordechai. A new emphasis was added to Jewish history. We had to find God's hand not in the splitting sea or heavenly fire, but in everyday events.
>
> —Resisei Laylah[550]

900.14c   Dichotomy

The purpose of man is to achieve his own potential growth, spiritual and otherwise. To that end, as man's implicit demand for increased freedom has grown, there has been a contraction of here-and-now Divine omniscience. The path is cleared for man to achieve fuller growth. The Deity, who is omnipotent and just, assumes an increased state of contracted omniscience and omnipresence, to allow man to quest for his own limitless possibilities.

Thus the crucial dichotomy: On the one hand, holy quest for potential is the underlying motif of the cosmos. It flows through every fiber of life to the ends of the universe. On the other hand, the Divine consciousness is increasingly contracted out of the here-and-now.

> He [the Divine] is everywhere but at the same time above and outside everything. When man who has just beheld God's presence turns around to address himself to the Maker of creation in the intimate "Thou," he finds the Master and Creator gone, enveloped in the cloud of mystery, winking to him from the awesome "beyond."
>
> —Soloveitchik[551]

900.20   INCREASE IN EVIL

As the contraction of real-time Divine consciousness continues, (as mankind ascends in knowledge and freedom) there is a commensurate lower incidence and level of direct particular Providence—for the sake of the general Providence of allowing mankind to reach its full potentialities.

As mankind in general ascends in knowledge, more and more heinous evil goes unchallenged, as there is an ongoing contraction of here-and-now Divine consciousness, a Hiding of the Divine Face.[552] The consequence is a greater level of evil—as the evil is real-time and the Divine consciousness is increasingly not.[553]

900.20a   Omnipotence and Omnimercifulness

Divine omnipotence can counter evil, and the imperatives of Divine benevolence indeed drive the Divine to counter evil. But the core Divine imperative of Holy Quest for Potential mandates Divine contraction so as not to allow the confrontation between the imperatives of Divine mercy and the imperatives of Divine potential. Contraction holds the two Divine imperatives at bay. We must conclude that a confrontation between the imperatives of Divine mercy and the imperatives of Divine potential would unleash the classic clash of the irresistible force meeting the unmovable object—yielding cosmic cataclysm.

900.20b   Evil and *Hester*

Evil and *Hester* are interlinked. The Midrash notes:

> As long as the seed of Amalek exists in the world, it is as though a cover hides the face of the Divine.
>
> —Pesikta[554]

Moses Hayyim Luzzatto directly interlinks kabbalistic Divine contraction (*tsimtsum*) and evil, although from a different perspective than ours. As Scholem notes in commenting on this point, "The metaphysical root of evil is inherent in the very act of privation that the act of *zimzum* [*tsimtsum*] involves." [555]

But is the contracted Divine consciousness impervious to the travail of Israel?

> There the angel of the Lord appeared to him in a flame of fire out of the midst of the bush; he [Moses] looked, and there was the bush burning with fire—yet the bush was not consumed.
>
> —Exodus 3:2

Among the several Midrashim on the burning bush which Nehama Leibowitz cites is the following:

> Don't you feel that I suffer anguish when Israel does? Know, therefore, from the character of the place from which I am speaking to you, out of the thornbush, that I, as it were, share their suffering.[556]

This is the same Midrash which Rashi selected as the basis for his exegesis. Leibowitz incorporates and ties together the themes of Israel's suffering, Divine *Hester,* and Divine suffering.

He who has decreed persecution and suffering on the seed of Abraham, and hid his face from them, for centuries, is not a cruel Deity, arbitrarily abusing His creatures. . . . He suffers with them, as the Psalm expresses it: "I will be with them in trouble" (Psalms 91:5).[557]

Twelve sentences following the first mention of the burning bush, the Divine relates His name to Moses: *Eheyeh Asher Eheyeh,* "I-Will-Be-That-Which-I-Will-Be." The God of Potential suffers alongside His children, through the millennia, just as the burning thornbush's travail is not quenched.

The Midrash explains the double usage of *Eheyeh:* "I will be with you in your current suffering, and I will be with you in your future travail."

A third-century Midrash pictures God as waking up in the middle of the night and roaring in pain like a wounded lion, for His Temple is burned, and His people are exiled.[558]

900.20c   Divine Intervention and Man's Freedom

A spectrum of viewpoints exists regarding the level and frequency of the Deity's intervention. Most would agree that intervention is in an inverse relationship to man's freedom; i.e., the more intervention, the less freedom. One could go even further and posit that even in a world which had hitherto experienced no intervention on a personal level, even a remote possibility of Divine intervention would negate the broad concept of man's freedom.

Thus, while some groups see a need to discern miracles to "prove" God's existence, in actuality the greater the limits Judaism places on possibilities of God's intervention, the surer footing it is on philosophically. Divine intervention contravenes concepts of man's freedom; possibilities of Divine intervention aggravate the problem of theodicy. Although Judaism is certainly receptive to the concept of miracles, in fact Judaism does not need miracles to prove the Deity's munificence. Creation, nature's wonder, and ongoing life-cycles are more than sufficiently wondrous. That is, the "mundane" is indeed miraculous in and of itself.[559]

To take matters one step further, one can fairly posit that in the context of an all-merciful God (*El Moleh Rachamim*), a God always watching in the here-and-now poses almost as severe a problem as a God intervening in the here-and-now. For the *rahamim* (mercy) aspect will presumably impel intervention at a given threshold (if Divine mercy is even remotely similar to human mercy). And intervention, or the possibility of intervention, leads us into the philosophical dilemmas noted above.

Emphasizing the concept of intervention raises a plethora of philosophical problems, many already interconnected with theodicy.[560]

Why is there evil extant at all, especially during periods of manifest Divine intervention?

Does man rule the earth or not?

To what extent will the intervening Deity violate the laws of nature?

Thus Divine intervention, while emotionally gratifying, is philosophically problematic.

900.20d   Knowledge and Evil

ascent in technology/knowledge → greater unleashed evil

Thus, if ascent in knowledge carries within it an implicit demand for greater freedom, intervention and its prerequisite here-and-now omniscience must be limited to whatever extent is consistent with other Divine imperatives and broader-scale Divine Providence. At the same time that increases in knowledge open the gates of freedom and potential, increases in knowledge also inexorably lead to more manifest evil,[561] as the Divine contraction of consciousness proceeds.[562] Furthermore, the pain is not distributed equally. Man pays a severe price for knowledge, freedom, and potential.[563]

The narrative of the expulsion from Eden is followed by the chapter of Cain's fratricide. Man, now the proud possessor of higher levels of knowledge, wastes no time in exercising the exclusive talent of fratricide.

> For in much wisdom is much vexations;
> And he that increaseth knowledge increaseth sorrow.
> —Ecclesiastes 1:18[564]

Thus, although the simple correlation is between knowledge and freedom, it would be a mistake to stop at that point. For the attainment of knowledge, which is a spur to greater freedom, in turn actualizes greater potential on all fronts—good and bad.[565]

As the freedom component of the Tree of Knowledge paradigm comes to the fore, Israel, in particular, must be strong on all fronts, moral and physical. As the primal crucible of God's will, it becomes subject to, and magnet for, greater negative forces. Israel therefore pays a high price for its particular status and for its freedom.

The fact, however, that the real-time consciousness of the Divinity is contracted to a great extent does not preclude entirely the possibility of the reversal of the process. The Divine intervened in all His majesty to remove Israel from the slavery of Egypt. Should mankind become enslaved beyond an unknown threshold, or should the evil or its consequences penetrate the veil of cosmic consciousness, a decontraction is not entirely precluded regardless of the damage to human freedom.[566] For freedom is of limited value if there are no living players left to practice.[567]

His hand is "stretched forth" to protect us from oblivion.

—Lamm[568]

900.20e   General Providence

In our schema, God manifests His care and concern for humanity—His Providence—by allowing mankind to develop in freedom and reach its fullest cosmic potentialities.[569] According to Aristotle, Providence extends only to entities that are eternal, e.g., the moon (Aristotle's assumption of the eternality of astronomical phenomena was, of course, incorrect.) Providence is manifested in laws of nature and is expressed in the constancy of these laws in their operation of the wonderment of creation. A state of *Hester* thus de facto brings Providence somewhat closer to the Aristotelian formulation.

> *Hester Panim* is not a rejection of the original *beri'ah* (creation); this would destroy the world. Instead it is the undoing of the restraints and controls of *yetzirah* (formation) while God still remains the sustainer of creation.
>
> —Soloveitchik[570]

If one wishes to challenge our thesis on the (incorrect) grounds that it denies Providence,[571] one might be missing the larger meaning of Providence. For the ultimate Providence may be in securing mankind's freedom and potential for (primarily spiritual) growth and ultimate perfection, an attainment conceivably possible only in an environment of proportionate contracted real-time omniscience.

According to Philo, the miracles worked by God in nature and the miraculous power of the freedom of the human mind are two forms of the same Providence by which God governs the world.[572]

900.20f   The Holocaust

It is therefore neither coincidence nor ironic that probably the most heinous mass crime against the Jews was effected through modern technology by technocratic superstars. For an age which manifests an exponential increase in knowledge also manifests a Divine *Hester.*

As man ascends intellectually in the days ahead, with all the wondrous positive potential inherent in this ascent, further challenges loom to the spirit of man.

> The Holocaust was an advance warning of the demonic potential in modern culture. . . . the strain of evil is deeply embedded in the best potentials of modernity.
>
> —Greenberg[573]

The realities of the Holocaust answer for that period, at least, the question of classic individual Providence. To insist on classic individual Providence for the Jewish children of Europe is simply to imply a God-turned-satanic controlling the cosmos.[574]

900.30   INVIOLABILITY

Quest for potential is an overarching and inviolate holy cosmic dynamic. A violation of quest for potential would be a violation of a core Divine dynamic—which was integral to creation itself, integral to the Divine essence, and integral to the potential of the cosmic order.

Holy Divine potential flows from the epicenter of the Divine through all life.[575] Therefore, it is not in the cosmic interest to limit potential. This inviolate core dynamic is reflected in man, God, and the universe at large.

Indeed, Divine contraction to foster man's growth and freedom is not only for the sake of man, but also for the sake of the Divine and the cosmic order. For the Divine is averse, as well, to a confrontation between the Mercy Face of God and the "Potential" core of the Divine. As man ascends the ladder of knowledge, implicitly demanding more freedom en route to greater potentiality, the Divine core of Potential preempts the

All-Mercy Face of the Divine, effecting a greater contraction of here-and-now Divine consciousness. For the inviolability and integrity of the holy core dynamic—"quest for potential"—must be vigilantly protected.

To undermine "quest for potential" would undermine the very core of the Divine and of Divine Creation. This is the true underlying message of the Jobian finale. Job's protestations of gratuitous suffering bring forth the Divine response in two complete chapters devoted to the Divine as the source of the wonder of creation. At the crux of Divine Creation—quest for potentiality—lies the elusive solution to the problem of theodicy.

The Divine "response" to Job begins as follows:

> Where wast thou
> when I laid the foundations of the earth?
> Declare if thou hast the understanding! . . .
> Whereupon were the foundations thereof fastened? . . .
> When the morning stars sang together,
> And all the creations of God shouted for joy . . .
> Canst thou bind the chains of the Pleiades,
> Or loose the bands of Orion?
>
> —Job 38:4–13

Upon closer observation and interpretation in light of our formulation, the dazzling Divine response is seen as one not of ultimate unfathomability, but rather as one of cloaked fathomability, concealed in the majestic spendor of Divine poetry. It is this same inviolate core dynamic, which was central to the Divine creation of the foundations of the earth and of the multiplicity of wondrous Divine creations, which ultimately allows gratuitous evil to go unchallenged in the millennia to come later.

The dynamic of "quest for potential" is crucial to the Divine, crucial to creation, and crucial to theodicy. This is implicit in the message of the Jobian finale. In retrospect, the solution to theodicy required the discernment of a dynamic of such all-transcending power; else the all-merciful, all-powerful Divine would have certainly found a way to counter gross evil. Only a dynamic of the overarching power and inviolability of "quest for potential" could initiate a contraction of Divine here-and-now consciousness, which in spite of the glorious potentialities flowing therefrom, would in turn also allow evil such widespread dominion.

PART III
Summation and Reprise

1010.00   UNIFIED FORMULATION: GENERAL BUTTRESS

We have presented a theodicy which preserves concepts of Divine omnipotence and benevolence in the context of a unified theology/philosophy. We have presented a unified metaphysics within the constraints of Jewish doctrine, consistent with its historical development and consistent with secular scientific thought.

The themes we have focused on are subtle, but are implicit in the biblical text. It is appropriate that our generation, which first saw its fellow Jews stare with horror into the dark abyss, and now witnesses the denizens of the entire planet standing on the precipice, should bring these themes to the surface.

When Jonah protests God's reversal of Jonah's prophecy that Nineveh would be destroyed, God replies:

> Thou hast had pity on the gourd, for which thou hast not labored, neither madest it grow; which came up in a night, and perished in a night: and should not I have pity on Nineveh, that great city, wherein are more than sixscore thousand persons that cannot discern between their right hand and their left hand, and also much cattle?
>
> —Jonah 4:10 f.

What are we to say in the face of far greater evil and destruction? In order to reconcile the evil of the past, our formulation reverses direction and looks to the ultimate purposes of man.[576]

> ... theodicy must be eschatological in its ultimate bearings. That is to say, instead of looking to the past for its clue to the mystery of evil, it looks to the future, and indeed to that ultimate future to which only faith can look.
>
> —Hick[577]

Our formulation views the cosmos as encompassing the interaction of many dualities. These contain potential for evil, which is the inexorable consequence of the creation of potential for good.[578] In this environment, man, God, and the cosmos all seek to achieve their potentials.

> Light is steadily pitted against the dark, and light will increasingly overcome the dark. In Rabbi Kook's words [in *Orot Hakodesh*]: "Nothing remains the same; everything blooms, everything ascends, everything steadily increases in light and truth. The enlightened spirit does not become discouraged even when he discerns that the line of ascendence is circuitous, including both advance and decline, a forward movement but also fierce retreats, for even the retreats abound in the potential of future progress."

> This vision of development "gives us ground optimism in the world" in the face of all discouragements.[579]

But in order to realize his ultimate quests, man must operate from a base of freedom—the ultimate Divine gift.

> But I prefer to live in a world in which man has the right to make choices, albeit wrong choices, rather than a world in which no choice at all is left to him. In other words, I prefer a world in which, on the one hand, a phenomenon such as Adolph Hitler may occur, and, on the other hand, phenomenon such as the many saints who have lived.
>
> —Frankl[580]

> God willed man to be free.
>
> —Soloveitchik[581]

> Out of distress I called upon the Lord; He answered me in freedom.
>
> —Psalms 118:5

However, the free will defense, in isolation from concepts of quest for potential and the motif of Divine contraction, ultimately fails. For the free will defense requires a radical reinterpretation of the central concepts of Divine omnipotence and omnimercifulness.

Only by tracking back to creation and discerning a core cosmic dynamic directly impacting theodicy, can a viable theodicy be constructed. This general imperative and line of attack was realized most acutely by the Lurianic kabbalists. However, in their earnest fervor they pressed way beyond areas of mortal competence and objective conjecture, and found themselves in the elusive arena of mysticism.

1020.00   PERSON TO PERSON

Over the millennia, man has often suffered most terribly. The price of freedom has indeed been a high one. Much of the suffering has been way beyond the ken of those who did not experience it.

When tragedy strikes, the aggrieved individual must first be comforted. Any attempt to explain away tragedy is fraught with peril, particularly on a person-to-victim level. To the family which has buried a youngster killed by a hit-and-run driver, there is little solace to be found in any quarter. While the family is in intense mourning, bystanders can only extend their hand in empathy and compassion.

However there are, as well, circumstances when a philosophical response is appropriate, if not mandated. The aggrieved, or the witness, may then find some small measure of consolation in the concept that reality need not negate his religious optimism, nor negate his belief in core doctrine. The Divine attributes of omnipotence, omniscience, and benevolence are intellectually defensible.

The witness to this tragedy, and ultimately the family itself, trying to reconcile the God of Israel with the severe tragedy of the youngster killed in the hit-and-run, may possibly find some measure of solace in the themes presented by this study. If there were no potential for tragedy, there would be no potential for triumph or growth. The two come wrapped inextricably together. And if there were no potential for growth and quest for ultimate potentiality, there might have been no creation at all. No triumph at all. No stars at all. No children at all. No love at all. No laughter at all. Literally.

The aggrieved may find some comfort in the concept that his pain is, rather, part of the high price humanity pays for its freedom, and for the possibility of ultimately realizing its full potential; that the individual's tragedy was unlikely to have been punishment, and at the same time did not occur for naught; that while the particular tragedy was not part of a specific Divine plan, the allowance of tragedy in general is a cosmic necessity, and on that level may be considered part of an ultimate schema. For man must operate at an increasingly higher level of freedom if he is to have bona fide potential for a higher good—in his quest towards ultimate potentiality.

Quest for potential is central to the Divine and central to creation. Unfortunately, the allowance for potential pain, however gratuitous and arbitrary, is apparently necessary to the cosmic order.

It is not that the cosmic order needs occasional tributes of pain and premature death. On the contrary, the cosmic imperatives would be maximized if all children could somehow live forever. The loss of the youngster to the hit-and-run tragedy is a very real cosmic loss. Cosmic quests, as well, are truncated by the loss of the youngster.

The cosmic order does not necessitate pain *per se*. It does necessitate, however, the possibility of pain. This was the "ransom" paid by "life" in its escape from the bottomless cosmic void. Man chose the Tree of Knowledge/Potential at Eden. He rejected zero-growth.

And as the battered, but still quite powerful, starship of mankind continues its zig-zag odyssey towards the infinite, the harsh price man pays for the possibility of reaching his destination is the potentiality for tragedy and pain. There would seem to be no alternative.

> The gods, if gods there be, cannot lift us to their side; we must make the painful climb ourselves.[582]

True, suffering and tragedy is personal and unique. And it is difficult to say how we ourselves would react to our own theodicy formulation in the face of overwhelming personal tragedy—nor do we wish to find out. And perhaps it is not even of consequence. Regardless, core doctrine, historical reality, and the dictates of logic, in concert with the mandatory internal intellectual cohesiveness of Judaism, almost inexorably lead us to our formulation as a viable philosophical approach.

As paradoxical as the situation may be, theodicies are generally more appropriate for the witnesses—near and far—to tragedy, than for the more direct victims in the throes of their sorrow. The victim to tragedy has entered his own universe, which outsiders may penetrate emotionally long before tapping into intellectually.

Buddhism would posit the wisdom that he who has been shot by an arrow has no use to inquire into the name of the archer, but rather must extract the arrow, heal the wound. Many rabbinic theologians would seem to posit that the arrow-shot victim's challenge does not go beyond finding out how to extract the arrow within the framework of health and halachic requirements.[583] Inquiry into questions of ultimate justice and purpose on the part of the arrow-shot victim, according to this viewpoint, is not appropriate.

However, philosophy and religion cannot isolate the victim into an airtight compartment. The tragedy of one individual, just as the spiritual upliftment of one individual, in varying degrees affects the whole. The whole, consequently, has an "interest" in the individual's suffering, transcending the immediate halachic response.

The victim of a remote and forgettable tragedy is at the center of concentric circles of "interested parties." Aside from the Divine "interest," these interested parties range from family, through friends and acquaintances, through witnesses and fellow-countrymen, through the remote party a thousand years later who never even heard of the country in which this nameless victim to tragedy belonged. Yet, all ultimately have an "interest" in the response to this nameless tragedy.

Thus, ultimately a philosophical response is in order, if not Divinely mandated as well. At that point, the vitality of the religio-philosophical response is a crucial question.

1030.00   OBSCURITY/AMBIGUITY OF GOD, ETC.

Theologians are often challenged by the following: If God exists and desires our adherence to a certain way of life, why does He remain hidden from man? Why is God's theological system so obscure to us?

The questions are valid ones. Secularists would argue that the balance of evidence has shifted against a compelling religious case. The religious responses center around concepts of freedom, to the effect that in order for man to have true freedom of choice, he must have equally a secular and religious path open to him.[584] If the religious path were overly compelling, he would have no true choice.[585]

As Norman Lamm points out, the Baal Shem Tov interprets a key biblical verse on *Hester Panim,* "And I will hide the hiding of My face from you" (Deuteronomy 31:18), as meaning that "the *Hester Panim* itself is in hiding! The obscurity itself is obscured."[586]

Note also the following:

> The Hebrew word for world, *olam,* comes from a root that means "hidden," for, in this world, the existence of God is hidden. . . . God does not drill faith into our minds and hearts; He places us in an *olam*—world of hiddenness and expects us to find our way to the truth because He has given us enough tools—just enough, barely enough—to find the truth if we really want to find it.
> —Scherman[587]

In a phrase with which Bonhoeffer has made us familiar, the world is *etsi deus non daretur,* as if there were no God. That is to say, the cosmic order is systematically ambiguous, capable of being interpreted either theistically or naturalistically. In such a world the awareness of God takes the form of the cognitive choice which we call faith.

—Hick[588]

The major components of our Unified Formulation, however, are not thoroughly obscure, and to a great extent stare us in the face in the Garden of Eden chapter. The enigma of the Garden lies essentially in discerning what is symbolic, what is literal, and what is shorthand notation. Indeed it is a philosophically exquisite parable—which works. The Garden of Eden tale is indeed the authentic Divine theodicy, and it fittingly leads off the biblical narrative—for theodicy is central to any monotheistic theology.

1040.00   MAN IS NOT ALONE BUT IS ESSENTIALLY ON HIS OWN

Man is not alone in the cosmos, but in his own sphere man is indeed currently essentially on his own. Rather than being despondent that some cherished idols of dependency have proven fragile, man's spirit should be exhilarated. He should be uplifted by the awesome potential he has been given in trust; by the confidence placed in him by his Deity; by the magnitude of his personal freedom.[589]

When on his own, man is truly an extension of, and in the image of, the Divine. As the Divine is free, so is man.

Man's mission is to approach the spiritual heights; to put man in a position to someday grasp the stars. The Divine has given him the blessing/curse of a base of freedom from which to make his quest. Only from this base of freedom does man have the chance of becoming wholly holy. Only when a truly free man accepts upon himself the *ol malchuth Shamayim* ("yoke of heaven") of the Covenant of Abraham and the Covenant of Sinai is the purity of *na-ase ve-nishma* ("we will agree to obey, and then we shall hear your directives") fully reaffirmed.[590]

No one is ever alone; the essence of the temporal is the eternal; the moment is an image of eternity in an infinite mosaic. God means: Togetherness of all beings in holy otherness.

—Heschel[591]

1050.00   MAN OF HALACHAH AND THE UNIFIED FORMULATION

Perhaps, then, for man of Halachah, pain and suffering on earth do carry an implicit reminder to suffering man of the ultimate quest for growth to potential from a base of freedom.[592] Man of Halachah is thereby constantly reminded and challenged that major aspects of his fate are indeed in his own hands.

The spiritual message of pain and suffering on post-Temple earth cannot simply be explained as admonitions or tests. Rather, the reverse: Man must be bold, spiritually and otherwise. He must push towards the bounds of the potential of "free man."[593]

Man of Halachah probably intuitively feels his mandate to fulfill his spiritual potential. He senses the awesome potential of his spirit. The fact that the attached philosophical formulation has not to our knowledge been previously articulated has not prevented him from intuitively grasping its essence.

Man of Halachah knows that God has not abandoned him, that his ultimate interests are indeed under the aegis of God. Potentially man can reach out to God, and God can potentially reach out to man.

A religion predicated on "free man" naturally shows an emphasis distinct to itself. The sanctification of freedom, as well as a careful delineation of an approach to life for man who is often "on his own," will be given high priority. The development of spiritual heights will take a clear priority over the obeisance aspects.

Judaism charts a route to these ends through *taryag mitzvoth* (the 613 precepts of Jewish Law) and a life lived in a prescribed manner within clearly delineated parameters. By walking within this prescribed path, and by building upon it according to individual needs and strengths, man builds upon his own spiritual potential and constructs a spiritual edifice which transcends the cosmos. Finite man, by spiritual extension, achieves a degree of infinitude.

If man indeed has such a wide latitude of freedom and choice, why then choose a religious approach, or any approach at all? If potential for spiritual growth is one of the primary motivators of the cosmos, and if a religious commitment is a route to spiritual growth, man has sufficient motivation for choosing a religious approach to life.

The Garden of Eden is generally considered a discrete event. Man tasted of forbidden "knowledge" and was "punished." But what if Eden is to be considered a continuing process, and what if the "punishment" came bonded with a gift? Man continues to ascend intellectually and to taste of more and more knowledge. The intellectual demands for freedom, responsibility, privacy, and selfhood continue to mature. As the *Shechinah* continues to contract Its real-time consciousness, negative forces have greater and greater leeway. But man's potential is at its highest level when his freedom is greatest.

Redemption must be achieved from a base of freedom, which also implies an environment of ascendant evil. As man's intellectual base advances, both of these criteria become more manifest. The Hasidic rebbe who consoled his flock, en route to their impending doom in a Nazi camp, by interpreting their travail as a harbinger of the coming of the Messianic age, was not necessarily out of line philosophically. For "redemption" cannot be seized from an environment of either slavery—or bliss. And out of the depths of evil, the potentialities of good can conceivably be snared.

Free man is obligated to protect his freedom and dignity.[594] When man—created in the image of God—yields, however slightly, on his dignity, he also yields on the dignity of the God who created him. When man allows himself to be dragged into slavery—and does not obsessively resist to the utter limits of the plausible—he also yields on Divine dignity.

Man, who has been granted the infinitely precious gift of freedom, must guard it with obsessive vigilance. Granted that we are geniuses in retrospect, nevertheless the lessons must be ingrained into the cumulative consciousness. For the Jew, in particular, has learned that, incredible as it might be to conceptualize, the forces of evil will, in one way or another, ultimately coalesce yet again to strike at man's freedom and dignity.

A new era of possibility

Judaism today is in a position without precedent. Major elements are in place for a bona fide Golden Age of Jewry quite capable of equaling the Golden Age of Spain in creativity, intensity, and scope. The American Jewish community and the State of Israel have each been impressive in their respective spheres. The American Jewish community is at a historical apex, and the State of Israel is at a 2000-year historical apex.

Each community has built up powerful, diversified, and continually expanding educational infrastructures along with well-developed intracommunity communications media. Each community is independently vibrant. An accelerated maturation process is also evident. Increased cross-fertilization between the two major Jewish communities alone, let alone the interaction with the secular world, complete with new and expanded Jewish Studies, Religion, and Bible departments at universities throughout the Western world, present excellent ingredients for achieving a critical mass of intellectual dynamism.[595]

Yet at the same time (naturally, we would maintain), man stands at the gates of self-annihilation. Should man succeed in destroying himself, and extinguish the possibility of reaching his human potential this time around, will the infinite potential of the primary essence be less infinite? Would the cosmic mandate fold back on itself towards the infinitely minute—only to be *boreh* ("creating") once again later on through the eons?

Or is the viability of the human race hopefully inherent in the initial actualization of God and the cosmos?

Will man seize his spiritual potential as his freedom ascends even higher and reaches its greatest level? Or, as man's knowledge ascends to new peaks, will man be seduced by the forces of evil into employing his newfound superknowledge for self-liquidation?

Is everything ultimately relatable by a multidimensional equation?

Do spiritual umbilical cords ultimately unite us all—mortal and immortal—traversing the cosmos?

Within a panoply of unknowns, mankind and individual man must, and certainly will, quest after their many and multivaried potentialities. It is the ultimate imperative of man created in the image of God.

1060.00   UNIFIED FORMULATION: WRAP-UP

The Unified Formulation fits well with the general trend of Jewish history, with the concept of the ascent of man, and with the intellectually vigorous thrust of Jewish history. It fits well with our concepts of freedom and privacy, while not limiting the potential total omniscience of the Primal Force. It reconciles manifest intervention in Pharaoh's Egypt and apparent nonintervention in Hitler's Europe. It validates the authentic views of those who went to their deaths at the hands of the Nazis fully believing in the God of Israel, and those who went to their deaths finally and completely rejecting the classic watching God of Israel. For in a sense both were correct.

God, indeed, is not sitting outside the crematorium watching while infants are being burned alive. Because it is an abomination to the essence of *El Moleh Rachamim*. It must presumed that God is in a state of contracted real-time consciousness for the higher purpose, elected by man, of allowing the totality of infants and men to grow up in a state of bona fide personal

freedom, so that they may grasp for the totality of their potentialities. The price, however, is often high, too high.

Man of reason, man of Halachah, and *homo religiosus* can all
relate to our formulation, albeit on different levels. Our formulation introduces an element of structure into a mysterious
world and almost incomprehensible existence. It offers hope
for the further ascent of man and his ultimate realization of
potential. Thus the theme of potential can be carried through
all stages of historical/religious development, both on a cosmic,
theistic, and human level.

The Unified Formulation is offered as a hypothesis to be
challenged, dissected, and debated within a spirit of positive-
ness towards all thinkers of good will, past and future. Like all
hypotheses, it should be challenged in a spirit of intellectual
and bona-fide religious vigor. Religious pseudo-dogma does
not yield one iota without a battle. However, when the day is
done, the Unified Formulation's integrated cohesiveness and
doctrinal validity will be sustained. For man seeking a religious
approach to life, it will, hopefully, be found to be a logically
compelling, consistent, and unified theological underpinning,
sufficiently finessed to reconcile the major problems in classic
secular philosophy.

Can Judaism survive with a God of contracted real-time
consciousness? Is our religious fervor not undercut? Can Judaism survive without the authoritarian God standing in the room
with us holding God's sledgehammer, watching our deeds and
thoughts in all times in all states? Can Judaism survive if prayer
is less efficacious than the literal meaning of the words might
indicate?

On the other hand, can Judaism truly be comfortable with
the formulation of an infinitely manifested omnipotent, omnimerciful, omnipresent God who observed, albeit in His mysterious ways, the debasement, enslavement, and murder of a
third of His people? What ultimate purpose did a God watching
in real-time calculate as the gas pellets were dropping, hun-

dreds of God's children nakedly, painfully, humiliatingly, and desperately being asphyxiated, hour after hour, day after day, year after year? Does Judaism just shrug its shoulders and go on to other, less intractable matters? Would the Patriarch Abraham, who argued so tenaciously for invidious Sodom, have been satisfied with consigning the Holocaust to the netherworld of the "unfathomable"?

We have attempted to make the case that potential/knowledge/evil/good/freedom/privacy/human dignity/Providence/Divine consciousness/ are all interlocked with each other in a cosmic dynamic geometric relationship, with man as the protagonist; that as man ascends in knowledge, and implicitly in his demand for greater freedom, the Divine Face of *Rachamim* (Mercy) is preempted by the Divine core of Potential.[596]

Man quests for God as the major component of his spiritual quest.[597] But he will also rape, pillage, and murder on the way to the Holy Land in the name of the Holy Crusade in 1096, and will send tens of thousands of his young to die in the marshes of Iraq in the 1980s, so that his Ayatollah's commands are obeyed. All in the name of God. All in the name of a great spiritual quest.[598] Man can be implacable in his resolution to serve his God. Nothing, but nothing, will get in his way.

Man quests for political liberty as part of his quest for freedom. He will electrify the world and launch a French Revolution in the name of liberty—and will then butcher his opponents. Man is implacable in his quest for "liberty" too.[599]

1070.00   REPRISE

In a sense, the post-Holocaust Jew is also the freest Jew in history. He has survived in spite of the fact that he is Jewish. His coreligionists have undergone some of mankind's most nefarious depravity. Indeed, depravity within depravity. Post-Holocaust Jew can be tempted to charge God with a breach of the covenant. Our commonly accepted image of the God of

Israel does not truly survive the Holocaust intact. Certainly, traditional concepts of reward and punishment were once again brutalized along with the innocent victims.

Yet if we postulate a God of Israel wholly directed towards opening the gates to man's infinite potential by granting him ascending levels of freedom as he ascends intellectually, and if we grant a God of Israel contracting His real-time consciousness to grant man this crucial freedom, then our outlook is clearer. A Deity exercising contraction of real-time consciousness for the greater good, man's freedom and potential, clearly—not inscrutably—commits no crimes of breach of covenant or complicity of silence. He is guilty only of the crime of increasing man's freedom—an option exercised by man at Eden.

The Nazi force, which subverted science for its nefarious ends, was a perversion of the dynamics of the Tree of Knowledge and of creation itself. It was anti-individualistic, anti-freedom, anti-privacy, anti-dignity. It claimed the right to enslave and terminate innocent life at will. It was a challenge to God Itself.

Ultimately this "thousand year Reich of Aryan supermen" would be ended by a secular nation-state whose coin of the realm bears the mottos "Liberty" and "In God We Trust." And a thousand years after the dismemberment of the Third Reich, a later generation of Jewish five-year-olds will undoubtedly be taking out their notebooks and learning the *aleph-bet*.[600]

The religion of Israel currently ranges over a spectrum of religious emphasis. In the outside world the Jew is challenged on all fronts. It would seem that man is quite on his own in a confusing world. Yet being on our own should not be demoralizing, but potentializing. More so than ever, the very great potential of the Jew occupies a crucial place in the future of mankind, as mankind itself occupies a crucial role in the future of the cosmic process. Post-Holocaust man is thus a victim of freedom, an inheritor of freedom, and challenged by freedom. Man must stare his freedom in the face and seize his awesome potential from out of it.

Man is on the lookout for Matterhorns to scale. He will build Towers of Babel, pyramids, sphinxes, Taj Mahals, and Temples. He will compose majestic symphonies and gossamer verse. He will quest on all fronts. He will formulate complex theological structures and target the transcendent.

Quests for spiritual growth and freedom may be inexorable, but in their inexorability, not without their price. We have presented what we feel to be a powerful formulation, but are not unaware of the ultimate unfathomability of ultimate matters. Indeed, the pain suffered has not been inconsiderable.

Man simultaneously wants total freedom and the total security of the womb. Yet mankind gave priority to freedom/potential at Eden, and it must be presumed that this is the only route for the cosmos to attain its full realization.

> One day when we came back from work [outside the concentration camp] we saw three gallows rearing up in the assembly place, three black crows. Roll Call. SS all around us, machine guns trained: the traditional ceremony. Three victims in chains—and one of them, the little servant, the sad-eyed angel. The SS seemed more preoccupied, more disturbed than usual. To hang a young boy in front of thousands of spectators was no light matter. The head of the camp read the verdict. All eyes were on the child. He was lividly pale, almost calm, biting his lips. The gallows threw its shadow over him. . . . The three victims mounted together onto the chairs.
>
> The three necks were placed at the same moment within the nooses. "Long live liberty!" cried the two adults. The child was silent.[601]

END[602]

APPENDIX

BAL TOSIF AND THEOLOGICAL DOGMA

Bal Tosif is the proscription against nonmandated additions to Jewish law.

All this word which I command you, that shall ye observe to do; thou shalt not add thereto, nor diminish from it
—Deuteronomy 13:1

Judaism, from its very inception, has been an intellectual revolution. Indeed, it defines an intellectual revolution. The progressive revelation of *Masorah* continues that thrust to this very day. Although some religious leaders feel threatened by, and consequently dismiss, intellectual inquiry, their fears are ungrounded.

Problems arise when rabbinic leaders confuse dogma with opinion. Problems arise when they sincerely but recklessly go beyond required boundaries, dictate new frills to codes not mandated by Halachah, or needlessly and dogmatically over-embellish the attributes of the Divine. Essentially, problems arise when rabbinic leaders needlessly limit the permissible range of opinion. At that point Judaism dilutes its internal intellectual strength, alienates adherents, and yields some of its intellectual primacy.

There is a natural, but intellectually destructive, tendency among religious groups to embellish their Deity's attributes and interventionist proclivities. There is a tendency to canon-

169

ize, as well, authoritarian theories that would best be left uncanonized.

It would be unfortunate for Judaism to yield the intellectual highground it maintains if, from the wide spectrum of viewpoints possible on omniscience and providence, it effectively canonized only the more aggressive and authoritarian theories, in spite of their apparent problems of internal consistency.

One of Judaism's strengths has been its self-limitation, its caution with regard to new restrictions, new obligations, new miracles, and new prophets.

Judaism regards the transgression of *Bal Tosif* seriously. A central thrust of this study is that it is as dangerous to overexpand the attributes of the Divine as it is to overly delimit His attributes. No service is done to God or to Judaism by attributing to God attributes or extensions of attributes which God neither manifests nor desires having attributed to Him.

> Add not unto His words,
> lest He reprove thee,
> and thou be found a liar.
>
> —Proverbs 30:6

We take the philosophical liberty of extending the proscription regarding overextending God's precepts, into a caution against theologically overextending infinite God's manifestations and interventions to areas from which the Deity demurs. Interestingly enough, the *Bal Tosif* proscription is initially cited by the Midrash with regard to the Garden of Eden itself. Eve's overextension of the proscription on eating from the Tree of Knowledge into a proscription on touching the Tree of Knowledge is cited as a major factor in her "ensnarement."[603]

There is a natural inclination among rabbinic elements of certain schools to "keep the masses in line," or to adopt the "most devout" formulation. However, no service is done God by overextending His edicts or by overextending His potentially infinite, but not necessarily manifested, attributes.

Those who stridently insist, as a matter of dogma, on a God who fully and always extends His infinite powers of potential omniscience in all planes of time err in several respects. First of all, they contravene specific text-proofs to the contrary. Secondly, even in the absence of the contravening text-proofs, the proponents of this maximalist line attempt to make the complex unnecessarily simplistic. Third, they are trapped in theodicy. Fourth, they directly contravene rabbinic luminaries, Gersonides and Maimonides in particular.

In an unnecessary attempt to defend God's powers, the overzealous throw theology into the throes of the theodicy and freedom dilemmas. By the needless overextension of basic doctrine, they set man up for disaster and set up doctrine for ultimate paralysis when it encounters reality and logical analysis.[604]

A heavenly voice said to him, "Do not be too righteous!"
—Kohelet 7:16

One can fulfill the imperative of belief in God without believing that God will necessarily always thwart undeserved evil.[605] The concept, prevalent in some quarters, as a matter of inviolate dogma of a steady-state, real-time omniscient, continuously intervening Deity has, unfortunately, caused much suffering to the Jewish people. Many sincere believers slackened up ever so slightly on their vigilance and self-reliance, confusing fate in retrospect with fate in prospect. For a sincere believer who is overly reliant on this inviolate dogma, may not quickly enough rise to thwart his looming enemy.[606]

The damage to the faith of sincere adherents unable to reconcile the common philosophical wisdom with the grossly evil reality defies all calculation. The alienation, as well, of potential adherents is equally beyond measure. A severe price has been paid over the millennia in this regard.

BIFURCATION: SUBJECTIVE VS. OBJECTIVE KEYS TO THE BOOK OF JOB

First Key

In section 70.02 our study bifurcates man's right to claim a rationally moral interaction between man and the Divine.[607] We posit as follows: On the "objective" level—when man is not immediately and directly involved—the inherent right exists. On the "subjective" level—where the individual finds himself in misfortune—the issue is not appropriate. In that situation, imperatives of faith override imperatives of logic.[608]

There are two salient episodes in Tanach which seem to preclude a blanket assertion that man in all cases can demand a rationally moral interaction: (1) the *Akedat Yitzchak* (Binding of Isaac), and (2) the Divine response to Job in the Jobian finale.

The *Akedat Yitzchak*

One may cite God's directive to Abraham to sacrifice his son, Isaac, and Abraham's willingness to do so. But if Judaism was to signal a significant departure from the idol worshipers, where is the differentiation? Are monotheism and efficacy sufficient differentiators? Where is the rational morality of the interaction?

Rashi avoids the whole problem by explaining that God did not instruct Abraham to slaughter Isaac, but rather only to bring him up to the mountain in order to prepare him as a burnt offering (as opposed to consummating the deed). This hardly conforms to the basic thrust of the narrative, however.

The answer rests partially on the "bottom line" point that Abraham was ultimately stopped from the sacrifice by God's angel. However, there are other factors. One might draw the lesson that this God would ultimately not demand child sacrifice, even from the progenitor of the religion, even when the child was a special gift of God.

Thus, if we focus first on the Divine, the initial directive was beyond moral comprehension, but God's final instruction to untie Isaac corroborates our faith in a moral interaction. Inasmuch as the entire episode was a test (*nisayon*), the climactic resolution, from the Divine perspective, was in Abraham's readiness to fulfill its directive.

But what about from Abraham's perspective? How could Abraham countenance child sacrifice? Immanuel Kant, to whom the imperatives of universal morality are absolute, condemns Abraham and argues that the Patriarch should have doubted the authenticity of the call. The Danish theologian Soren Kierkegaard sees in the *Akedah* evidence that faith can sometimes make demands that go beyond morality; the doctrine of the "teleological suspension of the ethical."[609] We demarcate this "sometimes."

Samson Raphael Hirsch points out that while it was God Himself who gave the initial directive of sacrifice, one angel alone was sufficient to countervene the directive in this case.

> If an angel had told him to sacrifice his son, he might not have believed him, because such an order was in utter contrast to everything God had told him in general, and especially in connection with his son, Isaac. But in order to refrain from sacrificing his son, it was enough to send an angel. For that purpose, and to explain the whole original commandment as being a test . . . no extraordinary revelation was needed. This fitted in fully with everything Abraham knew of God.[610]

Eliezer Berkovits (after Rashi) writes as follows:

> When God gave Abraham the command to sacrifice his son, Isaac, he said to him: *"Kach na eth bincha,"* which does not mean as usually translated, "Take now thy son." As has been pointed out in the Talmud (T. B. Tractate Sanhedrin 89b), the Hebrew word *na* indicates a request.[611]

Berkovits says the request was asking Abraham not to fail God. But perhaps the entire *Akedah* was a request and not a command. The moral issue, while still vexing, is then severely reduced.

Perhaps one may further argue that when it came to Isaac, the normal had long been suspended. From a natural perspective, Isaac should never have been born. If any given child is a Divine gift, then Isaac was certainly a super-Divine gift. Not only that, but Isaac is quasi-sanctified by God as Abraham's heir, the progenitor of an eternal people, as numerous as the sands and stars. Isaac had been wrapped up in the supranatural before he was even conceived. Isaac is historically unique. Looked at from this perspective, we may simply be unable to draw conclusions regarding moral interaction between God and man translatable to the more mundane.

However, from our moral perspective, Abraham's readiness to sacrifice his son, notwithstanding the most unique circumstances surrounding Isaac, notwithstanding the mores of the time, and notwithstanding the Divine directive, clearly indicates that the right to claim a rational morality in the human-Divine interaction is not a "given," across-the-board right.

Abraham's forthright and almost brazen remonstrations on behalf of Sodom, related a few chapters earlier in the text, show his profound understanding of, and God's receptiveness to, the moral underpinnings of the human-Divine interaction. Indeed, it shows Abraham's insistence on a rationally moral interaction. Clearly, Abraham was very much aware of God's moral commitment.[612] And perhaps it was on the strength of this previously requited faith in this ultimate moral commitment that Abraham proceeded.

But we must ultimately conclude that Abraham's readiness to sacrifice instructs an eternal lesson: The prophet, theologian, or any individual can only seek a rational interaction on issues in which he is not directly involved. When an individual, like our forefather Abraham, is at the vortex of the storm, he must ultimately act on faith in an ultimate morality.

*

Third parties to tragedy may cautiously question the moral/
philosophical underpinnings of the Divine/human interaction.
But primary parties to suffering leave the realm of those who
may intellectually challenge. They enter a new realm—that of
those whose faith is tested in the crucible of suffering.

Job

In the case of Job, we observe what on the surface appear to
be conflicting signals from the Divine on the issue of the
rationally moral aspect of the human-Divine interaction. In the
finale God seems to reproach Job's insistence on his right to
clear Divine justice: "Where wast thou when I laid the foundations of the earth? Declare if thou hast the understanding" (Job
38:4). Yet He reproves Job's friends as well for their dismissal
of Job's protestations. ". . . ye have not spoken of Me the thing
that is right, as My servant Job has" (Job 42:7).

Summary: Dual Keys

It would seem that at times the Divine importunes a challenge
that demands Divine adherence to "moral standards." The
seeming contradiction would seem to be clearly resolved by our
formulation: It is not the place of the sufferer Job to protest
God's "injustice"; but it may very well be the place of bystanders
to forcefully press the sufferer's case. This is the first crucial
key to the resolution of the arduous convolutions of the Book
of Job.

Thus, the Book of Job, which is an enigma wrapped in a
paradox, is unraveled by a combination of the Unified Formulation and the "Bifurcation" schema just noted. The Book of
Job is a counterpoint to the Garden of Eden narrative. The
Jobian theodicy, put forward by the Divine, fittingly links evil
to the wonderment and mysteries of creation. This is the
second key to Job. As "quest for potential" is the inviolate core
dynamic of the Divine and hence, of creation, the solution to
gratuitous evil indeed lies in the unrevealed, as of that time,

elusive crux of creation. The text proceeds to note two chapters of munificent potentialities unleashed by creation.

Does man have the right to "protest" evil, or should man attribute evil to mortal sin? The answer of the Book of Job is now clear. It is the mandate of the "friends" to protest seemingly gratuitous evil. It is the protagonist/sufferer Job's mandate to have faith in the ultimate cosmic necessity of the Divine's tolerance of evil.

PRAYER

Introductory

Prayer: the offering of petition, confession, adoration or thanksgiving to God.[613]

First it should be noted that the English word "prayer" is a somewhat misleading translation for the Hebrew *tefillah*.[614] "Prayer" implies request more than does *tefillah*. "Prayer" does not have the reflexive aspect embedded in *tefillah*.[615] "Prayer" is more universally applicable than the distinctively Jewish *tefillah*. "Prayer" is possibly not as metaphysically charged as the Hebrew *tefillah*. Therefore we will generally employ the Hebrew term *tefillah* for the balance of this section.[616]

There are many definitions and understandings of *tefillah*. Our concern is not to provide a full-scale analysis of the concept. Rather, it is to demonstrate that our formulation is reconcilable with *tefillah*. If *tefillah* as we know it is not easily reconcilable with our formulation, it does not necessarily follow that our formulation is wrong.[617] However, if our formulation is reconcilable with *tefillah*, an important hurdle is surmounted.

However, even if *tefillah* remains problematical, we will have advanced Jewish philosophy. For, we would be trading in the vexing, severe core challenge of the theodicy dilemma, and would remain with a pre-existing philosophical friction area with *tefillah*. The theodicy dilemma has always contained within itself, as one of several subthemes, the dilemma between the efficacy of prayer and evil befalling the innocent.

Tefillah: Structure and Purpose

Tefillah contains a plethora of elements—not all in consonance with each other.

The direct question would be as follows: If we are currently in a state of severely contracted real-time Divine consciousness, what is the purpose of *tefillah*? The direct answer would be twofold: (1) *tefillah* is first a cry that our words be heard in the here-and-now, and (2) most aspects of *tefillah* do not require a here-and-now Divine consciousness, as will be elaborated in the balance of this section.

Regarding the aspects which require a here-and-now Divine consciousness, the individual's cry must be that his *tefillah* pierce the veils of time and consciousness, that the gates of prayer be opened;[618] it entreats the Divine to manifest His consciousness in the here-and-now.[619]

> Open for me the gates of righteousness, that I may enter and praise the Lord.
>
> —Psalm 118:19

> May the Lord cause His face
> to shine upon thee
> and be gracious unto thee,
> May the Lord lift His face to thee
> and give unto you peace.
>
> —Numbers 6:24–26[620]

God's receptivity (or lack thereof) to prayer also finds echo in Hasidic[621] and kabbalistic literature.[622] "The mystical classic, the *Zohar*, points out that when the heavenly gates are closed to prayers couched in words, they remain open to prayers couched in tears (*Terumah*)."[623]

Prayer is fundamentally a twofold cry: first, a call that God hear our prayer in the here-and-now—that *Hester Panim* not be effected. We are *mevakesh penei Elohim* ("seekers of the face of God"), asking that God manifest His consciousness in the here-and-now.[624] We call for the *Rachok,* the "Far One," to become *Karov,* the "Near One."

Prayer is an attempt to pierce the veils of contracted consciousness.[625]

Hear my words, O Lord;
penetrate my thoughtful meditations;
Hearken unto the voice of my cry . . .

—Psalms 5:2–3

Incline Thine ear, O Lord, and hear;
open Thine eyes, O Lord, and see . . .

—Isaiah 37:15

Ye fast not this day
So as to make your voice to be heard on high.

—Isaiah 58:2

Rouse Thyself!
Why sleepest Thou, O Lord?

—Psalms 44:18[626]

From Thy Abode, our king, appear . . .

—Kedushah[627]

Prayer is also a cry that God intervene,[628] that God should, in effect, increase our dependence, inasmuch as the price we pay for our independence is too heavy.

Prayer is secondly a call that God hear and accept the specifics of our *tefillot* (prayers), our supplications and entreaties, our praise, our thanksgiving (*tachnunim, shevach, ve-hodaya*).

Though our *tefillot* are heard out-of-time, if the real-time consciousness of God is contracted to the point where the probability of short-term efficacy of *tefillah* is low, what then is the purpose of *tefillah?* As noted above, *tefillah* is extremely complex.

> Judaic dialectic plays mischievously with two opposites, two irreconcilable aspects of prayer. It [first] announces prayer as self-acquisition, self-discovery, self-objectification and self-redemption. . . . Yet there is another [second] aspect to prayer: prayer is an act of giving away. Prayer means sacrifice, unrestricted offering of the whole self, the returning to God of body and soul, everything one possesses and cherishes.
>
> —Soloveitchik[629]

> It [prayer] is an introspective process, a clarifying, refining process of discovering what one is, what he should be, and how to achieve the transformation.
>
> —Scherman[630]

> Prayer is the soul's yearning to define what truly matters.
>
> —Scherman[631]

> At times prayer is [partially] described as an unburdening of the soul, a pouring out of the heart.
>
> —Berkovits[632]

> It is a cry, an elementary outburst of woe.
>
> —Berkovits[633]

> It is an ultimate reliance on God.
>
> —Berkovits[634]

Embedded in *tefillah* are also other very important elements, for *tefillah* also goes by the term *avodah she-balev* ("service/offering of the heart").[635]
Pluralistic Jewish tradition incorporates the following elements within *tefillah:*

It is a thrust for spiritual upliftment.[636]
It is an exercise in spiritual growth.[637]

It is an appreciation of the munificence of creation.[638]
It is an aspiration for personal spiritual fulfillment.[639]
It is an aspiration for personal spiritual transformation.[640]
It is reflection.[641]
It is an exercise in humility, contemplation, and loss of selfhood.[642]
Man prays for the sake of the Divine (Hasidic).[643]
It is ritual.[644]

And independent of Divine contraction or decontraction, man quests for spiritual heights.[645] It is man's attempt to achieve a sense of unity with the Divine.[646]

> Out of the midst of the personal experience of God's hidden face one faces God as if His face were not hidden from one.
> —Berkovits[647]

> Do we stand overcome before the hidden face of God as the tragic hero of the Greeks before faceless Fate? No, rather even now we contend [like Job] with God, with the Lord of Being Himself whom once we, not our fathers only, chose for our Lord. We do not accept the world as it is but rather struggle for its redemption, and in this struggle appeal for help to our Lord, who on His part is once more, and still, One who hides. In this condition we await His voice, and whether it comes out of the storm or the stillness that follows it. And although His coming manifestation may resemble no earlier one, we shall nevertheless recognize again our cruel and merciful God.
> —Buber[648]

Tefillah is multifaceted and multileveled. Its efficacy is but one of many important components, and that aspect as well is not precluded,[649] although it is often limited, by our formulation.[650]

Study and *Tefillah*

Study and *tefillah* have intersecting goals and components.

We must bear in mind that all such religious acts as reading the Law, praying, and the performance of other precepts, serve exclusively as the means of causing us to occupy and fill our mind with the precepts of God, and free it from worldly business; for we are thus, as it were, in communication with God.

—Maimonides[651]

Intellectual redemption through study of Torah resembles in its structure, the redemption through prayer.

—Soloveitchik[652]

When *tefillah* and *talmud Torah* (study of Torah) unite in one redemptive experience, prayer becomes *avodah she-balev* (offering of the heart).

—Soloveitchik[653]

As the real-time consciousness of God continues to contract, study and ritual become more important.[654] In turn, the ritualistic/purely spiritualistic aspect of *tefillah* assumes an increasingly greater importance relative to the petitionary aspects of *tefillah*. Finally, within the "communication" realm of prayer, the "praise of God" aspect and the "expression of humility" aspect[655] assume an increasing importance relative to the literal efficacy aspect.[656]

Difficulties and Limitations

The difficult question, which theologians call the problem of the efficacy of prayer, actually includes a whole complex of issues. Does man have a right to intrude his own petty desires and limited objectives upon the will of the Almighty? Does the infinite wisdom of God stand in need of the instruction of man?

—Gordis[657]

Although it is the most fundamental and most universal form of religious expression, prayer is fraught with theological difficulties. Ostensibly, prayer is an attempt on the part of man to effect a change in God's conduct vis-à-vis man. God has afflicted man with, or allowed man to be afflicted by, sickness; man wishes God to restore him to good health. God has placed man, or allowed man to be placed, in a situation of poverty; man aspires to good fortune. He pleads with God to grant that which heretofore has been withheld. Is it not the height of audacity and unseemliness for man to presume to "pressure" God with prayer and argument in an attempt to dictate to God how He shall act! Moreover, the very act of prayer, unless it be completely futile, assumes that prayer is efficacious. The apparent implication is that the will of God is subject to change. Yet God and His will are one. Hence, God's will, which is identical with His essence, is itself eternal and immutable. Thus any change in the divine will is an impossibility. What, then, is the purpose of prayer?

—Bleich[658]

The notion that an individual who prays fervently, and with faith that the prayer will be answered, will necessarily receive a favorable response to his petition is not explicitly formulated in classical Jewish sources. . . .

Later scholars . . . stressed the contemplative and introspective nature of prayer and its effect upon man. The nineteenth-century writer, Rabbi Samson Raphael Hirsch, viewed prayer primarily as an occasion for introspection rather than as an attempt to communicate with the Active Intellect. . . . A similar description of prayer as an act of self-judgement in the ongoing conflict between man's good and evil inclinations, as well as a similar philological analysis of the term *tefillah,* is found in the preface of Rabbi Jacob Zebi Meklenburg's commentary on the prayerbook, Iyun Tefillah. The author of this work was a contemporary of Rabbi Samson Raphael Hirsch.

—Bleich[659]

Maimonides, in his Guide, regards prayer essentially as an exercise designed to enable man to achieve spiritual perfection rather than as an attempt to elicit a response on the part of God. Indeed, in his formulation of the principle, Maimonides carefully avoids any comment with regard to the efficacy of prayer. . . . Maimonides views prayer as an opportunity to contemplate the nature and grandeur of the Deity. This contemplation leads to intellectual perfection and the establishment of bond or contact between the human intellect and the Active Intellect.

—Bleich[660]

Samson Raphael Hirsch writes that "to ask for something, is only a minor section of *tefillah*."[661] Shem Tov ibn Falquera rejects the concept of a reacting God, negating this aspect in toto, and calling the idea that God is moved by human petition "false."[662]

Prayer is also religion's most problematic child.

—Stitskin[663]

We return to our initial point of departure: If petitionary prayer is efficacious throughout all time periods of Jewish history, given that we accept God as all-powerful and all-merciful why have the innocent suffered so greatly? Why were the desperate prayers on behalf of the innocents trapped by the Nazi cutthroats not answered? Surely none can argue that there were not more than a few innocents among the six million victims.

The greater the absoluteness of the claim of the efficacy of petitionary prayer, the more severe and intractable the unrelenting core challenge of theodicy looms to the entire structure of religious belief. The thrust of the Maimonidean position on prayer must therefore be sustained.[664]

NOTES

PART I

1. Germaine Tillion, *Ravensbruck* (New York: Anchor, 1975), p. 77, as cited in Fackenheim, *To Mend the World*, p. 213.
2. *New York Times*, January 23, 1985.
3. See *Encyclopaedia Judaica*, in addition to Philip Birnbaum, *A Book of Jewish Concepts*, for more detailed discussion of the Jewish-related terms.
4. Gordis, A Faith for Moderns, p. 8.
5. See Hick, *Evil and the God of Love*, p. 12. "What, then, are the various kinds of evil that have been identified in the literature of theodicy? There is, first, the important distinction just mentioned between moral and natural evil. Moral evil is evil that we human beings originate: cruel, unjust, vicious, and perverse thoughts and deeds. Natural evil is the evil that originates independently of human actions: in disease bacilli, earthquakes, storms, droughts, tornadoes, etc. In connection with these latter, it is a basic question whether events in nature which do not directly touch mankind, such as the carnage of animal life, in which one species preys upon another, or the death and decay of plants, or the extinction of a star, are to be accounted as evils."
6. Quoted by Lactantius (ca. 260 C.E.—ca. 340 C.E.).
7. See Glatzer, *The Dimensions of Job*, p. 37. "In 1791 Immanuel Kant (1724–1804) published in his essay 'On the Failure of All Philosophical Essays in the Theodicy,' . . . thus far no theodicy has succeeded in harmonizing the concept of moral wisdom in the rule of the world and man's worldly experience with the end of justifying the former. Our reason, says Kant, gives us no insight whatsoever into the relationship between the world of our experience and the supreme wisdom (of God)."
8. Schulweis, *Evil and the Morality of God*, p. i.
9. Hick, *Evil and the God of Love*, p. 6.
10. Cf. ibid., p. ix. " . . . so long as men live in this religiously ambiguous world the fact of evil will continue to haunt faith in the reality of an all-loving and all-powerful Creator."
11. Cf. Hick, "The Irenaean Theodicy," in idem, *Classical and Contemporary Readings in the Philosophy of Religion*, p. 508. " . . . theodicy has a negative rather than a positive function. It cannot profess to create faith, but only to preserve an already existing faith from being overcome by this dark mystery.

185

... The aim of a Christian theodicy must thus be the relatively modest and defensive one of showing that the mystery of evil, largely incomprehensible though it remains, does not render irrational a faith that has arisen, not from the inferences of natural theology, but from participation in a stream of religious experience which is continuous with that recorded in the Bible."

12. Camus, *Resistance, Rebellion and Death* (New York: Knopf, 1961), p. 71.

13. Voltaire addresses the same problem in his "Poem on the Lisbon Disaster," as cited in Schulweis, *Evil and the Morality of God*, p. 37:

> ... Did fallen Lisbon deeper drink of vice
> Than London, Paris, or sunlit Madrid?
> "All's well," ye say, "and all is necessary."
> Think ye this universe had been the worse
> Without this hellish gulf in Portugal?
> ... and as, with quaking voice,
> Mortal and pitiful, ye cry, "All's well,"
> The universe belies you, and your heart
> Refutes a hundred times your mind's conceit.

14. Weisel, cited generally in Fackenheim, *God's Presence in History*, p. 67.

15. Soloveitchik, *Halakhic Man*, p. 1.

16. Cf. Fackenheim, *To Mend the World*, p. 11. "The cruelty and the killing raise the question whether even those who believe after such an event dare to talk about God who loves and cares without making a mockery of those who suffered. Theologians refusing to face this question—and 'mutatis mutandis' philosophers as well—merely seek refuge from a unique scandal in an unreal realm of abstract thought."

See also Fackenheim, *The Jewish Return into History*, p. 32.

17. Cf. Berkovits, *Major Themes in Modern Philosophies of Judaism*, p. vii. "Judaism is awaiting a reformulation of its theology and philosophy."

Cf. Borowitz, *Choices in Modern Jewish Thought*, p. 276.

Cf. Greenberg, "Cloud of Smoke, Pillar of Fire," p. 24.

18. Fackenheim, *The Jewish Return into History*, p. 26.

19. There is a concept in Judaism of *makom hinichu lanu avoteinu le-hitgaber bam*, i.e., each generation has been left a portion of the Torah to reveal (in spite of the general, hierarchic, authoritative superiority of prior generations, due to their proximity to Sinai).

20. Berkovits, *With God in Hell*, p. 126.

21. See Schulweis, *Evil and the Morality of God*, p. 106.

22. See Frankl, *The Doctor and the Soul: From Psychotherapy to Logotherapy* (New York: Bantam Books, 1967), p. 25. "The meaning of the whole is no longer comprehensible and goes beyond the comprehensible."

23. See Hick, *Evil and the God of Love*, p. 8. "By what authority must we insist upon maintaining an unrelieved mystery and darkness concerning God's permission of evil?"

24. Cf. Schulweis, *Evil and the Morality of God*, p. 135.

25. Cf. ibid., pp. 1–3. "Far less attention is paid to the internal crises dwelling within the matrix of monotheistic faiths, specifically those that are engendered by the problem of evil. These are more devastating to traditional

faith than the challenges from without. . . . Could it be that the major irritants of traditional faith lie within the corpus of monotheism itself?"
Cf. ibid., p. 3.
Cf. ibid., p. 4. "For most people, the breaking point of traditional monotheistic belief lies not in Darwin or Einstein, but in Dachau and Hiroshima. . . . No challenge to traditional faith attacks every aspect of religious belief and conduct as thoroughly as the one fell blow from the hammer of gratuitous evil. . . . Appealing to God's mysterious ways will not assuage the disillusionment born of the shattered promise of the governing moral God of the Bible and liturgy. . . . The evil we have witnessed is radical. No patchwork will cover its agony."

26. See Luban, "The Kaddish," pp. 201, 207.

27. Gordis, *A Faith for Moderns*, p. 159.

28. See Schulweis, *Evil and the Morality of God*, p. 5. "Having extricated the problematic [philosophical theodicy] from the body of faith, many theologians undertake their defense oblivious to the consequences of their ad hoc solutions for the remaining corpus of monotheism. . . . Stephen Toumlin has observed that over matters of faith, one does not believe or disbelieve individual presuppositions: one accepts or rejects complete notions."

29. The most famous case in Jewish lore of an adherent who quit Judaism owing to the problem of theodicy is that of Elisha ben Avuyah, known as "Aher," originally a second-century Tanna and the teacher of Rav Meir. There are various traditions concerning Aher. According to Jewish lore, upon seeing the tongue of Rav Judah ha-Nahthom in a dog's mouth (during the persecutions following the Bar Kokhba revolt), Elisha ben Avuyah bitterly commented: "Is this the Torah and this its reward?" One version has Aher leaving Judaism upon seeing a child fatally fall out of a tree after following his father's directive to climb the tree to remove the chicks from the nest prior to taking the mother. According to a straightforward reading of the Torah, the reward both for honoring one's parents and for removing the chicks is long life. (On this particular theological point, see our discussion in section 100.07) See amplification in *Encyclopaedia Judaica*, s. v. "Elisha ben Avuyah," vol. 6, col. 668.

30. Schulweis, "Suffering and Evil," in *Great Jewish Ideas*, 198.

31. Cf. Schulweis, *Evil and the Morality of God*, p. 31.

32. Cf. ibid., p. 135. "For those who find consolation in the promise of a world controlled by an unfathomable Agent and of an ultimate reward, nothing can or should be said."
Cf. ibid., p. 115. "Theodicies, Kant wrote, offer an 'apology in which the defense is worse than the charge [and which] require no confutation, and may certainly be fully left to the detestation of everyone who has the least sense or spark of morality.' "
Cf. Friedrich Nietzsche, *The Joyful Wisdom* (New York: Ungar, 1964), bk. V, sec. 357. "To look upon nature as if it were proof of the goodness and care of a God; to interpret history in honor of a divine reason, as a constant testimony to a moral order in the world and a moral final purpose; to explain personal experiences as pious men have long enough explained them, as if everything were a dispensation or intimation of Providence, something planned and set

on behalf of the salvation of the soul; all that is passed; it has conscience against it."

33. Cf. Schulweis, *Evil and the Morality of God*, p. 2.

34. Fackenheim, *The Jewish Return into History*, p. 281.

35. See Berkovits, *Faith After the Holocaust*, p. 78. " . . . the ghettos were sheer luxury compared to the concentration camps, of which a German official reported home that Dante's hell was mere comedy compared to them."

36. See Waskow, "The Choice: Romanticism or True Messianism?" in Fleischner, *Auschwitz*, p. 307. "It is not new for Jews to contemplate a Holocaust, not only to seek in agony to incorporate Holocaust within the tradition, but also to seek in anger to make the tradition transform itself in the dark light of Holocaust."

37. See Fackenheim, *God's Presence in History*, p. 74. "Auschwitz was the supreme, most diabolical attempt ever made to murder martyrdom itself and, failing that, to deprive all death, martyrdom included, of its dignity."

38. Jung, *Psychology and Religion*, in *Collected Works*, vol. 2 (Princeton, N.J.: Princeton University Press, 1958), cited in Schulweis, *Evil and the Morality of God*, p. 1.

39. Schulweis, *Evil and the Morality of God*, p. 1. "The implosion sparked by the holocaustal events of our century has exposed serious cracks within the monotheistic faith system itself. Not that the outcry of innocence in the face of genuine evil is new. But the cultural environment in which it is heard is new. In a traditional society the murmurings of Job could be smothered by theodicies attributing hidden sins to man and inscrutable ways to God. In a society open to other alternatives besides acquiescence to the mystery of God's ways and promises of a happy epilogue, repressed resentments against traditional theodicies burst out afresh."

Cf. Greenberg, "Cloud of Smoke, Pillar of Fire," p. 8.

Cf. ibid., p. 11.

Cf. ibid., p. 20. "For both Judaism and Christianity (and other religions of salvation—both secular and sacred) there is no choice but to confront the Holocaust, because it happened. . . . So evil is the Holocaust, and so powerful a challenge to all other norms, that it forces a response."

Cf. Fackenheim, *To Mend the World*, p. 198. "Theodore Arno once remark[ed] . . . that after Auschwitz a poem is impossible."

40. Buber, "The Dialogue between Heaven and Earth," as cited in Fackenheim, *To Mend the World*, p. 196.

Cf. Borowitz, *Choices in Modern Jewish Thought*, p. 191.

41. Cf. Schulweis, *Evil and the Morality of God*, p. 100. "The silence (of a watching God) is more appalling than the apostasy which announces His demise."

42. Berkovits, *Faith After the Holocaust*, p. 69.

43. Cf. Wiesel, *The Fifth Son*, p. 19. "Absolute Evil was opposed by a Good that was only theoretical, therein lay the tragedy."

44. Hick, *Evil and the God of Love*, pp. 3–4. See also footnote: "It seems that God does not exist; because if one of two contraries be infinite, the other would be altogether destroyed. But the name God means that He is infinite

goodness. If, therefore, God existed, there would be no evil discoverable; but there is evil in the world. Therefore God does not exist."

45. Schulweis, *Evil and the Morality of God*, p. 7.

Cf. ibid., p. 1. "True depths of tragedy become apparent when two equally divine principles come into conflict."

46. Gordis, *The Book of God and Man*, p. 155.

Cf. Hick, *Evil and the God of Love*, p. 7.

Cf. ibid., p. 6.

Cf. ibid., p. 10.

Cf. Soloveitchik, "B'sod ha-yachid v'hayachad," pp. 333–343.

47. Cited in Schlesinger, "Logical Analysis and the Beliefs of an Orthodox Jew." A somewhat related talmudic philosophy is *gam zo l'tovah* ("this too is for a good purpose").

48. See outline of talmudic discussion on this viewpoint in Ramban, *Gate of Reward*, chap. 4, in idem, *Writings and Discourses*, vol. 2, p. 454.

Cf. Dov Noy's "The Jewish Theodicy Legend," in *Fields of Offerings*, a festschrift for Professor Raphael Patai, edited by Victor Sanua, (Fairleigh Dickinson University Press/Herzl Press, 1985), which, according to the review by Harris Lenowitz in *Midstream*, October 1985, "demonstrates that the folk-religious response to untimely (and it never really seems to be timely) death among Jews is the moral recommendation to the questioner not to question, for lack of knowledge is certain."

49. See outline of talmudic discussion on this viewpoint in Ramban, *Gate of Reward*, chap. 4, in *Writings and Discourses*, vol. 2, p. 451. See also T. B. Berachot 7a.

50. See also T. B. Berachot 69b. "As Rav Huna says: 'Whatever the Merciful One does, it is for good.'"

51. The scriptural citation "God said to Moses, 'Thou canst not see My face. I will remove My hand and thou shalt see My back.'" (Exodus 33:20) is used by some to buttress the idea of explanation or demonstration of justice in the next world. See Tanhuma B, *Ki Tissa* 58b, as cited in Montefiore and Loewe, *A Rabbinic Anthology*, p. 555.

See also T. B. Berachot 16.

52. Countered by Deuteronomy 24:16. "The children shall not be put to death for the fathers. Every man shall be put to death only for his own sin."

Supported by Exodus 34:7. "Visiting the iniquity of the fathers upon the children."

Supported by Exodus 20:5. "God visits the sins of the fathers upon the children."

Clarified by Sanhedrin 27b. "This means that He will do so only if they hold fast to the deeds of their fathers."

Resolved, according to Makkot 24a, by Ezekiel 18:20. "The soul that sins, that soul [alone] shall die."

53. See T. B. Shabbat 55a end. "R. Ammi said: No death without sin; no suffering without iniquity. [But at the end of the discussion on R. Ammi's statement it was held that, after all], There is a death without sin, and there is suffering without iniquity."

54. See also T. B. Berachot 5a. "If a man sees that he is afflicted with

suffering, he should examine his deeds, as it is said, 'Let us search and try our ways, and return unto the Lord [Lamentations III 3:40].' "

55. See T. B. Berachot 5a. "If he [an individual who suffers] searches but finds nothing (objectionable), he should attribute his affliction to neglect of the study of Torah." See also T. B. Berachot 7a.

56. See Besdin, *Reflections of the Rav*, p. 35.

Note also that Buber's theme of the "eclipse of God" would fall into this category.

57. See R. Samuel b. Nahmani in the name of R. Jonathan in T. B. Baba Kama 60a.

58. " 'Nevertheless,' said Rav Abba, 'his [Hanina's] son died of thirst,' 'because . . . God deals particularly strictly with those near to him' (Yeb. 121 b; R. T. p. 349)." As cited in Montefiore and Loewe, *A Rabbinic Anthology*, p. 553.

59. See Sifre Deuteronomy, *Re'eh*, no. 53, fol, 86a, as cited in Montefiore and Loewe, *A Rabbinic Anthology*, p. 549. See also Chagigah 15a. See also outline of talmudic discussion on this viewpoint in Ramban, *Gate of Reward*, chap. 9, in *Writings and Discourses*, vol. 2, p. 504.

60. See outline of talmudic discussion on this viewpoint in Ramban, *Gate of Reward*, chap. 1, in *Writings and Discourses*, vol. 2, p. 425.

61. See Isaiah 57:1. "The righteous [individual] is taken away from the evil to come." See also Baba Kama 60a.

62. See outline of talmudic discussion on this viewpoint in Ramban, *Gate of Reward*, chap. 4, in *Writings and Discourses*, vol. 2, pp. 440, 452–453. See also Berachot 7a. See various commentaries on Psalms 73:2–19.

See also Sifre Deuteronomy, *Va'ethchanan*, no. 32, fol. 73b, as cited in Montefiore and Loewe, *A Rabbinic Anthology*, p. 544.

Note also: "Rav Shimon ben Lakish said: . . . as salt enhances meat, so chastisements purify the sins of man" (T. B. Berachot 5a).

63. See also Leviticus 26:37. "And they shall stumble one upon the other." However, Sanhedrin 27b clarifies as follows: "So are they not all responsible one for the other? Only if one could have prevented the other's misdeeds, and if he did not do so."

64. "Raba (some say Rav Hisda) said . . . If a man who suffers searches his ways for sin, and then for neglect of Torah study, but find neither, let him be sure these are 'tribulations of love' " (T. B. Berachot 5a).

Cf. T. B. Kiddushin 39b.

65. "Whom God loves He chastens, even as the father chastens the son of whom he is fond" (Proverbs 3:12); "Happy is the man whom thou chastenest, O God, and whom thou teacheth from Thy Torah" (Psalms 94:12).

66. See Midrash Psalms on Psalms 73:1 (167a, no. I) as cited in Montefiore and Loewe, *A Rabbinic Anthology*, p. 544.

67. See Genesis 22:1. "And God tried Abraham." See Psalms 11:5. "The Eternal trieth the righteous." See outline of talmudic discussion on this viewpoint in Ramban, *Gate of Reward*, chap. 3, in *Writings and Discourses*, vol. 2, p. 445.

68. "Rav Shimon ben Yochai says: 'The Holy One, blessed be He, gave Israel three precious gifts, and all of them were given only through suffer-

ings. These are: The Torah, the Land of Israel, and the world-to-come' " (T. B. Berachot 5a).

69. See Rashi on Berachot 5a, in disagreement with Ramban, *Gate of Reward,* chap. 3, *Writings and Discourses,* vol. 2, p. 443.

70. Luban, "The Kaddish," p. 207.

71. Maharal, as explicated by Rabbi Mayer Schiller in an article in *Crown Heights Chronicle,* April 1985. p. 1.

72. See Gordis, *A Faith for Moderns,* p. 186.

73. See *Encyclopaedia Judaica,* s.v. "Kabbalah," vol. 10, cols. 583–587, for more elaboration.

74. In the Sayings of the Fathers (Avot 4:19) we find the adage, "It is not in our power to explain either the prosperity of the wicked or the afflictions of the righteous."
See also Hillel Goldberg, in *Tradition* 20, no.4 (Winter 1982):30.
See also Schulweis, *Evil and the Morality of God,* p. ii.

75. In the spirit of the folk etymology of the Talmud: T-Y-K-V (pronounced tay-ku).

76. Cf. Hick, *Readings in the Philosophy of Religion,* p. 86. David Hume provides an example of a classic perspective: "At least, you must acknowledge that it is impossible for us to tell, from our limited views, whether this system contains any great faults or deserves any considerable praise if compared to other possible and even real systems. Could a peasant, if the *Aeneid* were read to him, pronounce that poem to be absolutely faultless, or even assign to it its proper rank among the productions of human wit, he who had never seen any other production?"

77. Gordis, *The Book of God and Man,* p. 155.

78. T. B. Avot 4:15.

79. After discussion in T. B. Baba Batra 15a.

80. See Maimonides, *Guide for the Perplexed,* chap. 22.

81. Cf. Gordis, "The Temptation of Job," in Glatzer, *The Dimensions of Job,* p. 84. "Job's triumph lies in the fact that God speaks to him and does not ignore him. The confrontation of God is Job's vindication."

82. Cf. Greenberg, "Cloud of Smoke, Pillar of Fire," p. 34. "Rather, what is meaningful in Job's experience is that in the whirlwind the contact with God is restored. That sense of Presence gives the strength to go on living in the contradiction."

83. Cf. Glatzer, *The Dimensions of Job,* p. 38. Kant believed that "Man's intellect is subjective, finite, and therefore unable to know the unconditional, the infinite, the perfect-God."

84. Schulweis, *Evil and the Morality of God,* p. 9.
Cf. ibid., p. 95. "Once a radical qualitative difference between human and divine moral qualities is admitted, moral anarchy is let loose. Mill's objection is particularly pertinent to our discussion:
" 'If I know nothing about what the [Divine] attribute is, I cannot tell that it is a proper object of veneration. To say that God's goodness may be different in kind from man's goodness, what is it but saying, with a slight change of phraseology, that God may possibly not be good?' "

85. Berkovits, *God, Man and History,* p. 75.

86. Cf. Steven Ely, *The Religious Availability of Whitehead's God,* as cited in

Schulweis, *Evil and the Morality of God*, p. 59. "It is no help for present ills to know that God sees them in such a way that they are valuable for him. That my ill has an ideal counterpart in God does not help me very much as long as I am on earth and God is in heaven."

87. See Greenberg, "In Dust and Ashes," in Glatzer, *The Dimensions of Job*, pp. 222–224.

88. *Ani Ma'amin* (Jerusalem: Mosad Ha-Rav Kook, 1965), p. 206, as cited by Fackenheim, *The Jewish Return into History*, p. 281. Judaism does not easily acquiesce to a seemingly immoral interaction between the Divine and man.

89. Ramban, *Gate of Reward*, chap. 6, *Writings and Discourses*, vol. 2, p. 468.

90. Ibid. "With the enlightenment we have attained we can benefit ourselves by becoming wise and knowing God, blessed be He, through His manner and deeds. Moreover, we will believe and trust in his faith—in both the hidden and known matters. . . . We will recognize the fairness of the [Divine] judgment and the fairness of the [Divine] decision. Thus it is the duty of every person who worships God out of love and fear to search his mind in order to justify the Divine decision and to substantiate the judgment as far as his ability allows."

91. Interestingly enough, the Buddhist response to suffering bears a parallelism to mainstream rabbinic thought. See Kyokai, *The Teaching of Buddha* (Tokyo: Kosaido Printing Co., 1966), p. 84. "But if one carefully considers all the facts, one must be convinced that at the basis of all suffering lies the principle of craving desire. If avarice can be removed, human suffering will come to an end."

92. Berkovits, *Faith After the Holocaust*, p. 68.

93. See Glatzer, *The Dimensions of Job*, p. 287. "The aim of the Book of Job was to refute certain notions of retribution, of suffering as punishment."

94. See also the articles by Eliyahu Dessler (p. 26), Yitzchak Hutner (p. 39), and Mordechai Gifter (p. 56) reprinted in Wolpin, *A Path Through the Ashes*. All three view the Holocaust as *tochacha* (punishment). See Gifter, in particular: "The Churban should thus become a source of inspiration and encouragement for us. We are assured that we do have a Father in Heaven who cares for us and is concerned enough with our spiritual status to demonstrate His disfavor" (p. 59).

We are left numbed by the reasoning and can only comment that great minds sometimes make great mistakes.

95. Montefiore and Loewe, in *A Rabbinic Anthology*, p. 541, refer to this theodicy thrust as "The old view, now far off, and obsolete."

Cf. T. B. Berachot 16.

96. Lamm, *The Face of God*, sec. 2.

97. Cf. Borowitz, *Choices in Modern Jewish Thought*, p. 194. "That the Nazis' bestiality was just compensation for Jewish sins; that God must allow such evils so as to preserve human freedom; that it taught a valuable lesson to the world; that God tests our faith; that God has compensated the Jews for their suffering by giving them the State of Israel; or that the Holocaust brutality can be expunged by the bliss of the world-to-come, are all morally unbearable notions. No God who did such things would be worth worshipping. Further, to take refuge in traditional humility and say that God's ways are infinitely

beyond us, is an utter abdication of our human judgment and of the victims' human dignity."

98. Fackenheim, *God's Presence in History*, p. 39.

99. Cf. Gordis, *The Book of God and Man*, p. 145. " 'Yet he bore the sin of many' [Isaiah 52:13, 55:3, 4, 5, 12]. . . . Thus for the first time, the prophet affirmed the possibility of national suffering that was not the consequence of national sin, but on the contrary, a tragic, yet indispensable element in the process of the moral education of the race. For the first time the nexus between suffering and sin is severed."

100. Cf. Luzzatto, *The Way of God*, p. 101. "God gave suffering the power to dispel the insensitivity in man, allowing him to become pure and clear, prepared for the ultimate good at its appointed time."

101. See Cohen, *The Tremendum*, p. 51.

102. Berkovits, *God, Man and History*, pp. 75–76.

103. See *Encyclopaedia Judaica*, vol. 10, col. 594.

104. Glatzer, *The Dimensions of Job*, p. 221.

105. See Schulweis, "Suffering and Evil," p. 215.

106. See Schulweis, *Evil and the Morality of God*, p. 138.

107. Maimonides, *Guide* 3:5.

108. Stitskin, *Eight Jewish Philosophers*, p. 164.

109. See Ibn Daud, *Emunah Ramah*, pt. 2, Basic Principle 6, chap. 2, cited in Bleich, *With Perfect Faith*, p. 424. ". . . he who entrusts his spirit into the hand of God is supervised, since he tries to enter into the section of the notable substances, and the notable substances have supervision over existents in this world in general and over the human species in particular. Behold in all respects [the human species] is singled out by providence in great measure because of its diligence to entrust its spirit with Him. As we have said, 'If one comes to cleanse himself he is helped.' "

110. The motif of the "breaking of the vessels" is more specifically associated with Lurianic Kabbalah. There is considerable divergence among the elucidators of Isaac Luria's teachings as to his precise intent in many crucial matters, including this one. Luria's noted explicators Vital and Tishby provide various insights into the theme of the "breaking of the vessels." These explanations include the philosophically daring one that this "breaking," which is positioned as the direct source of evil on earth, was due to a Divine miscalculation. See articles in *Encyclopaedia Judaica* on Kabbalah and on Luria, as well as Scholem's chapter (7) on Lurianic Kabbalah in *Major Trends in Jewish Mysticism*.

[Vital was Luria's foremost disciple, while Tishby is a contemporary scholar, who uses the methodology of critical scholarship.]

111. See also Greenberg, "Cloud of Smoke, Pillar of Fire."

112. Fackenheim, *God's Presence in History*, p. 76.

113. Schulweis, *Evil and the Morality of God*, p. i.

114. Gordis, *A Faith for Moderns*, p. 211.

115. Hick, *Evil and the God of Love*, p. 15. ("All partial evil, universal good."—Alexander Pope, *Essay on Man*, Line 292.)

116. See ibid., p. 17. "Spinoza saw reality as forming an infinite and perfect whole—perfect in the sense that everything within it follows by logical necessity from the eternal divine nature—and saw each finite thing as making its own proper contribution to this infinite perfection. Thus every existing

thing occupies a place within the system of universal perfection, and our human notion of evil as that which ought not to be is merely an illusion of our finite perspective."

117. The kabbalistic theoretician Cordovero daringly offered the formula, a century before Spinoza, that "God is all reality, but not all reality is God," as noted in *Alima Rabati* (1881), fol. 24d, as cited by Scholem, *Major Trends in Jewish Mysticism*, p. 252.

118. Tillich, *The Eternal Now*, p. 45.

Cf. ibid., pp. 45–46. "There is an ultimate unity of all beings, rooted in the divine life from which they emerge and to which they return. All beings, non-human, participate in it. And therefore they all participate in each other. And we participate in each other's having and in each other's not having. . . . In every death we encounter, something of us dies, and in every disease, something of us tends towards disintegration."

119. See Schulweis, *Evil and the Morality of God*, p. 74.

Cf. ibid., p. 108.

120. See Hick, "Faith and Knowledge," p. 541. "In Leibniz's *Theodicy* (1710) we find the optimistic view that this is the best of all possible worlds—best not in the sense that it contains no evils, but in the sense that any other possible universe would have to contain more evil."

121. *Summa Theologiae* I, 22, 2 ad 2.

122. Hick, *Evil and the God of Love*, p. 10. Latin: *Si deus est, unde malum? Si non est, unde bonum?*

123. See Fosdick, *Living Under Tensions* (New York: Harper & Co., 1941), pp. 214–215.

124. This proposition *per se* is valid and important. In fact, we employ a slight variation on it as one of nine major propositions in our eventual formulation. The problem is rather in its employment as a stand-alone theodicy. The major challenge is as follows: Granted that evil has to exist as a counterpart to good, why does not omnipotent, omnimerciful God intervene to counter gross evil?

125. J. L. Mackie, "Evil and Omnipotence," *Mind* 64 (1955), as reprinted in Brody, *Readings in the Philosophy of Religion*, p. 157.

126. H. J. McCloskey, "God and Evil," *Philosophical Quarterly* 10 (1960), as reprinted in ibid., p. 168.

127. See Camus, "Letters to a German Friend," in his *Resistance, Rebellion and Death* (New York: Knopf, 1961) p. 32, as cited in Berkovits, *Faith After the Holocaust*, p. 71. "I know that heaven, which was indifferent to your horrible victories, will be equally indifferent to your just defeat. Even now I expect nothing from heaven."

128. See Schulweis, *Evil and the Morality of God*, p. 19. "The saddest proposition of religious philosophy is the Epicurean formulation of gods who exist and know but who do not care and do not intervene."

129. Bertrand Russell, as cited in Glatzer, *The Dimensions of Job*, p. 222. "In a world so full of contradictions I can not find God; I can more easily assume that it was created by a mischievous Mephistopheles in an exceptionally devilish mood."

130. Carl Gustav Jung, as summarized in Glatzer, *The Dimensions of Job*, p.

45, proposed that the God of Job, far from being a free Lord of creation, is a demiurge, amoral, inconsistent, touchy, suspicious, ruthless, brutal. This God envies man for what he, man, alone possesses: "a somewhat keener consciousness."

131. Kafka provides us with a naturally Kafkaesque theodicy: ". . . the fact that the voice does not reach us and that instead we perceive demonic noises, Kafka attributed not to the hostile power of a demiurge but to a strange derangement in the process of communication caused by intermediary forces." Cited in Glatzer, *The Dimensions of Job*, p. 48, quoting from Buber, *Darko shel mikra* (Jerusalem, 1964), p. 357. One might actually draw some parallels between Kafka's statement and some segments of kabbalistic literature.

132. See Kushner, *When Bad Things Happen to Good People*.

Kushner's main thrust is that the rabbinic response should focus on comforting the aggrieved, as opposed to providing specific theological responses to the aggrieved. Philosophically, Kushner posits in his book a nonomnipotent Divine. In subsequent lectures in 1985 in New York, Kushner modified his position to posit a Self-willed Divine nonomnipotence.

133. Rabindranath Tagore, "The Problem of Evil," *Hibbert Journal* 2 (1910): 705.

134. But if God is omnipotent, why did He not create beings who would not sin?

"If it is said: It would not have been difficult or laborious for Almighty God to have seen to it that all His creatures should have observed their proper order so that none of them should have come to his misery. If he is omnipotent that would not have been beyond His power and if He is good He would not have grudged it; this is my answer. The order of creatures proceeds from top to bottom by just grades, so that it is the remark of envy to say: That creatures should not exist, and equally so to say: That one should be different. It is wrong to wish that anything should be like another thing higher in the scale, for it has its being, perfect in its degree, and nothing ought to be added to it. He who says that a thing ought to be different from what it is, either wants to add something to a higher creature already perfect, in which case he lacks moderation and justice; or he wants to destroy the lower creature, and is thereby wicked and grudging." Augustine, *Confessions and Enchiridion*, p. 26.

135. See Hick, *Readings in the Philosophy of Religion*, p. 514. ". . . the ultimate source of evil lies in an original conscious turning away from God on the part of created personal life."

136. Hick, "Faith and Knowledge," in ibid., p. 515.

137. Hick, *Evil and the God of Love*, p. 369.

138. See Aquinas, *Summa Theologiae* I q. 22, art. 2. ". . . there would be no patience of martyrs if there were no tyrannical persecution."

139. Cited by Hertz, *Pentateuch and Haftorahs* (also cited by *Encyclopedia of Biblical Interpretation*, citing Hertz.)

140. Hick, *Evil and the God of Love*, p. 385.

Cf. Hick, "Faith and Knowledge," pp. 517–518. "Antitheistic writers almost invariably assume a conception of the divine purpose which is contrary to the

Christian conception. They assume that the purpose of a loving God must be to create a hedonistic paradise; and therefore to the extent that the world is other than this, it proves to them that God is either not loving enough or not powerful enough to create such a world. . . . Such critics as Hume are confusing what heaven ought to be . . . with what this world ought to be."

141. Schlesinger, *Religion and Scientific Method*, p. 47.

142. In countering another theodicy, Schlesinger writes in his article "Logical Analysis," "The laws of psychology could have been altered by the Almighty."

143. Aside from contravening the dictum God has laid down for man, *lifnei iver lo sitane michshol* ("before a blind man, place not an obstacle").

144. Hick, *Evil and the God of Love*, p. 386.

Cf. ibid., pp. 385–386. "What is the greatest difficulty in the way of such a theodicy? It is, I think, the stark question whether we can believe that the postulated end can justify the known means; whether all the pain and suffering, cruelty and wickedness of human life can be rendered acceptable by an end-state, however good? Madden and Hare put the straight negative: 'The price that is paid for spiritual growth . . . is often too high to be justly exacted.' " (See balance of paragraph, as well.)

Cf. ibid., p. 386.

145. Agus, *The Evolution of Jewish Thought*, p. 19.

146. Saadia Gaon, *Book of Beliefs and Opinions* 1:3.

147. See ibid., Prolegomena. "If both the scholar and student will follow this (the conceptual) path . . . the believer who blindly relies on tradition will turn into one basing his belief on insight and understanding."

148. "Yehudah Halevi argues (*Kuzari* 5:1) that a 'skeptical soul will be content only after speculative investigation when, subsequently, knowledge and tradition combine and become one and the same.' " Stitskin, *Eight Jewish Philosophers*, p. 20.

149. See Stitskin, *Eight Jewish Philosophers*, p. 126. "Maimonides regarded the works of Ibn Ezra superior to any other Jewish scholar. In his 'Letter of Instruction to His Son Abraham,' he admonished him as follows: 'As for you, my faithful son, I exhort you not to pay attention or distract your mind by concentrating on commentaries, treatises and books other than those of Ibn Ezra's which alone are meaningful and profitable to all who study them with intelligence, understanding and deep insight. They are distinguished from the writings of other authors, for Ibn Ezra was in spirit similar to our patriarch Abraham.' "

150. Abraham Ibn Ezra, *Introduction to Ecclesiastes*, translation extracts in Stitskin, *Eight Jewish Philosophers*, p. 127.

151. Abraham Ibn Ezra on Psalms 16:8, 11; 17:15, as cited in ibid., p. 123, and reprinted on p. 186.

Cf. Abraham Ibn Ezra, *Yesod Mora*, Introduction, as cited in ibid., p. 121. "Let me state at the outset that the preeminence of man over the beast is due to his rational soul, derived from on-high, which is destined to return to God who gave it."

152. Maimonides, *Guide* 1:2.

153. See Stitskin, *Eight Jewish Philosophers*, p. 110.

154. Soloveitchik, *Halakhic Man*, p. 79.

Cf. ibid., p. 89. "Halakhic man does not quiver before any man. . . . He knows that the truth is a lamp unto his feet and the Halakhah a light unto his path. . . . There can be no fear of God without knowledge and no service of God without the cognition of halakhic truth. . . . The old saying of Socrates, that virtue is knowledge, is strikingly similar to the stance of halakhic man."

Cf. ibid., p. 41. "Halakhic man differs both from homo religiosus, who rebels against the rules of reality and seeks refuge in a supernal world, and from cognitive man, who does not encounter any transcendence at all."

See also Soloveitchik, as quoted by Borowitz, *Choices in Modern Jewish Thought*, p. 238. "Precisely because of the supremacy of the intellect in human life, the Torah requires, at times, the suspension of the authority logos. Man defeats himself by accepting norms that the intellect cannot assimilate into its normative system."

155. See Schlesinger, "Arguments from Despair," *Tradition* 17, no. 4, p. 26. "I should like to maintain that the search for reasons fortifying belief—for those who are in need of such fortifications—is a legitimate search. It may of course be easier to avoid the rigors of this search and to abandon reasoning as the monopoly of non-believers. It may be easier to fantasize about the advantages of levitating far above the solid grounds of evidence and empirical confirmation. I believe that our task is to return to earth and to do battle in the arena of rational arguments no matter how arduous the task may seem."

156. See Fackenheim, *God's Presence in History*, p. 88. "The voice of Auschwitz commands the religious Jew after Auschwitz to continue to wrestle with his God in however revolutionary ways."

157. See Agus, *The Evolution of Jewish Thought*, p. 184. "Maimonides did not conceive the problem of theology to be the conquest of reason by faith, but the determination of the proper domains for the functioning of each faculty. In its own sphere of operation, reason is essentially jealous, brooking no rivals in the finality of its analysis and judgment. One cannot drive bargains and patch up compromises with reason, but having determined the field extending beyond its reach, we may allow the postulates of faith to prevail in that area of indetermination."

158. See Gordis, *A Faith for Moderns*, introductory "Warning to the Reader": "A reasonable faith will recognize the bounds of man's reason and will necessarily go beyond it in its vision of reality, but it will not scorn reason or contradict it, for it remains man's indispensable guide."

159. Cf. Bleich, *With Perfect Faith*, p. 10. "Bahya also posits an obligation to engage in philosophical investigation directed to the rational demonstration of the objects of belief: '. . . Scripture expressly bids you to reflect and exercise your intellect on such themes. After you have attained knowledge of them by the method of tradition which covers all the precepts of the law, their principles and details, you should investigate them with your reason, understanding, and judgment, till the truth becomes clear to you and false notions dispelled; as it is written, "Know this day and lay it to your heart that the Lord, He is God" (Deut. 4:39).' "

Cf. Stitskin, *Eight Jewish Philosophers*, p. 70. "Bar Hiyya . . . states that 'This biblical reference ["From my flesh, I shall behold God" (Job 19:26)] gives us permission to investigate the views of the classical philosophers and their theories of creation.' "

Cf. Bar Hiyya, *Sefer Hegyon ha-Nefesh*, chap. 1, as quoted in ibid., p. 80. "It is, therefore, incumbent upon every intelligent person endowed with reason and judgment to inquire and to investigate the unique and superior quality of mortal man."

Cf. ibid., p. 160. "Solomon ibn Gabirol (1021–1058), the first Jewish philosopher in Spain, begins his magnum opus, *Mekor Hayyim*, with the master addressing his pupil as follows: 'Inasmuch as by virtue of your native endowments and diligence you have acquired abundant knowledge in the study of the philosophic discipline, you may proceed to inquire about matters close to your heart, and especially about the supreme question concerning the aim of human life, why was man created?' "

Cf. Ibn Falaquera, *Sefer ha-Nefesh*, Introduction, as quoted in ibid., p. 138. "The scholars have also asserted that the mark of perfection is twofold: to love knowledge with utmost devotion and to choose the purest of activities with meaningful intentions."

160. See Gersonides, *Wars of the Lord*, Third Treatise, chaps. 3–6, as quoted in Bleich, *With Perfect Faith*, p. 463.

161. Saadia, *Beliefs ad Opinions*, Introduction.

162. Kook, *The Lights of Penitence*, in Bokser, *Abraham Isaac Kook*, p. 291. Cf. ibid., p. 371.

My soul aspires
For the mysteries,
For the hidden secrets of the universe.
It cannot be content
With much knowledge
That probes
The trivialities of life.

Cf. Kook, *Orot ha-Kodesh*, as cited in ibid., p. 9. "And as man grows in the scale of perfection, he draws upon all ideas, his own and those of others, for the kernel of abiding truth. He is made more perfect through them, and they through him."

163. Fackenheim, *Quest for Past and Future*, (Boston: Beacon Press, 1968) p.13.

164. Soloveitchik, *Halakhic Man*, p. 57.

Cf. ibid., p. 87. "Halakhic man, on the contrary, is very sparing in his recitation of the piyyutim, not, heaven forbid, on account of philosophical qualms, but because he serves his Maker with pure halakhic thought, precise cognition, and clear logic. . . . He serves the Creator by uncovering the truth in the Halakhah, by solving difficulties and resolving problems."

Cf. ibid., "Not so for halakhic man! When his soul yearns for God, he immerses himself in reality, plunges, with his entire being, into the very midst of concrete existence, and petitions God to descend upon the mountain and to dwell within our reality, with all its laws and principles."

165. Kadushin, *The Rabbinic Mind*, p. 14.

166. See ibid., p. 15. "Can we discern in the great array of ideas or concepts

any form of organization, or at least, any organizing principle? This is, we believe, the central problem in the study of Rabbinic Judaism."

167. See Greenberg. "Cloud of Smoke, Pillar of Fire," p. 27.

168. See Malbim: ". . . the whole of Judaism, apart from these two precepts [the existence and unity of God] is based on faith, faith in Moses as the messenger of God; faith that all that he commanded constituted the authentic message of God." As cited in Leibowitz, *Studies in Shemot*, p. 304. The aforementioned two precepts are attainable, according to the Malbim, Rambam, and others, by intellectual discernment.

169. See Buber, "What Should We Do About the Ten Commandments?" in his *Israel and the World* New York: Schocken, 1948, p. 86, as cited in Herberg, *Judaism and Modern Man*. "This affirmation—the 'leap of faith' that springs out of the decision for God—is not a leap of despair but rather a leap in triumph over despair."

170. See Soloveitchik, *Halakhic Man*, p. 79. "He does not require any miracles or wonders in order to understand the Torah. He approaches the world of Halakhah with his mind and intellect, just as cognitive man approaches the natural realm. And since he relies upon his intellect, he places his trust in it and does not suppress any of his psychic faculties in order to merge into some supernal existence."

171. Berkovits, *With God in Hell*, p. 123.

172. Bleich, *With Perfect Faith*, p. 6.

173. Ibid., p. 11.

174. As cited in Frazier, *Issues in Religion*, p. 259.

175. See Russell, *The Problems of Philosophy* (New York: Holt, 1912), p. 39. "All knowledge must be built on our intuitive beliefs; if they are rejected, nothing is left." Also, Pascal, *Pensées*, no. 274. "All our reasoning reduces itself to yielding to feeling." Both cited in Herberg, *Judaism and Modern Man*, p. 38.

176. See D. S. Shapiro, "The Meaning of Holiness in Judaism," *Tradition* 7, no.1 (Winter 1964–65): 48. "God is holy because he possesses in full all the attributes of goodness."

177. Philosophical opponents who challenge the rational-morality-of-God line of argument often erroneously cite Isaiah 55 as evidence of an inscrutable morality of God. "For my thoughts are not your thoughts, neither are your ways My ways, saith the Lord." The context of the oft-cited verse reveals no such intention. The succeeding verse explains its proper context.

For as the rain cometh down
and the snow from heaven,
And returneth not thither,
Except it water the earth,
And make it bring forth and bud,
And give seed to the sower and bread to the eater;
So shall My word be
that goeth forth out of My mouth;
It shall not return unto Me void
Except it accomplish that which I please,
And make the thing whereto I sent it prosper.

The intention is to convey the super-morality of God, not the supra-morality of God. If anything, reading the verse in context buttresses the rationalists. Isaiah is certainly the wrong prophet to cite in defense of an inscrutable morality of God.

178. Cf. Schulweis, *Evil and the Morality of God*, p. 120. "If the moral predicates mean one thing when applied to human beings and something incomprehensibly other when ascribed to God, no ethical universe of discourse can be said to exist. Not only is a critique of God's ways impossible, but a critique of man's conduct is similarly jeopardized. From the vantage point of a supramoral God, who knows whether our moral judgments of our society correspond to His moral criteria? . . . Biblical religion, in contrast to theology, opposes the rupture. 'I have not spoken in secret, in a place of the land of darkness; I said not unto the seed of Jacob: "Seek ye Me in vain." I the Lord speak righteousness. I declare things that are right.' (Isaiah 45:19)."

179. Cf. Berkovits, *Faith after the Holocaust*, p. 68. "This questioning of God with the very power of faith stands out at the earliest beginnings of the Jewish way in history. Abraham wrestled with God over the fate of Sodom and Gomorrah. We note how the man, who in the humility of his piety sees himself as mere 'dust and ashes' yet has the audacity to challenge God with the words: The judge of all the earth shall not do justice?!"

180. Schulweis, *Evil and the Morality of God*, p. 79.
Cf. ibid., p. 80.
Cf. ibid., p. 81. "The bilateral covenant signifies that there is no double standard, one for God and one for man. . . . Indeed, the qualitative sameness of the moral attributes enables man's moral *imitatio dei*."

181. Maimonides, *Guide* 3:51.

182. Hick, *Evil and the God of Love*, p. 98.

183. Also note that Ignatius' dictum has a direct parallel in Jewish literature—"even if right is left, and left is right."
Cf. John Stuart Mill, *An Examination of Sir William Hamilton's Philosophy*. "I will call no being good, who is not what I mean when I apply that epithet to my fellow creature, and if such a being can sentence me to hell for not so calling him, to hell I will go." As cited in Schulweis, *Evil and the Morality of God*, p. 26.

184. Shubert Spero, *Morality, Halakha and the Jewish Tradition*, p.86.

185. T. B. Sotah 14a; Genesis 3:21, 18:1, 25:11; Deuteronomy 34:6.

186. Sifrei Deuteronomy 49, 85a.

187. Exodus 15:2, Mekhilta 37a, Shabbat 133b.

188. E. Fackenheim, *Encounters Between Judaism and Modern Philosophy* (New York: Schocken, 1980), p. 48.

189. See Schulweis, "Suffering and Evil," p. 200.

190. Cf. Ibn Gabirol, *The Royal Crown*. "I will flee from Thee to Thyself, and I will shelter myself from Thy wrath in Thy shadow; and to the skirts of Thy mercies I will lay hold until Thou hast had mercy on me. I will not let Thee go until Thou hast blessed me." Cited by Schulweis, "Suffering and Evil."

191. "Though He slay me, yet I will trust in Him, but I will argue my ways before Him" (Job 13:15).

PART II

192. See comments of Berkovits noted in Schlesinger, "Logical Analysis."

193. See Glatzer, *The Dimensions of Job*, p. 73. "As in Jonah, the ultimate secret is seen to lie in the fact of creation."

194. Indeed, in the Jobian finale, when God challenges Job's remonstrations, God challenges Job on his comprehension of cosmic origins. This is elaborated on later in the text.

195. See Luban, "The Kaddish," p. 209. "Judaism does not frown on man's anxiety over evil. On the contrary it encourages man to be aware of his exitential dilemma, and to use his powers as a creative ethical fulcrum."

196. See Kellner's introduction to Abravanel, *Principles of Faith*, p. 20. "Abravanel . . . also notes that, if he has to choose principles for the Jewish faith, he would put forward only one, creation."

197. "Lord of the World" is a rhymed liturgical hymn. The author is unknown, although the hymn has been attributed to Solomon ibn Gabirol (11th cent.). See *Encyclopaedia Judaica*, vol. 2, col. 295.

198. See Davies, *God and the New Physics*, p. 47.

199. And indeed, why/wherefore does space/time exist at all? While quantum physics attempts to address and answer these points, the infrastructure of the "quantum" dovetails neatly with a philosophical formulation predicated on the centrality of "(holy) potential" in the cosmic order—the crux of our philosophical construct to follow. See Davies, *God and the New Physics*, chap. 3 (pp. 25–43).

200. See Wolfson, *Religious Philosophy*, p. 252. "In opposition to Philonism, emanationism denies that God, either after the manner of a potter created the world from a pre-existent matter, or after the manner of a stage-magician created it out of nothing. Emanationism maintains instead that, after the manner of a spider which spins its web out of itself, God caused the world to emanate out of His own essence."

201. See Staub, *The Creation of the World According to Gersonides*, p. 51.

202. Maimonides presents the view of the Kalam in *Guide* 1:73–74.

203. See *De Aeternitate Mundi*, ed. H. Rabe (Leipzig, 1899), pp. 7 ff., as cited in Staub, *The Creation of the World According to Gersonides*, p. 129, fn. 11.

204. *Guide* 2:13–30.

205. See Staub's discussion in *The Creation of the World According to Gersonides*, p. 130, n. 13.

206. See Stephen Toulmin, *Foresight and Understanding* (New York: Harper & Row, 1961), p. 42. "There must always be some point in a scientist's explanation where he comes to a stop: beyond this point, if he is pressed to explain further the fundamental basis of his explanation, he can say only that he has reached rock bottom."

207. Aristotle attributes this view to Empedocles and Heraclitus. Maimonides (*Guide* 2:13) treats this as a view of some of the rabbis. For fuller treatment, see Staub, *The Creation of the World According to Gersonides*, p. 129, fn. 8.

208. *Timaeus* 48e–53c. For fuller discussion, see ibid., p. 129, n. 9.

209. *Physica* 8.1–10; *De Caelo* 1.10–12; *Metaphysica* 12.6–10. Cf. *Guide* 2:13.

As cited by Staub, *The Creation of the World According to Gersonides*, p. 130, n. 14.

210. See Davies, *God and the New Physics*, p. 46.

211. See *Encyclopaedia Judaica*, s.v. "Kabbalah," and *Major Trends in Jewish Mysticism*, both by Gershom Scholem.

The valid question remains whether the voluminous extent, depth, obscure complexity, and mystical imagery, which they explored, dissected, and propounded, was not quite beyond "mortal competence," however spiritualized the writers. This is probably one of the reasons that the fate of kabbalistic philosophy, notwithstanding its preeminence at one time, is to be relegated to the very borderline of Jewish doctrine.

212. As previously noted, others use this same citation to support the idea of the unfathomability of God. But the extreme focus on creation and the lengthy dissertation on God's wonders lead us towards another conclusion.

213. The phrase *Eheyeh Asher Eheyeh* is commonly translated in the present tense, I–AM–THAT–I–AM. Note, however, that the literal and simple translation (*peshuto*) is future tense, as we translate it. Onkelos maintains the future tense, and Rashi's translation is clearly future-oriented—"I will be with them during this travail, as I will be with them in future travails." The main thrust of Nehama Leibowitz's explanation (in *Studies in Shemot*, p. 60) is also future-oriented. She cites Psalms 91:5, "I will be with them in trouble."

214. See below for citations regarding linkage of God's potential to man's potential.

Note that T.B Hagigah 11b admonishes against inquiry into origins or futures. However, the works of Maimonides and other medievals, aside from the kabbalists, stand as clear counterweights to this admonition.

215. See Isaac the Blind, "God beheld in Himself these essences, which would manifest themselves at the creation of the world." As cited in Scholem, *Origins of the Kabbalah*, p. 281. Scholem's footnote 172 says: "As quoted in *Sefer ha-Emunah weha-Bittahon*, chap. 18, and in somewhat better text, in the old miscellanies preserved in Ms. Christ Church College 198, fol. 25b."

Isaac the Blind, son of the Rabad, Provence, France, is referred to by Scholem as "the central figure in the oldest Kabbalah." Ibid., p. 252.

Cf. Isaac the Blind's commentary on the begining of *Midrash Konen*, as cited in Scholem, ibid., p. 287.

Cf. ibid., p. 451, citing a text of the kabbalists of Gerona. "Before God created the world . . . all things were mixed together and all the essences were hidden, for He had not yet brought them forth from potentiality to reality, like a tree in whose potency the fruit is already present." Scholem footnote 205 says: "Thus in Ms. British Museum, Margoliouth 752, fol. 36a. A very similar passage also in *Kether Shem Tob* in Jellinek, *Auswahl kabbalistischer Mystik*, 41."

Cf. Abraham Ibn Ezra in his commentary on Daniel 10:21. "And man alone is the foundation of the sublunar world and it is because of him that the world was created, his soul being linked to the Upper Soul." As cited in Stitskin, *Eight Jewish Philosophers*, p. 120.

Cf. Saadia Gaon, *Beliefs and Opinions* 4:1. "Although man is not the largest of the creatures, by virtue of his soul he encompasses the entire universe."

Cf. Bokser, *Abraham Isaac Kook*, p. 379.

Cf. Kant's argument in favor of the "principle of plentitude" (the principle that whatever can exist must somewhere actually exist, since otherwise the creative capacity of God would not be fully realized): "It would be absurd to represent the Deity as bringing into action only a small part of his creative potency." From Kant, *Allgemeine Naturgeschichte und Theorie des Himmels* (1755), pt. II, chap. vii, as trans. in A. O. Lovejoy, *The Great Chain of Being*, p. 140. Cited in Passmore, *The Perfectibility of Man*, p. 216.

216. We find it easier to posit Infinite Holy Potential as eternally preexisting all, as opposed to positing the classic God of Israel—an entity—as preexisting all.

Cf. Scholem, *Origins of the Kabbalah*, p. 348.

Later in the text (section 200.00) we call *Holy quest for potential* the underlying 'dynamic.' Subsequent to the First Printing, Haim Cohen, Former Justice, Supreme Court of Israel, suggested that the term 'abstract dynamic' or 'dynamic abstraction' might be closer to the intended mark. I agree, in particular, for the embryonic stages of *Holy quest for potential.*

217. See *Sefer Yesirah* (1562) fol. 63a, as cited in ibid., p. 341. "Before anything at all was created, God was unfathomable and limitless, alone and unique, capable of subsisting by Himself in the potency of existence."

Cf. ibid., pp. 282–283, 441.

Cf. Hirsch, *Chapters of the Fathers*, on Avot 5:1. "However, in this world . . . all the things that were made first were contributing factors in the creation of what came after them, and were, in fact, completed by the latter. . . . All things sustain and are sustained in their turn."

218. See Matt, *Zohar*, p. 24.

219. See Scholem, *Origins of the Kabbalah*, pp. 281–284, 438, 443.

Cf. ibid., pp. 431–432. "Asher ben David, too, expresses himself clearly in a theistic and personalistic vein, identifying '*en-sof*' with the personally conceived supreme primordial cause."

Asher ben David was the nephew of the aforementioned Isaac the Blind and grandson of the Rabad. He "carried on the traditions of his father and uncle during the first half of the thirteenth century in Provence and at the same time served as one of the most important links with the mystical centers newly forming in northern Spain, above all in Gerona." Ibid., p. 252.

220. See Hirsch, *Timeless Torah*, p. 16.

221. See Hirsch, *Chapters of the Fathers*, on Avot 5:1. "Man is the final work of creation, the goal and summit of the whole, in whom all creation culminates."

222. Note also the statement of the Sages. "For the sake of Israel, Moses, [and the precepts of] challah, tithing, and first fruits, was the world created." See also Hirsch, *Timeless Torah*, p. 5.

223. The possible argument, alluded to by Maimonides, that every potentiality needs an agent to actualize it, is inapplicable to our context for at least three reasons differentiating our case: (1) infinite potential, (2) potential within potential ad infinitum, and (3) holy potential.

224. Maimonides notes (*Guide* 2:26) in particular from *Rabbi Eliezer*: "Whence were the heavens created? He took part of the light of His garment, stretched it like a cloth . . ."

225. See "The Creation of Elohim," in Matt, *Zohar*, pp. 49–50.

Note in particular the "radical" position of the *Zohar* at the conclusion of the chapter:

With the Beginning
the Concealed One who is not known
created the palace
the palace is called *Elohim*
the secret is:
"With Beginning _____ created *Elohim*"
(Genesis 1:1)

226. See Greenberg, *Perspectives: Voluntary Covenant*, p. 2.
227. See Scholem, *Major Trends in Jewish Mysticism*, pp. 207, 208, 214.
228. See ibid., p. 207. Cf. Maimonides, *Guide* 3:20. Cf. Matt's "introduction" to Moses de Leon, in *Zohar*, p. 33.
229. See Hirsch, *Chapters of the Fathers* on Avot 5:1. "By ten utterances was the world created . . ."
230. Note Agus, *The Evolution of Jewish Thought*, p. 287.
231. See Scholem, *Major Trends in Jewish Mysticism*, pp. 213–214.
232. See ibid., pp. 213–214.
233. Ibid., p. 214.
234. Matt, *Zohar*, p. 34.
235. See Scholem, *Origins of the Kabbalah*, pp. 81–84, 437.
Cf. ibid., p. 450. "In their conception of the emanation, the kabbalists of Gerona unite the two motifs of the emergence from potentiality to actuality on the one hand, and of the maturation of the organic process, on the other."
CF. Azriel of Gerona, *Commentary on Talmudic Aggadoth*, p. 110 (lines 13–14 in particular), and idem, *Perush Eser Sefirot*, p. 4 (sec. *gimel*).
On a very closely related track, the Book of Bahir deals with the aeons, or powers, of God. Scholem notes: "Each *middah* [aeon] is a particular spiritual potency." Ibid., p. 82.
236. Hayim Vital, *Ets Hayim* (Warsaw, 1891), XI, 7, p. 107, as cited in Scholem, *Major Trends in Jewish Mysticism*, p. 269, n. 76.
237. Scherman, "An Overview: Kaddish," p. xii.
238. Specifically, when a woman gives birth to a male she becomes "impure" for seven days; to a female, fourteen days (Leviticus 12:6).
239. Or HaChaim, Leviticus 12:2.
240. Soloveitchik, *Halakhic Man*, p. 107.
241. See Agus, "The Meaning of Prayer," in Millgram, *Great Jewish Ideas*, p. 235. "The Tetragrammaton (YHVH), whatever its original meaning and pronunciation, is understood to be a formula, combining the future, the past and the present."
Cf. Hick, *Readings in The Philosophy of Religion*, p. 72. "that His true name is He that is, or, in other words, Being without restriction, all Being, the Being infinite and universal."
242. See Whitehead, "Process and Reality," in Alston and Nakhnikian, *Readings in Twentieth-Century Philosophy*, p. 151. "Viewed as primordial, he [God] is the unlimited conceptual realization of the absolute wealth of potentiality."
Cf. Berkovits, *Major Themes in Modern Philosophies of Judaism*, p. 21. "God is *m'huyab hamziut*, He is absolute and exists of his own uncreated intrinsic necessity."
243. See Berg, *Kabbalah for the Layman*, p. 72.
244. See Bokser, *Abraham Isaac Kook*, p. 4. "Rav Kook saw the whole universe stirred by the pulsating energies emanating from the divine source of all existence."

Cf. Steinsaltz, *The Thirteen Petalled Rose*, p. 39. "All these *Sefirot* are infinite in their potency, even though they are finite in their essence."

Cf. *Shem Olam*, p. 41, as cited in Agus, *The Evolution of Jewish Thought*, p. 285. "The primal man consists in his turn of ten *sefiroth*, which were conceived as being both God and not-God. 'For that which is infinite and boundless could not make that which is finite and definite; therefore, it was necessary to postulate ten *sefiroth* in the middle, which are both finite and infinite.' "

245. Soloveitchik, *Halakhic Man*, p. 132. (Soloveitchik cites Maimonides, *Guide* 2:32. "Prophecy is a certain perfection in the nature of man. This perfection is not achieved in any individual from among men except after a training that makes that which exists in the potentiality of the species pass into actuality.")

Cf. ibid., p. 132. "In truth, Greek philosophy was also familiar with the notion of a process of development from relative nothingness to a perfect existence. What is more, this problem is practically the central issue in Greek ontology. The dispute between Heraclitus and Parmenides concerning the nature of being—whether it is perpetual development and movement or fixed, perfect existence—still made itself felt in the analyses of the Platonic and Aristotelian schools and their successors."

246. See Lamm, *The Face of God*, sec. 5, comments on "Survivalist Hester."

247. Kook, "Light of Penitence," in Bokser, *Abraham Isaac Kook*, p. 376.

248. To draw a parallel with architecture: Aristotelian philosophy concerning the origins of the universe can be compared to a classic structure: the upper structure, i.e., the universe, is supported by the foundation—God. Our formulation can be compared somewhat to an infinitely expanding geodesic dome—with all elements supporting each other. (A geodesic dome, often employed as a roof for large stadiums, is composed of a framework of light, straight-sided polygons in tension. It was originally conceived by Buckminster Fuller.)

249. See Agus, *The Evolution of Jewish Thought*, p. 74. "In the Hellenistic world there was current the Stoic conception of *anima mundi*, the soul of the world, which pictured the Deity as the sum and substance of the laws prevailing in the universe. The rabbis did not think of God as the world's soul, in the sense of being the expression of the totality of its powers and functions."

Cf. ibid., p. 87. "Philo rejected the Aristotelian concept of the Deity as the unmoved mover, since it implied the eternity of the world and denied the miracle of creation. Similarly, Philo repudiated the Stoic view of God as a material principle, immanent in physical nature, revealed in reason and expressed in the laws which govern all events in the universe. The Stoics believed the fundamental energy of the universe to be a quasi-rational logos, conscious, inflexible, and benevolent. . . . Scripture emphasizes the spiritual character of God's being and His difference from the material world."

250. Stephen Hawking, a physicist, observes: "It may be that the universe really did not have a beginning. Or maybe the 'space-time' forms a closed surface without an edge like the surface of the earth but in two more dimensions." From WNET's production "The Origin of the Universe" (approximately 5478 on standard-speed VHS tape).

251. Soloveitchik, *Halakhic Man*, p. 131.

252. Stitskin, *Eight Jewish Philosophers*, p. 120

253. See Genesis Rabbah, chap. 30, on the verse ". . . walk before Me, and be wholehearted" (Genesis 17:1)—"in the view of Rabbi Johanan we need His honor; in the view of Rabbi Simeon be Lakish He needs our honor." As cited in Heschel, *Man Is Not Alone*, p. 243.

254. See Soloveitchik, *Halakhic Man*, p. 91. "Halakhic man cannot be cowed by anyone. He knows no fear of flesh and blood. For is he not a creator of worlds, a partner of the Almighty in the act of creation?"

Cf. Berkovits, *Faith After the Holocaust*, p. 60. "Man, according to his own strength, continues the work of creation and becomes, urged on by God's call, a humble associate of the Creator."

255. See Bokser, *Abraham Isaac Kook*, pp. 27–28. "As long as the striving for divine ideals and their effectuation in the course of a continuous historical existence does not manifest itself in the nation, the divine Presence is in exile, and the life-force released by the service of God is in a state of weakness" (*Ikve Hatzon*, "Daat Elohim," in *Eder Hayakar*, pp. 130–141).

256. "Of course, man needs God. But God, 'in the fullness of His reality,' needs man. He who says 'Thy will be done' may say no more, but truth adds for him 'through me whom Thou needest.' " (Martin Buber, *I and Thou* (New York: Charles Scribner's Sons, 1958), p. 83. "God thus responds to a man's dealings with the beings and things of the universe by pouring His divinity into all of nature. In this sense, it is man who 'turns the world into a sacrament.' " Idem, *mamre* (Melbourne University Press, 1946), p. 105. As cited in Schulweis, *Evil and the Morality of God*, p. 99.

Cf. Gordis, *A Faith for Moderns*, p. 260.

Cf. Soloveitchik, *Halakhic Man*, p. 99. "The dream of creation is the central idea in the halakhic consciousness—the idea of the importance of man as a partner of the Almighty in the act of creation, man as creator of worlds."

See also the contemporary discourses of Rav Shlomo Chaim Hakohen Aviner in *Tal Hermon: Iyunim BaTorah* editor A. Kleinspitz, privately printed in Jerusalem by Ateret Kohanim. See section on *Bereshit*. Translation of selected segments follows:

". . . All that God created needs completion by us, as is written '*asher ba-rah Elokim la-a-sot.*'"

". . . It is possible to say that all that we do is a continuation of . . . '*na-a-seh ha-adam*'. We complete the creation of man."

257. Midrash Rabbah, Lamentations 1:6.

258. See Fackenheim, *God's Presence in History*, p. 23.

259. There is a midrashic concept that there are three partners in the creation of a child—man, woman, and the Divine.

260. Heschel, *Man Is Not Alone*, p. 241.

Cf. ibid., p. 242. "God is a partner and a partisan in man's struggle for justice, peace and holiness, and it is because of His being in need of man that He entered a convenant with him for all time."

Cf. Heschel, *God in Search of Man*, p. 413. "To be is to stand for, and what man stands for is the great mystery of being His partner. God is in need of man."

261. Pesikta, ed. Buber, XXVI, 166b, as cited in Heschel, *Man Is Not Alone*, p. 243.

262. See below in this section on the Torah's tolerance of the consumption of animals.

263. Ramban, *Commentary on the Torah*, vol. 2, p. 448.

264. Inasmuch as the boiling of a kid goat in its mother's milk was also apparently a pagan rite, the thrice-cited proscription of this practice is also taken in some quarters as a general injunction against paganism.

265. The usual explanation is *hakaras ha-tov*—acknowledgment of God's good. Our interpretation would be a further refinement of this general explanation.

266. *"Arami oved avi . . ."*

267. See also T. B. Berachot 40b.

268. Newtol Press, "Kosher Ecology," *Commentary* 79, no. 2 (February 1985).

269. Sifrei, Shoftim, sec. 203.

270. Pesachim 56a.

271. Chullin 7b; Tosefot Baba Kamma 115b, based on Avodah Zarah 30b. See Robert Gordis, "Ecology in the Jewish Tradition," *Midstream*, October 1985, p. 22.

272. See also Leibniz, who posits that the universe as a whole must display a "perpetual and very free progress . . . such that it advances always to still greater improvement." Translated in Wiener, *Leibniz: Selections*, p. 354, as cited in Passmore, *The Perfectibility of Man*, p. 215.

273. See Book of Bahir, excerpt from secs. 64–67, as cited in Scholem, *Origins of the Kabbalah*, p. 77. "The potency of one is [also] in the other. . . . all thirty-six potencies are already found in the first . . . and the potency of each one is found in the other."

Cf. ibid., *Origins of the Kabbalah*, p. 462, citation from *Megillath ha-Megalleh*.

274. Soloveitchik, "The Lonely Man of Faith," p. 31.

275. See Scholem, *Origins of the Kabbalah*, p. 289. "The divine power spreading from the sefiroth into Creation . . . also descends below the human domain to living beings of a lower order, even to plants."

276. "That they may know from the rising of the sun from the east, and its setting westward, that there is none beside Me; I am the Lord, and there is no other." (Isaiah 45:6).

277. See Kant, *Idea of a Universal History*, First Proposition, as cited in Passmore, *The Perfectibility of Man*, p. 216. "All the capacities implanted in a creature by nature, are destined to unfold themselves, completely and conformably to their end, in the course of time."

"Who can fail to discover that the hand of the Lord is behind all this!" (Job 12:9).

278. See Soloveitchik, "The Lonely Man of Faith," p. 32 (citing Bereshit Rabbah 59): "Our sages said that before Abraham appeared, *majestes dei* (the glory of God) was reflected only by the distant heavens and it was a mute nature which 'spoke' of the glory of God. It was Abraham who 'crowned' Him the God of the earth, i.e., the God of men."

279. See Scholem, *Origins of the Kabbalah*, p. 339, expounding on the views of the "Gerona circle" of kabbalists. "In this view, primordial man is . . . only a configuration of the supreme potencies."

280. See Schulweis, *Evil and the Morality of God*, p. 129. "Akiba, the rabbinic sage, is asked by Tinneius Rufus, the pagan, 'Whose works are greater, those

of God or those of man?' Akiba replies that the works of man excel, and as evidence places before him sheaves of wheat and dishes of cakes. Akiba regards the latter as greater not because he would denigrate God. For Akiba God and the human being are not contending forces. The sheaves represent the nonhuman givenness—the product of seed, water, soil, and sun; the cakes represent the transformation of that givenness, the actualization of the potential for the sake of the sustenance of humanity. It is bread and wine, not sheaves and grapes, which are sanctified in praise of the transaction which with human hands brings the natural process to controlled perfection. The ideals are not the final reality already extant in some realm of being. Rabbinic wisdom expresses the faith which calls for transformation. 'Everything needs to be acted upon. The lupine must be soaked, the mustard seed sweetened, the wheat ground, and man must be perfected. Everything requires repair.' "

281. According to Herder, men of different ages are linked by a "golden chain of improvement." Herder, *Ideas*, bk. IX, chap. 1, p. 231, as cited in Passmore, *The Perfectibility of Man*, p. 223.

282. See the discussion of Soloveitchik in *Peli, On Repentance*, p. 14.
    Cf. ". . . a man's reach should exceed his grasp, / Or what's a heaven for?" Browning, *Andrea del Sarto*.

283. There are two places where Scripture relates the creation of man. The first is near the end of Genesis 1; the second, in Genesis 2. There has been considerable discussion on the differences in wording and nuance between the two chapters. See Soloveitchik's classic "The Lonely Man of Faith."

284. Ibid., p. 15.

285. See Herbert Spencer, *Social Statics*, ed. cit., pt. I, chap. II, #4, 65, as cited in Passmore, *The Perfectibility of Man*, p. 241. "Progress . . . is not an accident, but a necessity."
    See also Stephen Hawking, *A Brief History of Time*, p. 121. "Why did the universe start out with so nearly the critical rate of expansion that separates models that recollapse from those that go on expanding forever, so that even now, ten thousand million years later, it is still expanding at nearly the critical rate? If the rate of expansion one second after the big bang had been smaller by even one part in a hundred thousand million million, the universe would have recollapsed before it ever reached its present size."

286. Faith is described as "the queen of virtues" by Philo, *On Abraham*, XLVI, 270 (Loeb ed., vol. 6, p. 133), as cited in Passmore, *The Perfectibility of Man*, p. 61.

287. Bokser, *Abraham Isaac Kook*, p. 229.

288. Gordis, *The Book of God and Man*, p. 147. Cf. idem, *A Faith for Moderns*, p. 208.

289. Aquinas, *Summa Theologiae*, vol. I, q. 6, a. 1, p. 110.

290. Greenberg, *Perspectives: The Third Great Cycle of Jewish History*, p. 1.

291. Berkovits, *God, Man and History*, p. 81.

292. Berdyaev, *The Destiny of Man*, p. 136.
    Berdyaev elegantly straddles the Aristotelian position of creation out of

primal matter, and the position of those (including traditional Jewish think-ers) who posit creation *ex nihilo* ("out of nothingness").

293. In Aquinas' *De Potentia Dei*, potency (power) and act are important principles; however, Aquinas' meaning, emphasis, and thrust are different from ours. For summary, see article on Thomas Aquinas in *Encyclopedia of Philosophy* (New York: Macmillan, 1967), vol. 8, p . 110.

294. Soloveitchik, "The Lonely Man of Faith," elaborating on the verse "Holy, holy, holy is the Lord of hosts; the whole earth is full of His glory" (Isaiah 6:3).

295. To our knowledge, the Aristotelians, while considering, at least pe-ripherally, the concept of potential, do not seem to have proffered or developed the concept of holy potentiality, specifically: Holy Potential within potential within potential . . . *ad infinitum.*

296. See also Merton, *The New Man,* p. 31, and his footnote on page 56: "In the Biblical concept [as opposed to the Nietzschean], man is raised above himself by supernatural gifts for which his nature has a passive and obedien-tial potency, gifts by which these hidden potentialities receive a supereminent realization."

297. See also ibid., p. 27.

298. "Rabbi Kook in his introduction to his commentary on the *Siddur Olat Riyah,* writes that man's soul is continually in a state of worship. It expresses the soul's yearning for inner fulfillment from a state of potentiality to actuality." Stitskin, *Studies in Torah Judaism,* p. 86.

299. See Herder, *Sammtliche Werke,* ed. B. Suphan, 33 vols. (Berlin, 1877–1913), vol. 5, p. 98, as cited in Barnard, *J. G. Herder on Social and Political Culture,* p. 28. "The essence of life is never fruition, but continuous becom-ing."

However, note that Herder also seemingly posits in the opposite direction in *Ideas for a Philosophy of the History of Mankind,* bk. VIII, chap. IV, as cited ibid., p. 304. "Everything that exists strives towards self-preservation; from the grain of sand to the solar system it strives to remain what it is."

300. Adherents of Ayn Rand take note!

301. Teilhard de Chardin, *The Future of Man,* p. 11.

302. To clarify terms: Light is in an inverse relationship to dark, i.e., the more light, the less dark. Judaism is mutually exclusive with human sacrifice. If one is within Judaism, one does not engage in human sacrifice. If one engages in human sacrifice, one is not within Judaism.

303. Agus, *The Evolution of Jewish Thought,* p. 293.

304. See Scholem, *Major Trends in Jewish Mysticism,* p. 261. "In other words, the cosmic process becomes two-fold. Every stage involves a double strain, i.e., the light which streams back into God and that which flows out from Him, and but for this perpetual tension, this ever repeated effort with which God holds Himself back, nothing in the world would exist."

Cf. Scholem, *Origins of the Kabbalah,* pp. 438–440.

305. Cited by Kaellis in "The Crescas Dispute." *Midstream,* December 1986, p. 47.

306. See Altizer, *The Descent into Hell,* pp. 120–121, 131.

307. See the Chinese classic, the *Book of Changes.*

308. See Leibowitz, *Studies in Bereshit* p. 17. ". . . it is the allegorical, hidden meaning of the garden of Eden and tree of knowledge that we must seek."

309. See the analogous but quite different formulation in Merton, *The New Man*, p. 108. "St. Bernard puts this 'sapor mortis,' this taste for death, at the very heart of original sin. It is the exact opposite of the wisdom, the 'sapida scienta' or existential ('tasting') of knowledge of the Divine good. The two are incompatible with one another. They cannot exist together. Consequently, having acquired the one, Adam necessarily lost the other."

310. See Philo, *On the Unchangeableness of God* 143 (Loeb ed., vol. 3, pp. 81 ff.). "Wisdom is a straight high road, and it is when the mind's course is guided along that road that it reaches the goal which is the recognition and knowledge of God. Every comrade of the flesh hates and rejects this path and seeks to corrupt it. For there are no two things so utterly opposed as knowledge and pleasure of the flesh." In Lewy et al., *Three Jewish Philosophers*, p. 52.

Cf. Fackenheim, *The Jewish Return into History*, p. 263. "Philosophical reflection may find it necessary to choose between a God who is divine only if he is omnibenevolent and omnipotent, and a world which is truly world only because it contains elements contradicting these divine attributes, namely, evil and human freedom."

311. Berkovits, *God, Man and History*, p. 79.

312. See Merton, *The New Man*, p. 110. "Adam, by his proud act, his insistence on improving his wisdom and science by adding to it the knowledge of evil, inevitably lost the full experience of goodness that was freely given to him by God. . . . These deprivations [the consequences of eating from the literal 'tree of knowledge'] were not merely the revenge of an irate God—they were inherent."

313. Thus "miracles" are consistent with a period of limited Divine intervention, e.g., the Exodus, but not consistent with a period of perceived contraction of the Divine, e.g., the mid-twentieth century.

314. See Cohen, *The Tremendum*, pp. 27–28. "It is of the nature of the human that we live on two sides always: one illuminated, the other remaining in darkness. . . . These bivalences of the human exist . . . these contrarieties inhere in the human . . . bifurcated creature in a bifurcated universe, man doubled in a universe that is doubled, fractured man, prisoner of contradiction in a universe no less cut in two."

315. Midrash Bereshit Rabbah 14 addresses the question of why there is a seemingly extraneous consonant *y* (*yod*) in the Hebrew *Vayyizer* in the phrase "Then the Lord God formed the man" (Genesis 2:7). The consensus is that the connotation is for two formations, with variations of that theme offered: (1) Adam/Eve, (2) the celestial/the earthly, (3) good/evil, and (4) this world/the next world. We would parallel (3) and offer (5) Tree of Life/Tree of Knowledge; i.e., two possible world paths were open to man.

Cf. Midrash Rabbah, Genesis 21:5–6. " 'Behold, the man has become as one of us.' . . . Said R. Akiba to him . . . How then do you interpret *Mimmennu*? It means that the Holy One, blessed be He, set two ways before him, life and death, and he chose the other path." (Commentary: "that which God did not wish him to choose," viz., death. Th.: R. Akiba treats *mimmennu* as third-person singular ["of himself"], not first-person plural ["of us"], translating: "Behold, the man has become as one who knows good and evil of himself, of his own free will, and thereby has himself chosen the path of death.")

316. Midrash Rabbah, Genesis 49, no. 20.

317. See Augustine, *Confessions and Enchiridion*. "For God would never have created any, I do not say angel, but even man, whose future wickedness He foreknew, unless He had equally known to what uses in behalf of the good He could turn him, thus embellishing the course of the ages, as it were an exquisite poem set off with antitheses. For what are called antitheses are among the most elegant of the ornaments of speech. They might be called in Latin 'oppositions,' or, to speak more accurately, 'contrapositions.' " As cited in Hick, *Evil and the God of Love*, p. 24.

318. The theme of the parallel of the relationship of God: Israel, in particular, with father: son is amplified below.

319. See Herder, *Ideas for a Philosophy of History*, bk. IV, pt. VI, as cited in Barnard, *J. G. Herder on Social and Political Culture*, p. 265. "Man is the first of nature's creatures to be set free; he stands erect. He can weigh up good against evil, truth against falsehood; he can explore possibilities and choose between alternatives."

320. See Merton, *The New Man*, p. 13.

Cf. Kaplan, *The New World of Philosophy*, p. 108. "[Existentialism maintains that] In every choice I am responsible for the fate of mankind. . . . This is why Kierkegaard says we choose only 'in fear and trembling,' why he speaks of the 'dizziness of freedom,' why Sartre says that man is 'condemned to be free.' "

321. See Abravanel as cited in Leibowitz, *Studies in Bereshit*, p. 18. ". . . the whole perfection of man lay in his possession of the capacity to choose freely between evil and good. Otherwise he could not have been human and God could not have commanded him: 'from all the trees of the garden you may eat but of the tree of knowledge of good and evil you may not eat thereof'; since a command can only apply to one who possesses a free choice and will."

322. See the question posed by the third-century Syrian philosopher Porphyrius (in his controversy with the Christians): "Is it not very odd that [what is described as] the punishment for disobedience should be the attainment of a perfection which he [man] had never possessed, namely—intelligence?" As cited by Heinemann in his "Abarbanels Lehre vom Niedergang der Menscheit," *Monatsschrift fuer Geschichte und Wissenschaft des Judentums*, 1938, pp. 381–400, as cited in Leibowitz, *Studies in Bereshit*, p. 26.

323. See the question posed by Abravanel: "If it is maintained that the eating of the tree [of Knowledge] did harm because it involved the knowing of evil, surely it was, at the same time beneficial, in involving the knowledge of good?" As cited in Leibowitz, *Studies in Bereshit*, p. 17.

324. See Seltzer, *Jewish People, Jewish Thought*, p. 756. "Jewish observance can be described only in polarities: on the one hand, stability, repetitiveness, and regularity, but on the other hand, inwardness, spontaneity, freedom."

325. See Buber, *The Prophetic Faith*, p. 103. "The unformulated primal theological principle of the Garden of Eden story about the divine-human relationship [is] . . . that created man has been provided by the Creator's

breath with real power of decision and so is able actually to oppose YHVH's commanding will." As cited in Herberg, *Judaism and Modern Man*, p. 84, n. 15.

326. Man foresook a low-risk/low-reward-potential existence, for a high-risk/high-reward-potential existence.

327. While Luzzatto's treatment of Providence is very different from ours, he notes: "God arranged matters so that man's chances of achieving ultimate salvation should be maximized." Luzzatto, *The Way of God*, p. 125.

Cf. Bertrand Russell, "A Free Man's Worship," in idem, *Mysticism and Logic* (New York: Norton, 1929), p. 48. "A strange mystery it is that nature, omnipotent but blind, has brought forth at last a child, subject still to her power but gifted with sight, with knowledge of good and evil, with the capacity of judging all the works of his unthinking mother. . . . Man is yet free, during his brief years, to examine, to criticize, to know and in imagination to create. To him alone in the world with which he is acquainted, this freedom belongs and in this lies his superiority to the resistless forces that control his outer life."

328. See Hick, "Faith and Knowledge," pp. 518–519.

Cf. Berkovits, *God, Man and History*, p. 146. "By creating man as a being in need of spiritual, intellectual, and ethical freedom in order to fulfill himself, God took a chance with His creature."

329. Berkovits, *God, Man and History*, p. 79.

330. Miguel de Unamuno, cited in Lamm, *Faith and Doubt*, p. 34.

331. Abravanel challenges in parallel: "A command is not given to animals or one lacking intelligence. With his intellectual faculty man differentiates between truth and falsehood, and this was possessed by him [prior to partaking of the tree] in his pristine perfection and purity." As cited in Leibowitz, *Studies in Bereshit*, p. 18.

332. Parallel to some kabbalistic formulations of *Adam Kadmon*.

See Scholem, *Major Trends in Jewish Mysticism*, p. 265. "The decisive point is that according to this [Lurianic] doctrine, the first being which emanated from the [Divine] light was *Adam Kadmon*, primordial man."

Note to reader: Although there are parallels between Lurianic "primordial man" and our Primal Man, according to many interpretations of *Adam Kadmon*, there would be very major differences. See complete discussion in Scholem's *Major Trends in Jewish Mysticism* and related sources.

333. Erich Fromm asserts that man's humanity begins when he leaves Eden.

334. See Wiesel, *The Fifth Son*, p. 71. "In our [Jewish] tradition it is the woman who represents continuity; it is she who carries and projects the future of our people. And that is how it should be. Don't you agree?"

335. Tishbi on the Zohar posits that *e-lana d'mavsa* (the Tree of Death) is embedded in the Tree of Knowledge.

336. See Hick, *Evil and the God of Love*, p. 12. "The working vocabulary of theodicy, compared with that of some other branches of theology, is in a state of imprecision. In English 'evil' is usually, although not always, used in a comprehensive sense, and we then distinguish under it the moral evil of wickedness and such non-moral evils as disease and natural disaster. In German 'Ubel' is a general term, covering both moral and non-moral evil,

though it can also be used specifically for the latter; whilst 'Buse' refers more definitely to moral evil. In French 'le mal' can be used to refer to all types of evil."

337. See Berdyaev, *The Destiny of Man*, pp. 30, 158.

338. See Schulweis, *Evil and the Morality of God*, p. i. "The Gothic word 'evil' refers to the force in the universe that gives rise to wickedness, sin, misfortune, disaster. The presence of evil, its reality, makes a hole in the heart of the believer."

339. See Sarna, *Understanding Genesis*, pp. 30–31.

340. See Berg, *Kabbalah for the Layman*, p. 85.

Cf. Bokser, *Abraham Isaac Kook*, p. 267. "there is a conception [in the Kabbalah] of a negative counterforce paralleling institutional religion, the ideal essence of religion."

Cf. Zohar, *Parshat Terumah* 129b. ". . . the glory of the Holy One, blessed be He, is more greatly exalted [by the Kaddish] than through any other prayer, because it causes the 'other side' to wane and its empire to decline." As cited in Luban, "The Kaddish," p. 210.

Cf. Zohar 1:4a. We are here "to turn darkness into light."

Cf. Scholem, *Major Trends in Jewish Mysticism*, p. 263. "Throughout this process the two tendencies of perpetual ebb and flow—the Kabbalists speak of *hithpashtuth*, egression, and *histalkuth*, regression—continue to act and react upon each other. Just as the human organism exists through the double process of inhaling and exhaling and the one cannot be conceived without the other, so also the whole of Creation constitutes a gigantic process of divine inhalation and exhalation. In the final resort, therefore, the root of all evil is already latent in the act of *Tsimtsum*."

Cf. Scholem, *Origins of the Kabbalah*, p. 293.

There is a theme in kabbalistic literature that when the Ten *Sefirot* (of holiness) were created, alongside them came into existence Ten *Sefirot* of impurity (*de-mis'avusa*).

341. Maimonides cites and approves this general proposition in *Guide* 3:10 (Dover ed., p. 266).

342. Baal Shem Tov, *Kesser Shem Tov*, cited by Agus, "The Meaning of Prayer," in Millgram, *Great Jewish Ideas*, p. 221.

343. Bokser, *Abraham Isaac Kook*, p. 21.

344. John Milton, *Areopagitica*, p. III, as quoted in *Commentary*, January 1985, p. 46.

345. In disagreement see the viewpoint related in Hick, *Evil and the God of Love*, p. 19. "In the first place, good and evil are not objective realities (*entia realia*), but mental entities (*entia rationis*), formed by comparing things either in respect of their conformity to a general idea or merely in respect of their utility to ourselves."

346. See Scherman, "An Overview: The Period and the Miracle," p. xxvii. ". . . the many comments of the sages make it abundantly clear, however, that Amalek is the very embodiment of evil on earth."

We decline to take the route of attributing evil to "Satanic forces," implying a source other than the Divine, and then not explaining the origins of the Satanic. As Hick notes, "The puzzles attending human imperfection, free will, and sin are reiterated, but not further illumined, by transferring them to a superhuman plane." *Evil and the God of Love*, p. 13.

Cf. Cohen, *The Tremendum*, p. 33.

Cf. Augustine, "The Problem of Evil," in Hick, *Readings in the Philosophy of Religion*, p. 19.

347. See Heschel, *Man's Quest for God*, p. 98. "The soul is clean, but within it resides a power for evil, 'a strange god' (T. B. Tractate Shabbath 105b) that seeks constantly to get the upper hand over man and to kill him . . . (T. B. Tractate Sukkah 52b)."

Cf. Hick, *Readings in the Philosophy of Religion*, p. 184. "When powers are at war with one another for the rule of the world, the boundary between them is not fixed but constantly fluctuating. This may seem to be the case on our planet as between the powers of good and evil when we look only at the results; but when we consider the inner springs, we find that both the good and the evil take place in the common course of nature."

Cf. Cohen, *The Tremendum*, p. 51.

348. Soloveitchik, *Halakhic Man*, p. 102.

349. See Maccoby, "Christianity's Break with Judaism," p. 40. "In the Hebrew Bible this world, having been created by God, is regarded as good, and as the scene of the human drama, where all things will eventually find a solution. At the opposite extreme is the literature of the gnostic sects that flourished around the time of the emergence of Christianity; in its view this world is evil, the creation of an evil Power."

350. Hick, *Evil and the God of Love*, p. 25.

Cf. Maccoby, "Christianity's Break with Judaism," p. 42. "In the Hebrew Bible this world . . . is regarded as good, . . . where all things will eventually find a solution. At the opposite extreme [are] the Gnostic sects. . . . The Pseudepigrapha and the Dead Sea Scrolls, both of which envisage a war between good angels and bad angels, and which may be thought of as a first step away from the unified, humanistic outlook of both the Hebrew Bible and rabbinic Judaism, nevertheless represent a milder form of dualism than that in either gnosticism or Christianity."

351. See Mamlak, "Gershon Mamlak Responds," *Midstream*, November 1984, p. 32. "The history of Israel is one uninterrupted outcry against all forms of evil-doing."

352. See Greenberg, "Cloud of Smoke, Pillar of Fire," p. 36. "Karl Barth, Roy Eckardt, and Eliezer Berkovits have suggested that Israel suffers for the nations' anger at God. Because Israel is God's people, 'other nations are constantly enraged by its existence, revolting against it, and wishing its destruction.' Or, as Eckardt puts it: 'In the existence of the Jewish people, we are confronted by God's electing grace, by His mercy as the only basis of human life. By our antagonism to Jews we show that we really do not like this fact.' . . . By its existence, Israel testifies to the God who promises the ultimate redemption and perfection in an unredeemed world. Thus it arouses the anger of all who claim already to have found absolute perfection. Whenever there are Christian claims to absolute spiritual salvation, or Stalinist or Nazi claims to absolute social and political perfection, or capitalist or superpatriot

claims to ultimate national loyalty, then Jews naturally become the object of suspicion and rejection."

353. See Stitskin, *Eight Jewish Philosophers*, p. 77. "Another view offered by many philosophers and drawn from Platonic sources is that evil is a negative property. It is the absence of good, just as blindness is the absence of vision, deafness the absence of hearing and darkness the absence of light. This understanding of evil as a negative property does not mean that evil is an illusion and can be disregarded. It implies rather that it is not created by God directly. God produces the positive, the good forms, and determines them to last a definite span of time. When this time comes to an end, the forms disappear and pain and evil take their place just as darkness comes when light goes out."

354. T. B. Pesachim 50a teaches us that "in this world we must bless God for both good and evil. But in the world-to-come we will realize that there is nothing but good."

355. See Stitskin, *Eight Jewish Philosophers*, pp. 77–78 (in his chpater on Abraham Bar Hiyya). "There is ample evidence in Scripture that God is the cause of evil as well as good. . . . Justice denotes the good and evil distributed in this world according to the law of justice. Thus, God is the author of both good and evil in the world."

356. Maimonides, *Guide* 3:10 (Dover ed., p. 266). The development by Maimonides in chapter 10 of the *Guide* stresses that God directly creates only good, and only indirectly evil. It would seem to us that any differences between our position and Maimonides' position on this point are primarily semantic ones. (We trust that the devotees of Maimonides now breathe easier.)

357. Aquinas, *Summa Theologiae*, I, q. 49, a. 1.

358. Augustine, "The Problem of Evil," in Hick, *Readings in the Philosophy of Religion*, p. 21.

359. See Berkovits, *God, Man and History*, p. 78. "It is a commonplace by now to say that without evil goodness would not be possible either. In a world without temptation, man could never be holy. . . . Without the forever-lurking inclination to selfishness and discord, there can be no ethical ideal and practice."

360. See Schulweis, *Evil and the Morality of God*, p. 47. "Without good, evil could not exist; without evil, goodness would be impoverished. Paradoxically, if there is evil, there is God. Leibniz echoes this logic in his declaration that to permit the evil, as God permits it, proves to be the greatest goodness" (Leibniz, *Theodicy*, pt. II, par. 121).

361. See Hick, *Evil and the God of Love*, p. 368. ". . . not only may it not be possible for God to create a world including freedom but no evil, but it may also not be possible for him to create a world containing freedom and containing less evil than the existing world."

362. See Heschel, *God in Search of Man*, p. 377. "If not for the will of God, there would be no goodness; if not for the freedom of man, goodness would be out of place in history."

363. See also Teilhard de Chardin, *The Future of Man*, p. 93. "Evil . . . the inevitable reverse side—or better, the condition—or better still, the price—of an immense triumph."

364. "Why has God created both wicked and good? So that the one should atone for the other." Pesikta Rabbati 201 a init., as cited in Montefiore and Loewe, *A Rabbinic Anthology*, p. 542.

365. Schulweis's paraphrase of T. B. Yoma 69b in *Evil and The Morality of God*, p. 137.

366. See Wolfson, *Religious Philosophy*, pp. 18–19. ". . . our hypothetical scriptural philosopher would say that not only Maimonides and St. Thomas . . . but also all other scriptural philosophers would admit that God does not change impossibilities. In support of this he would refer offhand to Origen (*Cont. Cels.* III, 70; V, 23) and St. Augustine, (*Cont. Faust. Manich.* XXVI, 4–5) among Christian philosophers, to the Mutakallimun, among Muslim philosophers (Ibn Hazm, *Fisal fi al-Milal* [Cairo, A.H. 1317–1327], IV, 192 11. 13–14; Ghazali, *Tahafut al-Falasifah*, XVII [ed. Bouyges], 24, p. 292, 11. sff); to Maimonides (*Moreh Nebukim* I, 73, Prop. 10) and Saadia (*Emunot ve-De'ot*, II, 13, p. 110, 11. 4–7) among Jewish philosophers. He would also add, in passing, that all these scriptural philosophers had been re-echoing a sentiment expressed in the same words and illustrated by the same examples by such pagan philosophers as Alexander Aphrodisiensis (*De fato* 30) and Plotinus (*Enneades* VI, 8, 21) and others. (Cf. chapter on 'Omnipotence' in R. M. Grant, *Miracles and Natural Law in Graeco-Roman and Early Christian Thought*, pp. 127–134)."

Cf. *Benedict de Spinoza: His Life, Correspondence, and Ethics* (trans. R. Willis), p. 299. "To ask of God, however, why he did not give Adam a more perfect will were as absurd as to inquire why a circle had not been endowed with the properties of a sphere." As cited in Hick, *Evil and the God of Love*, p. 21.

367. See Wolfson, *Religious Philosophy*, p. 20. "For God does not change the laws of nature in vain, nor does He, like a stage magician, perform miracles to amuse or to impress the spectators. . . . Now, in the wisdom of God, the world is so ordered that to attain that purpose of miracles there is only a need for a change of the laws of thought or of the laws of mathematics. . . . St. Thomas' explanation of why God cannot do that which implies a contradiction by saying that a contradiction implies the notion of non-being and is therefore not 'the proper effect' (*proprius effectus*) of God's power. (*Cont. Gent.* II, 22, Item)."

Cf. Schlesinger, *Religion and Scientific Method*, p. 43.

368. Maimonides, *Guide* 3:15 (Dover ed., p. 279).

369. Gordis, *A Faith for Moderns*, p. 264.

370. See Aristotle, *Nicomachean Ethics*, I. 7 (as translated by J. A. K. Thomson [London, 1953; reissued, Harmondsworth; Penguin Classics, 1955], p. 39). "We ought not to listen to those who counsel us 'O mortal, remember your mortality.' " Cited in Passmore, *The Perfectibility of Man*, p. 47.

See Greenberg, "Cloud of Smoke, Pillar of Fire," p. 7. "Rather, the decisive truth is that man is of infinitive value and will be redeemed. Every act of life is to be lived by that realization."

371. Talmudic dictum: "Whoever destroys even a single soul should be considered the same as a man who destroyed a whole world. And whoever saves even one single soul is to be considered the same as a man who has saved a whole world."

372. See Fackenheim, *The Jewish Return into History*, p. 10. "When God created the world, He decreed: 'The heavens are the heavens of the Lord; but the earth He has handed over to the children of man' (Ps. 115:16). Yet when He was about to give the Torah, He rescinded the first decree and said: 'Those who are below shall ascend to those on high, and those who are on high shall descend to those that are below, and I will create a new beginning,' as it is said: 'And the Lord came down upon Mt. Sinai' (Exod. 19:20), and later 'And unto Moses He said: "Come up unto the Lord"'' (Exod. 24:1) [Exodus Rabba, XII, 3]."

373. Maimonides posits the primacy of man in the Bible by pointing out that the terms *zelem* and *demuth*, which have reference to the Divine intellectual faculty, apply not to God's qualities but to man's.

"I mean because of the divine intellect conjoined with man, that it is said of the latter, that he is in the image of God" (*Emunoth v'Deot* 2:9).

"The major concern of the Torah is not to describe God's attributes but man's, in the sense of projecting man as possessing as his proporium something that is strange, not found in anything else existing under the sphere of the moon, namely, intellectual apprehension" (*Guide* 1:1).

T. B. Sanhedrin 4.5.

374. Kook, "Lights of Holiness," in Bokser, *Abraham Isaac Kook*, p. 194.

375. *Sefer ha-Gilgulim* 6, cited in Agus, *The Evolution of Jewish Thought*, p. 326.

376. Buber, *Good and Evil*, p. 135.

377. Berkovits, *God, Man and History*, p. 145.

378. Hermann Cohen, *Die Religion der Vernunft aus den Quellen des Judentums*, as cited in Berkovits, *Major Themes in Modern Philosophies of Judaism*, p. 31.

379. Stitskin, *Eight Jewish Philosophers*, p. 4.

Cf. ibid., pp. 15–16, 18, 35. "Personalism, on the other hand, puts the mark on the human potential and insists that man is neither a tragic creature nor a perfect being.

"The notion of man as a potential is attested to by biblical, rabbinic and philosophic traditions. The biblical delineation of the creation of man in the divine image (*zelem elokim*), is an endowment in a state of potentiality to be actualized when man stakes his existence on the penetration into his being of concepts, essences, and empirical experiences. Every person is sacred because this divine potential is present in him. . . .

"As potential beings, we are given a Torah not only as a prescription of laws to follow, but as an exposition to analyze, to study and explicate in order to develop our human intellect. . . .

". . . personalism posits a realm of the spirit where the self exists in an undefined, functional, developmental situation. . . .

". . . The overriding motive for commitment in personalism is grounded in a positive affirmation of life which stresses the gradual unfolding of the spirit and is based upon man's limitless pontentialities for self fulfillment."

380. See Saadia Gaon, *Opinions and Beliefs*, fifth treatise.

Cf. Goethe: "When we take man as he is, we make him worse; but when we take man as if he were already what he should be, we promote him to what he can be." Cited in Frankl, *From Death Camp to Existentialism*, p. 110.

381. Hick, *Readings in the Philosophy of Religion*, p. 515.

382. Pascal, *Pensées*, no. 434, as cited in Herberg, *Judaism and Modern man*, p. 69.

383. Jean-Paul Sartre, *L'être et le néant* (Paris: Gallimard, 1943), P. 655; Ralph Harper, *Existentialism* (Cambridge: Harvard University Press, 1948), p. 104. As cited in Herberg, *Judaism and Modern Man*, p. 31.

384. Merton, *The New Man*, p. 122.

385. See Greenberg, *Perspectives: Voluntary Covenant*, p. 17. "The purpose of the Jewish covenant is to realize the total possibility of being. It is not like a utilitarian contract designed to achieve limited ends where, if the advantage is lost, the agreement is dropped. The Jewish covenant is a commitment, out of faith, to achieve a final perfection of being."

Cf. Luzzatto, *Mesillat Yesharim*, p. 335. "The deterrents to Holiness are a lack of true understanding and much association with people; for earthiness finds its counterpart and takes on new strength, and the soul remains trapped within it, unable to escape. However, when one dissociates himself from them and remains alone, preparing himself for the reception of His Holiness, he is conducted along the path which he wishes to travel; and, with the help that God gives him, his soul grows strong within him, overcomes his physical element, unites itself with the Holiness of the Blessed One and perfects itself in it. From this level one proceeds to an even higher one, that of The Holy Spirit, his understanding coming to transcend the bounds of human nature. It is possible for one to reach such a high degree of communion with God as to be given the key to the revival of the dead, as it was given to Elijah and Elisha."

Cf. Luzzatto, *The Way of God*, p. 95. ". . . the purpose of the creation of the human species is that man should become worthy of attaining true good, namely, being drawn close to Him in the World to Come. . . .

". . . This preparation involves two aspects, one concerning individuals, and the other, humanity as a whole.

"The preparation of the individual is his attainment of perfection through his deeds. That of humanity as a whole involves the preparation of the entire human race for the World to Come."

Cf. Kaplan, *If You Were God*, p. 75.

Cf. Herberg, *Judaism and Modern Man*, p. 96, citing Schechter, *Some Aspects of Rabbinic Theology*, p. 199, and Buber, *Prophetic Faith*, pp. 102, 114. "This obligation under which man is placed is a great and fearful one, for it is nothing less than a call to perfection. 'Walk before me and be perfect' (Gen. 17:1), are the words in which Scripture records God's injunction to Abraham, and his words to Abraham are his words to all of us. It is a call to holiness: 'You shall be holy for I the Lord your God am holy' (Lev. 19:2). It is, in short, a call to the imitation of God."

Cf. Moses Ibn Ezra, *Arugat ha-Bosem*, as cited in Stitskin, *Eight Jewish Philosophers*, p. 115. ". . . it behooves man to seek its wisdom. Plato supplemented his definition of philosophy with the notion that the aim of philosophy is for man to become like God as far as possible."

Cf. Hick, "Faith and Knowledge," in idem, *Readings in the Philosophy of Religion*, p. 518. "But if we are right in supposing that God's purpose for man is to lead him from human Bios, or the biologial life of man, to that quality of Zoe, or the personal life of eternal worth."

Cf. Leibniz, *Principles of Nature and Grace* (1718), trans, from *Philosophische Schriften*, ed. Gerhardt, VI, 606, in A. O. Lovejoy, *The Great Chain of Being* (Cambridge, Mass., 1936), p. 248. "Our happiness will never consist but in a perpetual progress to new pleasures and new perfections." As cited in Passmore, *The Perfectibiity of Man*, p. 48.

Note also the following viewpoints on the theme:

A major current in Jewish thought is that the Torah is the purpose of creation. See Agus, *The Evolution of Jewish Thought*, p. 62.

"Man's purpose on earth, they [the Essenes] postulated, is to refine his soul, keeping it pure from the taints of greed, lust and worldly ambition." Ibid., p. 103.

"Luzzatto defines the purpose of man's life as being the attainment in the hereafter of the joy of 'contemplating the radiance of the Shechinah, which is the one true joy.' " Ibid., p. 322, citing *Iggerot Ramanal*, II, 232.

"Behold, the fear of the Lord, that is wisdom; and to depart from evil is understanding" (Job 28:28).

"Fear God, and keep His commandments; for that is the whole man" (Koheleth 12:12–13).

"Man's task is to make the world worthy of redemption." Heschel, *God in Search of Man*, p. 380.

386. Bokser, *Abraham Isaac Kook*, p. 372.

387. See Stitskin on Abraham Ibn Ezra in *Eight Jewish Philosophers*, p. 121. "Once the soul perceived its own true nature it will apprehend how to actualize its potential by the power of intellection and come near to God."

388. This is an important Hasidic theme.

389. Note Martin Luther's comment,"No one is without some commission and calling." J. N. Lenker, ed., *The Precious and Sacred Writings of Martin Luther* (Minneapolis, 1903). vol. 10, *Church Postil Gospels: Advent, Christmas and Epiphany Sermons*, p. 243, as quoted in Passmore, *The Perfectibility of Man*, p. 13.

Thus in the theological debate concerning Noah's righteousness, we would side with the "relativists."

390. G. Scholem, *Major Trends in Jewish Mysticism* p. 278. His note 105 reads as follows: "The idea is based on the mystical intepretation of an Aggadah on Adam, cf. Midrash Tanhuma, Parshat ki Tissa, #12 and Exodus Rabba par. 40."

391. Soloveitchik, *Halakhic Man*, p. 40.

392. Bleich, expounding on Maimonides, in *With Perfect Faith*, p. 5.

393. Heschel, *Man's Quest for God*, p. 95.

394. Berkovits, *Faith After the Holocaust*, p. 59.

395. Stitskin, *Eight Jewish Philosophers*, p. 5.

Cf. ibid., p. 25. ". . . if the ultimate aim of man, according to Maimonides is yediat Hashem—'knowledge of God'—this can be attained by a process of self-authentication which leads to a knowledge of God. Martin Buber likewise asserted that 'God does not wish to be defined by us, but simply to be realized by us.' "

396. Bokser, *Abraham Isaac Kook*, p. 232.

397. Steinsaltz, *The Thirteen Petalled Rose*, p. 46.

398. See Mamlak, "Gershon Mamlak Responds," *Midstream,* November 1984, p. 30. ". . . with the loss of its potentialities Judaism's covenantal mission has been obscured, and the self-image of Jews damaged."

399. See ibid., p. 33. "With Judaism realizing its potentialities as 'A Light unto the Nations,' Redemption will affect and transform all human communities."

400. Kaplan, *If You Were God*, p. 17. "It was in this spirit that Judaism gave birth to both Christianity and Islam. [Although far from perfection], these religions are a step in the right direction. (Kuzari, 4:23, Tshuvos Rambam, 58)."

401. Kook, *Orot Yisroel* 5:2, as cited in Bokser, *Abraham Isaac Kook*, p. 24.

402. Greenberg, *Perspectives: Voluntary Covenant*, p. 2.

403. See G. F. Moore, *Judaism* vol. 1, p. 384. "The maintenance of the world is a kind of continuous creation: God in his goodness makes new every day continually the work of creation."

Note that the concept has some convergence with Hartshorne's "process theology."

404. Bokser, *Abraham Isaac Kook*, p. 267 (scriptural citation is Exodus 3:14).

405. Ibid., p. 230.

406. Gordis, *A Faith for Moderns*, p. 208.

407. See Steinsaltz, *The Thirteen Petalled Rose*, p. 39. "All these *Sefirot* are infinite in their potency, even though they are finite in their essence."

408. On the importance of freedom—other perspectives.

See Spinoza in his preface to the *Tractatus (Tractatus Theologica-Politicus,* trans. R. H. M. Eleres [London, 1909]), in which he sums up his argument as the attempt to prove that freedom of religion is indispensable to the genuine piety of the individual: "not only can such freedom be granted to the public peace, but also without such freedom, piety cannot flourish nor the public peace be secure." Cited in Agus, *The Evolution of Jewish Thought*, p. 301.

Cf. Wolfson, *Religious Philosophy*, pp. 196, 198. "Two theories of completely undetermined freedom of the will were advanced in Greek philosophy in opposition to the rationalized conception of fate which prevailed in the philosophies of Plato, Aristotle, and the Stoics. One of these theories, the Epicurean, was based upon the denial of causality, maintaining that the rise of the world as well as the occurrence of everything within it was due to chance. The other, the Philonic, was based upon the belief in the possibility of the suspension of causality, maintaining that God, who in His working of miracles intermits the process of causation which He himself implanted in the world, has endowed the human will with a similar miraculous power enabling it to act in a free and undetermined manner.

"In the general history of the philosophy of religion, whether Christian, Muslim, or Jewish, it is the Philonic conception of freedom that prevailed, though sometimes with certain modifications. . . .

". . . The formula for the Philonic theories would be: given a world in which God is either the remote or the immediate cause of all that happens, and given also a God who in a miraculous manner sometimes either breaks the chain of secondary causes or deviates from the continuity of His own direct creation, one could logically maintain that man's will was endowed by God with part of His own miraculous power to act in a manner free and undetermined."

Cf. Descartes, *Traité des passions de l'âme* III, 152. Free will "in a certain sense renders us like God in making us masters of ourselves." As cited in ibid., p. 260.

Cf. Wolfson on Descartes in ibid., p. 198. "The freedom with which Descartes endows man's will is the Philonic, miraculous kind of freedom. He repeatedly speaks of it as something which we 'have received from God' or as something which God 'has given' to us.' "

Cf. Harvey Cox, *The Secular City* (New York: Macmillan, 1966), p. 72. "A God who emasculates man's creativity and hamstrings his responsibility for his fellow man must be dethroned."

Cf. St. Augustine, in McKeon, *Selections from Medieval Philosophers*, p. 13, ". . . since without it [free will] man can not live rightly, there is cause enough why it should have been given."

Cf. Borowitz, *Choices in Modern Jewish Thought*, p. 245.

409. See Greenberg, *Perspectives: The Third Great Cycle in Jewish History*, p. 4.

410. See Mishnah Avot 3:16.

Note: At least three different words are used in the Pentateuch for "freedom": *chafshi, dror,* and *cherut*. See Pelkovitz, "*Cherut*," *Amit*, April 1985.

Cf. Hirsch, *Timeless Torah*, p. 4.

411. Ramban, *Gate of Reward*, in *Writings and Discourses*, vol. 2, p. 445.

412. Hirsch, *Timeless Torah*, p. 21.

413. Soloveitchik, *Halakhic Man*, p. 136.

414. Agus, *The Evolution of Jewish Thought*, p. 154.

415. See Abravanel, *Principles of Faith*, p. 149. " . . . so it was His pleasure that man should have liberty of will, and all his acts should be left to his discretion; that nothing should coerce him or draw him to aught (*Hilkot Teshuva*, V. 4, p. 873). . . . This makes it clear that Maimonides did not consider choice as a principle of the Torah, but as a great principle of human action." Cf. Stitskin, *Eight Jewish Philosophers*, p. 19. " . . . personalism maintains that the most essential human values are to be found only in personal choice and self-fulfillment. The efficiency of our social structure must be judged in terms of the free existence it supports."

416. Irving Younger, "What Good Is Freedom of Speech?" *Commentary*, January 1985, p. 49.

417. Berkovits, elucidating on Buber in *Major Themes in Modern Philosophies of Judaism*, p. 143.

418. Soloveitchik, "The Lonely Man of Faith," p. 29.

419. See Bloch, as quoted in Fackenheim, *God's Presence in History*, p. 57. "He [God] is the herald of freedom."

420. Variations on this theme are not uncommon in the writings of Jewish theologians who are "freedom maximalists." The theme is echoed in the writings of St. George of Nyssa and St. Bernard. See Merton, *The New Man*, p. 63.

421. See Lamm, *Faith and Doubt*, p. 86. "This power of free choice and the gift of wisdom, by which Saadia means the whole range of human talents

from the technological and the social to the scientific, constitute the true eminence of man"

422. Christian theologians would cite the powerful episode from Dostoevsky's *The Brothers Karamazov*. In the piece, Ivan tells Alyosha about a story he has written. It is set in Seville during the Inquisition. An auto-da-fé is in progress. One hundred heretics are to be burned alive. So great an event warrants the presence of the Grand Inquisitor himself, a saintly old priest of ninety. Meanwhile, a man appears. Saying nothing, he heals the blind and restores a dead child to life. The Grand Inquisitor orders the man arrested. When the prisoner is brought to his study, the Grand Inquisitor speaks to him. "I know you," says the Grand Inquisitor. "You came once before and promised freedom. That is why you were crucified." (It should be noted, however, that there are elements of interpretation of this episode which are clearly anathema to Jewish doctrine.)

423. Philo, *The Unchangeableness of God*, 45–49 (Loeb ed., vol. 3, pp. 33 ff.), in Lewy, et al. *Three Jewish Philosophers*, p. 30.

Cf. Wolfson, *Religious Philosophy*, p. 259. "Philo, who was the first to formulate the philosophic basis of this kind of undetermined human freedom, says that God endowed the human mind with a proportion 'of that free will which is His most peculiar possession and most worthy of His majesty,' and that by this gift of free will the human mind 'has been made to resemble God. (Immut. 10, 47–48.)"

424. Belkin, *In His Image*, p. 108.

Cf. ibid., pp. 111–112. "The rabbinic opposition to imprisonment as a penalty is not a result of a 'liberal' approach to punishment or a 'modern' concept of penology. It is an outgrowth of the religious principle that man, created by God, is endowed with inviolable rights, among them the right to liberty, which can be abridged only by Him in Whom all rights originate. Obviously, this is a far-reaching consequence of the belief in the sacredness of the human personality, one of the pillars upon which the Jewish democratic theocracy rests. This concept recognizes man's right to freedom and guarantees the preservation of each man's individuality. Needless to say, this guarantee is not limited to personal liberty. It insures all men against any form of slavery or subjugation."

425. Gordis, *A Faith for Moderns*, p. 212.

426. Ibid., p. 203.

Cf. Schulweis, *Evil and the Morality of God*, p. 99.

Cf. Mishnah Sotah 5:5 to the effect that Job served God from love and not from fear.

427. See Bokser, *Abraham Isaac Kook*, p. 161. "The aspiration after freedom of thought has a good as well as a bad aspect, a dimension of the holy and a dimension of the profane. The good aspect is manifested when it is directed beyond the zone of the imagination and physical lusts."

428. Cohen, *The Tremendum*, pp. 92–94.

429. " 'And the tablets were the work of God, and the writing was the writing of God, *ch-r-t* on the tablets' [Exodus 32:16]. Do not read *charut* [engraved on the tablets]; read *cherut* [freedom on the tablets]!" Mishnah Avot 6:2.

430. See Fackenheim, *To Mend the World*, p. 24. " . . . a Grace that gives commandments also gives the freedom to obey them."

Cf. Buber, *Eclipse of God*, p. 105. "Man is created by God with an autonomy enabling him to 'stand over against God.' "

Cf. Cohen, *The Tremendum*, p. 92. "The world is complemented by man whose essential character is freedom. It is not reason that makes man little lower than angels, but freedom and speech."

Cf. Borowitz, *Choices in Modern Jewish Thought*, pp. 258, 272.

Cf. Herberg, *Judaism and Modern Man*, pp. 73, 92, 101.

Cf. Merton, *The New Man*. "All the powers of the soul reach out in freedom and knowledge and love" (p. 19); ". . . at the first moment of his existence, Adam breathed the air of an infinitely pure freedom—a freedom which was poured into his soul directly by God in his creation" (p. 54); ". . . man's freedom was to be without limit" (p. 55).

431. Ibid., pp. 42, 63, 230.

432. See Agus, *The Evolution of Jewish Thought*, p. 42.

433. See Bokser, *Abraham Isaac Kook*, p. 21, citing *Olat Rayah* (Jerusalem: Mosad Harav Kook and Agudah Lohotzoat Sifre Harayah Kook, 1949), vol. 2, pp. 262 f. "The love for freedom is forged in part in the crucible of suffering under servitude."

434. See Berkovits on Buber in *Major Themes in Modern Philosophies of Judaism*, pp. 75–76. "The dialogue, the human responsibility to respond to the Voice presupposes freedom. Without freedom man could render no answer; without freedom there can be no relation. . . . The world of the It is indeed one of unfreedom. The man who has encountered the Thou knows of freedom. I and Thou confront each other in freedom. . . . The freedom of one's own being, as well as that of Being, is vouchsafed in the spontaneous reciprocity of the relation. . . . Freedom and destiny embrace each other in order to reveal to man the meaning of his life."

435. Ibn Ezra and Rav Yehuda Halevi (*Kuzari* 1:12) both grapple with this point. See Leibowitz, *Studies in Shemot*, p. 308, and associated footnotes, for citations and excerpts.

436. See Greenberg, *Perspectives: Voluntary Covenant*, p. 25.

437. See Merton, *The New Man*, p. 109. "For there is no full and total experience of God that is not at the same time an exercise of man's fundamental freedom (of spontaneity) and of God's mercy."

438. See also ibid., pp. 9, 11, 12.

439. See T. Y. Berachot 2:14 (15b). "On the day the Temple was destroyed, the Messiah was born."

440. See Tillich, *The Eternal Now*, p. 17. "[Man] has the freedom for good or evil. Only he who has an impenetrable center in himself is free. Only he who is alone can claim to be a man. This is the greatness and this is the burden of man."

Cf. Borowitz, *Choices in Modern Jewish Thought*, p. 237.

441. See Berkovits on Buber in *Major Themes in Modern Philosophies of Judaism*, p. 117. "Only in the utmost affirmation of his spiritual independence and responsibility can man commit himself in faith."

Cf. Hick, "Faith and Knowledge," p. 517.

442. See Greenberg, *Perspectives: Voluntary Covenant,* p. 3. "Knowing that the Jews will permanently represent that party of final redemption, the Divine is willing to release all of humanity to exercise its freedom."

443. See Heschel, *God in Search of Man,* p. 409. ". . . the grand premise of religion is that man is able to surpass himself. Such ability is the essence of freedom. According to Hegel, the history of the world is nothing more than the progress of the consciousness of freedom."

444. See Cohen, *The Tremendum,* p. 98. "In short, freedom within history is the continuation of creation made articulate by revelation."

445. See Bokser, *Abraham Isaac Kook,* p. 215. "The inner essence of the soul, which reflects, which lives the true spiritual life, must have absolute inner freedom. It experiences its freedom, which is life, through its originality in thought, which is its inner spark that can be fanned to a flame through study and concentration. But the inner spark is that basis of imagination and thought. If the autonomous spark should not be given scope to express itself, then whatever may be acquired from the outside will be of no avail."

446. Soloveitchik, *Halakhic Man,* p. 137.

447. Heschel, *God in Search of Man,* p. 411.

448. Berkovits, *God, Man and History,* p. 143.

449. Berkovits, *Faith after the Holocaust,* p. 63.

Cf. Hannah Arendt as cited in Fackenheim, *To Mend the World,* p. 20. ". . . every free action is unprecedented . . . all events worthy of the name are initiated by free actions."

450. See Abbé Turgot's 1750 Sorbonne lecture in *Oeuvres, de Turgot,* ed. Gustave Schelle, 5 vols. (Paris, 1913–23), vol. 1, p. 215, as cited in Passmore, *The Perfectibility of Man,* p. 195. ". . . the total mass of the human race, between calm and agitation, good and bad, marches always, however slowly, towards greater perfection."

451. See Herder, *Ideas for a Philosophy of the History of Mankind* (1784–91), bk. III, pt. IV, as printed in Barnard, *J. G. Herder on Social and Political Structure,* p. 265. "Man has to learn everything. This is his destination, his 'instinct.' "

452. See Herder, *Ideas,* bk. XV, chap. i, p. 442, as cited in Passmore, *The Perfectibility of Man,* p. 223. "The whole history of nations is to us a school, for instructing us in the course, by which we are to reach the lovely goal of humanity and worth."

453. See Bronowski, *The Ascent of Man,* pp. 19–20, 24. "Among the multitude of animals which scamper, fly, burrow and swim around us, man is the only one who is not locked into his environment. His imagination, his reason, his emotional subtlety and toughness, make it possible for him not to accept the environment but to change it. . . . [That] man from age to age has remade his environment, is a different kind of evolution—not biological, but cultural evolution. . . . Man ascends by discovering the fullness of his own gifts (his talents or faculties) and what he creates on the way are monuments to the stages in his understanding of nature and of self—what the poet W. B. Yeats called 'monuments of unageing intellect.' "

Cf. Ibid., p. 437. "We are a scientific civilisation: that means, a civilisation in which knowledge and its integrity are crucial. Science is only a Latin word for knowledge."

454. See Kaplan, *If You Were God,* p. 76.

455. Teilhard de Chardin, *The Future of Man,* pp. 32–33. ". . . the sum of knowledge retained and transmitted by education from one generation to the next constitutes a natural sequence of which the direction may be observed.

". . . In the passage of time a state of collective human consciousness has been progressively evolved which is inherited by each successive generation of conscious individuals, and to which each generation adds something. . . . a sort of generalised human personality is visibly in process of formation upon the earth. It seems that where man is concerned the specific function of education is to ensure the continued development of this personality."

456. See ibid., p. 70. ". . . the movement of the cosmos towards the highest degree of consciousness is not an optical illusion, but represents the essence of biological evolution."

457. Note that if Teilhard is essentially correct, then our formulation is buttressed still further, for we later posit a contraction of Divine consciousness, which we could symmetrically juxtapose against man's ascent in consciousness.

458. Schulweis on Aquinas in *Evil and the Morality of God,* p. 15.
Cf. ibid., p. 16. "A contemporary version of such a religious-metaphysical position is articulated in Michael Novak's fidelity to the drive to understand. Intellectual passion serves him as the keystone of human salvation. To contribute toward the 'merging intelligibility of a world process' is a moral and creative *imitatio dei.* For him, as for his mentor, B. J. F. Lonergan, God is the radical why behind the drive to understand, the source of understanding and of intelligibility in man."

459. See Whitehead, *Religion in the Making,* p. 160. "The universe shows us two aspects: on one side it is physically wasting, on the other side it is spiritually ascending."

460. See Berkovits, *Faith after the Holocaust,* p. 63. "Freedom and Law are the two foci of human existence in time and history."

461. See Greenberg, *Perspectives: Voluntary Covenant,* p. 2.

462. In discussing the concepts of contingency and freedom, Spero notes, in his *Morality, Halakha and the Jewish Tradition:* "The limits on man's freedom to carry out his desires that are imposed by the physical environment, are constantly being eroded by the expansion of scientific knowledge and technology." (In our Unified Formulation it is not just physical knowledge and freedom which are expanding, but a knowledge and freedom as broadly defined as possible.)

463. See also Teilhard de Chardin, *The Future Man,* p. 75. "Evolution, by the very mechanism of its synthesis, charges itself with an ever-growing measure of freedom."

464. See Agus on Abrabanel in *The Evolution of Jewish Thought,* pp. 296–297. ". . . man's ascent toward the Deity consists in the acquisition of knowledge of physical reality and in the cultivation of a sympathetic under-

standing of the entire range of creation. Every increment of knowledge is a step on the infinite road of love."

465. See Stitskin, *Eight Jewish Philosophers,* p. 136. "Knowledge and intellectual excellence, according to personalistic doctrine, is more than a mere search for truth. It is a means of ecstatic union of the human spirit with the divine spirit."

466. See Midrash Rabbah 1:4–8 (on Proverbs 3:19). "The Lord, for the sake of wisdom [i.e., the Torah], founded the earth."

467. See Abraham Ibn Ezra, "Introduction to Ecclesiastes," in Stitskin, *Eight Jewish Philosophers,* p. 128.

468. See ibid., p. 129.

Cf. ibid., p. 124. "The search for *taame ha-mitzvot* (the reason for the *mitzvot*) is the practice and intellection over them by which the *neshamah* rises to the Divine Presence. To fathom the divine wisdom and establish patterns of thought and behavior is conducive to coming near to God. They provide the best specific means for actualizing man's potential. . . .

". . . Mere observance without a quest for the reason behind practice is insufficient. The quest is crucial to the *neshamah*'s ultimate transcendence and nearness to God."

Cf. ibid., p. 126. "Maimonides regarded the works of Ibn Ezra superior to any other Jewish scholar. In his 'Letter of Instruction to His Son Abraham,' he admonished . . . [that] Ibn Ezra's [works] alone are meaningful and profitable to all who study them. . . . Ibn Ezra was in spirit similar to our patriarch Abraham."

469. Schulweis, *Evil and the Morality of God,* p. 42.

470. Maimonides, *Guide* 3:54.

Cf. R. N. Flew, *The Idea of Perfection in Christian Theology,* as cited in Schulweis, *Evil and the Morality of God,* p. 42. "The attainment of perfect intellection is the highest aspiration of Thomas' man. For him, as for Maimonides, the active, moral, social life is important but auxilliary to the contemplative ideal."

471. See Wolfson on Spinoza in *Religious Philosophy,* p. 260. According to Spinoza, "Freedom is power, the power of reason by which man may control and guide the forces of his own nature, just as by the same power of reason he can control and guide the forces of external nature."

472. Amplified below in Section 900.10.

473. See Scherman, "An Overview: The Period and the Miracle," p. xxx. "[David] was not permitted to build the Temple because his people could not measure up to this level of purity and righteousness (Yalkut Shimoni II Samuel 145)."

474. Kook, *Orot Hakodesh,* vol. 3, quoted in Bokser, *Abraham Isaac Kook,* p. 24.

475. Steinsaltz, *The Thirteen Petalled Rose,* p. 47.

476. See Genesis 3:21. "And the Lord God made for Adam and his wife garments of skin and clothed them."

477. Lamm, *Faith and Doubt,* pp. 302–303. (He cites Mendel, *Derech Mitzvotecha,* p. 59f.

478. Ibid., p. 301.

479. See Sartre, "Existentialism and Humanism," in Frazier, *Issues in Religion*, p. 356. ". . . man is condemned to be free. Condemned, because he did not create himself, yet is nevertheless at liberty, and from the moment that he is thrown into this world he is responsible for everything he does."
480. Berkovits, *Faith after the Holocaust*, p. 61.
481. Herberg, *Judaism and Modern Man*, p. 13.
482. Note Soloveitchik, "The Lonely Man of Faith." "For the sake of clarification of the double equation humanity = dignity and dignity = glory-majesty, it is necessary to add another thought. There is no dignity without responsibility."
483. See Pierre Teilhard de Chardin, *The Future of Man*, p. 70.
484. See Fackenheim, *To Mend the world*, p. 253. "The *Shekhina* is in exile. God Himself is in a state of *Tzimtzum*—a retreat from the world."
485. See Schulweis, *Evil and the Morality of God*, p. 41.
486. Schematic formal development of our formulation, to recap and show the development of our formulation so far in schematic terms:

[let ↑ *mean "increases in . . ."]*
[let → *mean "implies" or "leads to" or "necessitates"]*

↑ *knowledge* → ↑ *freedom*
↑ *freedom* → ↑ *privacy*
　　　　　　 ↑ *selfhood*
　　　　　　 ↑ *responsibility*
↑ *freedom* → ↑ *contraction of here-and-now Divine consciousness*
therefore:
↑ *knowledge* → *contraction of here-and-now Divine consciousness*

----

487. See Greenberg, *Perspectives: Voluntary Covenant*, p. 2.
488. Fackenheim, *God's Presence in History*, p. 21.
489. See Paul A. Schilpp and Maurice Friedman, eds. *The Philosophy of Martin Buber*, p. 32, as cited in Schulweis, *Evil and the Morality of God*, p. 25. Buber goes on to explain that there is nothing astonishing in the fact that an observant Jew, "when he has to choose between [a merciful, caring] God and the [sometimes seemingly severe] Bible, chooses God: The God whom he believes, Him in whom he can believe."
490. N. Lamm, in "The Religious Meaning of the Six Day War," *Tradition* 10, no. 1 (Summer 1968): 7–8. "Between these two poles there are, according to the Sages of the Talmud, two intermediate states. In the lower state, there is no relationship. Nonetheless, God does preserve Israel; His 'hand is stretched forth' to protect us from oblivion. Other than mere survival, there is no real redemptive meaning to the vicissitudes of our history. But the second state, penultimate to *nesiat panim*, is that of 'in a dream I address him.' "
491. See Bleich, *With Perfect Faith*, p. 203. "God, as an infinite being, has no beginning in time; since He is the uncaused First Cause, God must always have existed. As an infinite being, God's existence is subject to no limitations.

. . . According to Maimonides, time is an object of creation. If this is so, it follows that God cannot conceivably exist in time. God, the Creator of time, is transcendental; He stands above the process of time . . . . God is neither eternal nor noneternal; He is totally removed from all time processes and all time concepts. Eternity, like all other attributes, can be attributed to God only in a negative sense. In ascribing eternity to God one can only intend to convey the idea that God is not limited by time. . . . Nevertheless, God is independent of all time. A being which is dependent upon time is limited in power. God, who is omnipotent, is eternal."

Cf. Bleich on Saadia in *With Perfect Faith,* p. 496. "Saadia accepts both the principle of Divine omniscience and the reality of human freedom. . . . This can best be understood in light of the proposition that God transcends time."

Cf. Stitskin in *Studies in Torah Judaism,* p. 85, where God is described as "ineffable, removed, incomprehensible."

Cf. Anselm, *Proslogium,* chap. XIX and XX. "Thou wast not, then yesterday, nor wilt thou be tomorrow . . . but simply thou art outside all time." Cited by Kretzmann, "Omniscience and Immutability," in Brody, *Readings in the Philosophy of Religion,* p. 371.

492. The Midrash Shemuel of Samuel b. Isaac of Uceda is cited in Jacobs, *Principles of the Jewish Faith,* p. 328, as putting forward the idea that God is outside of time and therefore sees all events in an eternal, as opposed to human, "Now."

493. *Guide* 3:20.

494. Aquinas, *Summa Theologiae,* pt. I, article 13, reply objection 3.

Cf. ibid., 14, 13 ad 3. "To us, because we know future contingent events as future, there can be no certainty about them; but only to God, whose knowing is in eternity, above time." As cited in Kenny, *Aquinas: A Collection of Critical Essays,* p. 261.

495. Many Jewish thinkers approach the concept of God's omniscience against the backdrop of the concepts of *din va-mishpat* (judgment and justice) and *sachar va-onesh* (reward and punishment). Both concepts are firmly grounded; consequently one might conclude that *din va-mishpat* and *sachar va-onesh* require a real-time omniscience. This reasoning is flawed. In order for the Deity to judge my action of May 1 it is not necessary for the Deity to be consciously watching me in real-time May 1.

496. Gersonides, *Wars of the Lord,* Third Treatise, chap. 4, as cited in Bleich, *With Perfect Faith,* p. 450. (See also Feldman translation in Jewish Publication Society edition)

497. Philo, *On the Posterity of Cain* 13–20 (Loeb ed., vol. 2, pp. 335 ff.), in Lewy et al., *Three Jewish Philosophers,* p. 67.

498. See Greenberg, *Perspectives: Voluntary Covenant,* p. 19.

Cf. Hick, *Readings in the Philosophy of Religion,* p. 518. ". . . this characterization of God as the heavenly Father is not a merely random illustration but an analogy that lies at the heart of the Christian faith."

Cf. Moore, *Judaism,* vol. 2, pp. 201–211. "The idea of the Fatherhood by God is very ancient, older even than the idea of God as King." Millar Burrows, *An Outline of Biblical Theology* (Philadelphia: Westminster, 1946).

Cf. Sigmund Freud, "The Future of An Illusion," in Frazier, *Issues in*

Religion, p. 106. "Men cannot remain children for ever; they must in the end go out into 'hostile life.' "

499. Luzzatto, *The Way of God,* p. 171.

500. See complete citation from Soloveitchik in Besdin, *Reflections of the Rav,* pp. 35–38. Soloveitchik's definition (p. 36) is as follows: "*Hester Panim,* however, is a temporary suspension of God's active surveillance."

We will focus this definition further to mean contraction of active Divine surveillance in the here-and-now.

There is, of course, a spectrum of variations on this theme, ranging from those who define *Hester* as a complete blockage of surveillance (and intervention), through those who define *Hester* as blockage of intervention but not of surveillance, through those who define *Hester* as neither a blockage of surveillance, nor of intervention.

It should be noted that the citation of *Hester* from the Pentateuch, cited shortly in our text, contains the double phraseology "and I will foresake them, and I will hide my face from them," which lends itself more naturally to our definition, which involves contraction of omniscience as well as ruling out intervention.

Towards the other end of the range from our definition is one which posits that in a state of *Hester* the Divine exclusively employs strict *din* (justice), as opposed to *mishpat* (justice tempered with mercy). However, this explanation does not flow readily from the text or from an approximate translation of the words, and seems to us to be a forced attempt to preserve a concept of surveillance-cum-intervention even during *Hester.* When employed as a theodicy it is forced to take the position that man in general is deserving of considerable punishment. It is therefore essentially covered within Group II theodicies.

501. See Maimonides, *Guide* 3:51, in reference to Deuteronomy 31:17. "It is clear that we ourselves are the cause of this hiding of the face, and that the screen that separates us from God is of our own creation. This is the meaning of the words, 'And I will surely hide my face in that day.' "

502. See Glatzer, *The Dimensions of Job,* p. 62. "Job believes now, as later Deutero-Isaiah (Isa. 45:15) did under the influence of Isaiah (8:17), in 'a God that hides Himself.' This hiding, the eclipse of the divine light, is the source of his abysmal despair. . . . Deutero-Isaiah expressed (40:27) the despairing complaint of the faithful remnant which thinks that because God hides Himself, Israel's 'way' also 'is hid' from Him, and He pays no more attention to it.

503. Berkovits, *God, Man and History,* p. 64.

Cf. Berkovits, *Faith after the Holocaust,* p. 65. "The El Mistater, in his very hiding, is Savior. . . . what we make of his absence will ultimately determine the quality of our Judaism for generations to come."

Cf. ibid., p. 172. "Cox does argue that 'the Biblical God's hiddenness stands at the very center of the doctrine of God'—Cox, p. 258."

Cf. Berkovits, *Major Themes in Modern Philosophies of Judaism,* p. 218. ". . . talmudic and midrashic tradition does speak of the *Galut ha'Shekkinah* (cf. T. B. Tractate Megillah, 29a), the exile of the *Shekkinah.*"

504. Scholem, *Major Trends in Jewish Mysticism,* p. 260.

505. *Sefer ha-Iyyun,* cited by G. Scholem in *Encyclopaedia Judaica,* vol. 10, col. 588 s.v. "Kabbalah," as "the basic source of the ẓimẓum doctrine."

506. Steinsaltz, *The Thirteen Petalled Rose,* p. 37.

507. See Scholem in *Encyclopaedia Judaica,* s.v. "Kabbalah," vol. 10, col. 594.

508. Midrash Genesis Rabbah 19:13, as cited in Luban, "The Kaddish." p. 231, fn.

Cf. Scholem in *Encyclopaedia Judaica,* s.v. "Kabbalah," vol. 10, col. 587.

Cf. Berg, *Kabbalah for the Layman,* p. 84. "The creator veils his Or Ein Sof (Eternal Light) in order to allow this world to exist in its present form."

509. Soloveitchik, *Halakhic Man,* p. 108.

510. See also Merton, *The New Man,* pp. 123 and 127. "One, who infinitely hidden and transcendent . . ."; "the Lord is hidden in the clouds of an infinite and inexorable transcendency."

511. Kaplan, The Infinite Light, p. 57.

512. Luzzatto, *The Way of God,* p. 123.

513. Steinsaltz, *The Thirteen Petalled Rose,* p. 37.

514. Buber, "God and the World's Evil," in Noveck, *Contemporary Jewish Thought,* vol. 4, p. 256.

515. Besdin, *Reflections of the Rav,* p. 35.

516. See ibid., p. 37. "The Holocaust, in contrast, was *Hester Panim.* We cannot explain the Holocaust but we can, at least, classify it theologically, characterize it, even if we have no answer to the question, 'why?' The unbounded horrors represented the *tohu vavohu* anarchy of the pre-*yetzirah* state. This is how the world appears when God's moderating surveillance is suspended."

517. According to Soloveitchik, "The State of Israel, however, reflects God's return to active providence, the termination of *Hester Panim.*" Besdin, *Reflections of the Rav,* p. 37.

518. See also Maimonides, *Guide* 3:51.

Cf. Lamm, *The Face of God,* sec. 5.

519. "Hester minimalists" retain essentially complete Divine surveillance even during Hester. "Hester maximalists" posit a complete blockage of Divine surveillance during Hester.

520. See Schechter, *Aspects of Rabbinic Theology,* chap. 14, "Sin as Rebellion." Specifically, p. 219: ". . . sin and disobedience are conceived as defiance and rebellion."

521. Asserted by Fackenheim in *To Mend the World,* p. 196.

522. See Buber, *Eclipse of God,* p. 23.

Cf. ibid., p. 127. "What is it that we mean when we speak of an eclipse of God which is even now taking place? Through this metaphor we make the tremendous assumption that we can glance up to God with our 'mind's eye,' or rather being's eye, as with our bodily eye to the sun, and that something can step between our existence and His as between the earth and the sun. That this glance of the being exists, wholly unillusory, yielding no images yet first making possible all images, no other court in the world attests than that of faith. It is not to be proved; it is only to be experienced; man has experienced it. And that other, that which steps in between, one also experiences, to-day. I have spoken of it since I have recognized it, and as exactly as my perception allowed me."

Cf. ibid., p. 129. "The eclipse of the light of God is no extinction; even to-morrow that which has stepped in between may give way."

Cf. Buber, "A God Who Hides His Face," in Glatzer, *The Dimensions of Job*, p. 63. "The just creator gives to all His creatures His boundary, so that each may become fully itself."

523. See Buber, as quoted in Berkovits, *Major Themes in Modern Philosophies of Judaism*, p. 108. "There is no trace of freedom or creatorship for man in the biblical encounter. The essential experience there is human worthlessness and powerlessness that, nevertheless, is redeemed by the love of God. Man may stand upright in the encounter because he is held up; he may hear because the spirit from God sustains him; he can speak because the dew from God revives him. The situation is not a dialogical one. Man is not a partner of God in the actuality of the I-thou. He is altogether a creature, if ever there was one. As long as the actuality of the revelation lasts, man has no freedom. He cannot deny his Thou, he cannot disobey him. Only when the encounter has passed, is he dismissed into a measure of self-hood and independence; only then can he deny and disobey."

524. Berkovits, *Major Themes in Modern Philosophies of Judaism*, p. 116.

525. Berkovits, *God, Man and History*, pp. 145–146.

Cf. Berkovits, *Major Themes in Modern Philosophies of Judaism*, p. 107. "Rabbi Joshua, the son of Levi, explained: 'At the impact of each word at Sinai, their souls left the Israelites.' For so we read, 'My soul failed me when He spoke.' (Daniel 10:8–9) But if their souls departed at the first Word, how could they receive the next one? —God brought down on them the dew with which He will quicken the dead and thus revived them. For so does the psalmist declare, 'A bounteous rain didst Thou pour down, O God; when Thine inheritance was weary, Thou didst confirm it.' (Song of Songs 5:6) According to the Bible, and to the biblical tradition, man can indeed not endure the encounter with God. It is true, as Buber says, that in revelation man is revealed to himself; but in exactly the opposite sense in which Buber understands it. It is man's nothingness that is first of all revealed to him in the presence of God. He cannot but realize that, in his own right, he is indeed but 'dust and ashes.' He is not annihilated, but he is at the brink of nothingness. He is brought back into existence by the love of God. His I is returned to him as a gift of God."

Cf. ibid., p. 106. "About his encounters with the Divine, Ezekiel reports: 'I fell upon my face, and I heard a voice of one that spoke.' The context shows that this falling upon the face is due to human weakness. The force of the vision saps the strength of the prophet. He cannot stand up and confront the Divine. Most impressively is the nature of the experience described by Daniel when he says: 'So I was left alone and saw this great vision, and there remained no strength in me; for my comeliness was turned in me into corruption, and I retained no strength. Yet I heard the voice of His words; and when I heard the voice of His words, then I was fallen into a deep sleep on my face, with my face toward the ground.' Far from entering into a relation of mutuality in the encounter with the Divine, man becomes aware of his utter helplessness in the presence of God."

526. Scholem, *Major Themes in Jewish Mysticism*, p. 261.

527. Steinsaltz, *The Thirteen Petalled Rose*, p. 37.

528. Schulweis, *Evil and the Morality of God*, p. 79.

529. See also section 800.30 above.

530. See Spero, *Morality, Halakha and the Jewish Tradition*, p. 247, who believes that delimiting foreknowledge minimizes the problem: "Eliminate the time factor and you seem to eliminate the problem." Actually, limiting foreknowledge alone, and leaving here-and-now knowledge, does not sufficiently minimize the problem. But Spero's general proposition (just quoted) is an essential truth.

531. Ibn Daud, *Emunah Ramah*, Basic Principle 6, chap. 2, in Bleich, *With Perfect Faith*, p. 421.

532. Ibid., p. 416.

Cf. ibid., p. 417. "Gersonides resolves the matter in a similar, but somewhat different, manner. He argues with Ibn Daud that man is free and that God's knowledge is limited in a certain sense. God has absolute knowledge of universals, which are eternal and not subject to change. God's knowledge of particulars is somewhat different. He knows them in one sense but does not know them in another. . . . God knows particulars insofar as they are ordered, but He does not know them insofar as they are contingent upon human choice. God knows them only to the extent that they are ordered by nature. This is not an imperfection in the nature of God because He knows the contingent in its true nature."

Cf. ibid., p. 417. "Crescas adopts precisely the opposite position. Confronted, as were Ibn Daud and Gersonides, with what he perceived to be a contradiction between divine omniscience and human freedom, Crescas was prepared to sacrifice the notion of human freedom in order to affirm God's omniscience."

Cf. *Encyclopaedia Judaica*, s.v. "Ibn Daud, Abraham ben David Halevi."

533. Kenny, *Aquinas: A Collection of Critical Essays*, p. 256

534. Ibid., p. 257.

Cf. Aquinas, *Summa Theologiae*, Ia 14, 3, 3. "Aquinas' statement of the difficulty is as follows: 'Whatever is known by God must be; for whatever is known by us must be, and God's knowledge is more certain than ours. But nothing which is future and contingent must be. Therefore, nothing which is future and contingent is known by God.' " Cited in Kenny, *Aquinas*, p. 258.

535. Berkovits, *God, Man and History*, p. 146.

536. See also Saadia Gaon, *Opinions and Beliefs* 4:4. "What God foreknows is the final denouement of man's activity after it turns out after all his planning, anticipation, and delays."

537. See *Emunah Ramah* pt. II, Basic Principle 6, chap. 2. According to the author, since man is free, and free to choose, those events which are the result of man's freedom of choice are not, in fact, known beforehand by God. For, according to Ibn Daud, that would obviate the free choice.

538. *Wars of the Lord*, III, chaps. 1–6, similarly argues that God does not know the contingent. "But He does not know which of the two possible alternatives will be actualized from the point of view that they are contingents.

The reason for this is that if it were so, there could be no contingency in this world at all." (chapter 4)

Note that Saadia, Abraham ibn Daud, and Gersonides would seem to be in disagreement with Akiva as cited in Mishnah Avoth 3:19: "Everything is foreseen, yet freedom of choice is given."

539. See, for example, Leviticus 26 (in *Parshat Bechokotai*) and Deuteronomy 28 (in *Parshat Ki-Tavo*).

540. See Kaplan, *The Infinite Light*, p. 27.

541. "Do not try to measure the immeasurable with words, nor with the plummet of thought to sound the unfathomable." Saying of the Buddha, cited in Kaplan, *The New World of Philosophy*, p. 242. (One might cite this proposition to challenge our entire endeavor; to which we reiterate, that our primary purpose is not to demarcate the Divine, but rather to explore the relationship between the Divine and man.)

542. Maimonides, *Guide* 58 (Dover ed., p. 81). "Then I will show that we cannot describe the creator except by negative attributes."

543. See Bleich, *With Perfect Faith*, p. 109. "It remained for Maimonides to assert the complete denial of all attributes. For Maimonides, all attributes, insofar as they purport to describe God, rather than His effects, involve a plurality. The only attributes which may be ascribed to God are negative ones. They do not tell us what God is, but what He is not."

544. See Fackenhaim, *God's Presence in History*, p. 4. "In a well-known Midrash it is asserted that what Ezekiel once saw in heaven was far less than what all of Israel once saw on earth. . . . In the sharpest possible contrast, the Israelites at the Red Sea had no need to ask which one was the King: 'As soon as they saw Him, they recognized Him, and they all opened their mouths and said, "This is my God, and I will glorify Him" ' (Exod. 15:2). Even the lowliest maidservant at the Red Sea saw what Isaiah, Ezekiel, and all the other prophets never saw."

545. See Maccoby, "Christianity's Break With Judaism," p. 41. ". . . rabbinic Judaism, unlike the Pseudepigrapha, has come to terms with the ending of prophetic inspiration. . . . the Pseudepigrapha themselves testify to the end of prophecy; otherwise why should they adopt the name of prophets of the past rather than prophesying in the names of their true authors?"

Cf. ibid. "Rabbinic Judaism acknowledges that prophecy has ended, but does not regard this as wholly a loss. Now begins the age of the rabbi—in his way as considerable a figure as the prophet. . . . when Rabbi Eliezer tried to decide a halakhic matter by appeal to a voice from Heaven, he was sharply declared out of order, as was Rabbi Johanan ben Dahabai when he attempted to introduce legal rulings heard from ministering angels 'behind the Curtain.' "

546. Fackenheim, *To Mend the World*, p. 196.

547. Greenberg, *Perspectives: Voluntary Covenant*, p. 7. More accurately, prophecy ended with the beginning of the Second Temple period.

548. Cohen, *The Tremendum*, p. 43.

549. T. B. Berachot 32b.

550. *Resisei Laylah* (probably by Zadok ha-Kohen of Lublin) chap. 56, as cited in Scherman, "An Overview: The Period and the Miracle," p. xxxv.

551. Soloveitchik, "The Lonely Man of Faith," p. 31.

552. See Merton, *The New Man*, p. 13.

Cf. Teilhard de Chardin, *The Future of Man*, p. 12. "Even the striving after progress contributes to the sum of evil."

553. See Luban, "The Kaddish," p. 208.

554. See Pesikta deRav Kahana, Zochor; Tanhuma (Buber) *Ki Tetze* 18; Tanhuma, *Ki Tetze* 11; Midrash Hagodol, Exodus 17:16. As cited in Luban, "The Kaddish," p. 207.

555. See *Encyclopaedia Judaica*, s.v. "Kabbalah," vol. 10, col. 594.

556. Shemot Rabbah 2:7.

557. Leibowitz, *Studies in Shemot*, p. 60.

558. See Fackenheim, *To Mend the World*, p. 29.

559. See also Henry Drummond, *The Lowell Lectures on the Ascent of Man* (London, 1894), chap. 10, p. 428. A God who gradually reveals His nature to man "is infinitely grander than the occasional wonder worker, who is the God of an old theology." As cited in Passmore, *The Perfectibility of Man*, p. 251.

560. Even independent of the freedom problem of intervention—and the associated problems of man's responsibility, privacy, and selfhood.

561. Edward Peters, Henry C. Lea Professor of Medieval History at the University of Pennsylvania, in his book *Torture* (New York: Basil Blackwell, 1985) notes, according to *New York Times* book reviewer Sally Moore (Sept. 15, 1985), that "technological developments and a dulling sense of civic sensibilities have made it [torture] more horrible today—more freely practiced and more efficiently rationalized than ever before."

562. See Agus on the "Qabbalists" in *The Evolution of Jewish Thought*, p. 286. "In the endless chain of being, things get 'coarser' and more evil in proportion to their 'remoteness' from the source and in direct relation to the number of 'garments' in which the holy spark is hidden."

563. See Luban, "The Kaddish," p. 207.

564. See Camus, *The Rebel*. "The real passion of the 20th century is servitude." As cited in Berkovits, *With God in Hell*, p. 135.

565. See Suzuki, "The Nature of Zen," in Frazier, *Issues in Religion*, p. 163. "Growth is always attended with pain. . . . The growth of the organism called society is also marked with painful cataclysms, and we are at present witnessing one of its birth-throes."

566. See Gordis, *A Faith for Moderns*, p. 261. "That there is a Providence governing the *collective affairs* of mankind at work in the history of the race *(hashgahah kelalit)*, is not so difficult to believe. It was the Prophets of Israel who first proclaimed the teaching of God in history and formulated the law of righteousness, working its way out in the world and determining the lot of nations and civilizations."

567. See Nachmanides on Exodus 2:25, as translated in Ramban, *Commentary on the Torah*, vol. 2, p. 4. "At first He hid His face from them and they were devoured, but now G-d heard their groaning and He saw them, meaning that He no longer hid His face from them; He knew their pains and all that was done to them, as well as all that they required."

568. Note again Lamm, "The Religious Meaning of the Six Day War," *Tradition* 10, no. 1 (Summer 1968): 7–8. "Between these poles there are,

according to the Sages of the Talmud, two intermediate states. In the lower state [closest to complete *Hester*], there is no relationship. Nonetheless, God does preserve Israel; His 'hand is stretched forth' to protect us from oblivion."

Cf. Lamm, *The Face of God*, sec. 5.

569. Gordis, *A Faith for Moderns*, p. 261.

570. Besdin, *Reflections of the Rav*, p. 36.

571. See Berkovits, *With God in Hell*, p. 116. "As they were leading Rabbi Shalom Eliezer Halberstam, the Ratzfirter Rebbe, to be killed, an SS officer approached him and said: 'I see your lips are moving in prayer. Do you still believe that your God will help you? Don't you realize in what situation the Jews find themselves? They are all being led to die and no one helps them. Do you still believe in divine providence?' To which the Rebbe replied: 'With all my heart and all my soul I believe that there is a Creator and that there is a Supreme Providence.' "

572. Wolfson, *Religious Philosophy*, p. 260.

573. Greenberg, "Cloud of Smoke, Pillar of Fire," p. 37.

Cf. ibid., p. 38. "The Holocaust warns us that our current values breed their own nemesis of evil when unchecked—even as Nazi Germany grew in the matrix of modernity."

Cf. ibid., p. 15 (recounting the Holocaust). "In Zlutomir, Minsk, Firiatin, Mariampole, Nemirov, Stalinodorf, and Kiev among others, children were thrown alive into the killing pits or beaten over the head and dumped into the pits—to save bullets. In Berditchev the ground was turned into muck by the blood of the victims, and some wounded drowned in it. In Firiatin and Berditchev the ground settled and turned from the cries and writhings of those still alive and superficially buried. No assessment of modern culture can ignore the fact that science and technology—the accepted flower and glory of modernity—now climaxed in the factories of death. . . . There is the shock of recognition that the humanistic revolt . . . is now revealed—at the very heart of the enterprise—to sustain a capacity for death and demonic potential."

Cf. ibid., p. 17. "One of the most striking things about the Einsatzgruppen leadership makeup is the prevalence of educated people, professionals, especially lawyers, Ph.D.'s and yes, even a clergyman."

574. See Berkovits, *With God in Hell*, p. 92. "Nazi Germany was the deification of the diabolical; the religious befouling of all purity and innocence. Jews rightly saw in it the rebellion of Kohot haTumah (a phrase well understood in the context of Judaism, which can only be weakly rendered in English as 'the forces of impurity'), the satanic relishers of destruction."

Cf. Cohen, *The Tremendum*, p. 20. "In the time of the human tremendum, conventional time and intelligible causality is interrupted. In that time, if not redemption, then the demonic tears the skein of events apart and man (and perhaps God no less) is compelled to look into the abyss."

Cf. ibid., p. 48. "The Holocaust, in its immediacy, constellates everything that we mean by evil and, as such, is a perfected figuration of the demonic."

575. See also Teilhard de Chardin, *The Future of Man*, p. 74. "Life has paradoxically flourished in the improbable. Does not this suggest that its

advance may be sustained by some sort of complicity on the part of the 'blind' forces of the Universe—that is to say, that it is inexorable?"

See also above (section 400.40 "Universal Laws") for related discussion on "Inviolability."

PART III

576. See Schulweis, *Evil and the Morality of God,* p. 61. "In Wieman's evolutionary theodicy, the eye is fixed upon the future, whose promise of growth rescues the apparent evils of the past."

577. Hick, "Faith and Knowledge," p. 521.

578. Note that while our formulation has some common themes with the Irenaean, the two diverge on many fronts. Among other differences: According to the Irenaean, the choice is God's, not man's. According to the Irenaean, the purpose is growth, not quest. According to the Irenaean, there is a full-time real-time omniscience, not a contraction. According to the Irenaean, the theodicy is independent of creation, not integral to the cosmic process.

579. As written or cited by Bokser in *Abraham Isaac Kook,* p. 21.

580. Viktor Frankl, "The Philosophical Foundation of Logotherapy," in Strauss, *Phenomenology: Pure and Applied* (Pittsburgh: Duquesne University Press, 1961), p. 55, as quoted in *Tradition* 19, no. 4 (Winter 1981).

581. Soloveitchik, "The Community," p. 13.

582. Kaplan, *The New World of Philosophy,* p. 243, expanding on Buddhist and Nietzschean doctrine.

583. See also Soloveitchik, "B' sod hayachid v'hayachad," p. 233.

584. See Berkovits, *God, Man and History,* p. 146. " . . . the encounters had to be extremely rare in history, in order to leave room for doubting, and, thus, to safeguard man's spiritual freedom, which is the most noble quality of faith. God is hiding from man most of the time so that man may believe in Him without compulsion."

Cf. ibid., p. 147. "Such indirect and, therefore, not altogether convincing intervention in the affairs of men, which the human being is free to recognize or to reject, may well be one of the ways in which God discharges His responsibility to His creation."

585. See Emanuel Rackman, "Replies to Gershon Mamlak," *Midstream,* November 1984, p. 26. "The medieval philosophers did debate whether belief in God was one of the 613 mitzvot. But if it is not, then there may be good reasons why it was not included. Philosophically speaking, if God had commanded belief in Him, then one's freedom to choose not to believe would have been curtailed. And perhaps God wanted to expand, rather than limit, man's exercise of his free will."

Cf. Scherman, "An Overview: The Period and the Miracle," p. xxv. "Often, the prophet himself may not understand the full import of the Heavenly words conveyed through his lips. The classic example is the prophet Jonah. His prophecy was—'and Nineveh will be overturned.' To him it was clear that he was foretelling the destruction of the great city. Nineveh would be overturned just as Sodom and Gomorrah were overturned. When the population repented and was spared, Jonah thought that he would be branded a false prophet. But Jonah did not know the true meaning of his own prophecy [Sanhedrin 89b]. Nineveh was indeed overturned, but in the moral, ethical, and religious sense."

Cf. ibid., p. xxvi. "When God wants His people to understand His words clearly, He makes them known clearly. But countless prophecies, including those foretelling the coming of the Messiah, the ultimate redemption, and the end of the days, were not meant to be explicitly clear. . . . Every Torah school child 'knows' that God told Abraham of a four-hundred year exile that would begin with the birth of Isaac. But this knowledge did not become absolute and public until future events will illuminate the apparent obscurities of the Torah like a flash of lightning."

586. Lamm, *The Face of God*, sec. 4.

587. Scherman, "An Overview: The Period and the Miracle," pp. xxxiv–xxxv.

588. Hick, *Evil and the God of Love*, p. 373.

589. The theme of man depending on himself, while maintaining his belief in God, is, of course, not brand-new in Judaism. The entire Megillat Esther is a case in point of Jews apparently even stretching beyond the limits of Halachah to protect their people in what is, in retrospect, sanctified by the Jewish historic consciousness.

Cf. Tillich, *The Eternal Now*, p. 17.

590. Title of a book by A. J. Heschel (Jewish Publication Society, 1951).

591. Heschel, *Man Is not Alone*. p. 127.

592. See Luban, "The Kaddish," p. 207. "God uses problems to provoke us to reflect on our inadequacies and propel us to develop our potentiality."

593. See Greenberg, *Perspectives: Voluntary Covenant*, p. 16. "If the Jews keep the Covenant after the Holocaust, then it can no longer be for the reason that it is commanded or because it is enforced by reward or punishment."

594. See Soloveitchik, "The Community," p. 13.

595. See my article "The Quantification of Jewish Education: A Strategic Error," *Midstream*, December 1983.

596. Cf. See Buber, in Noveck, *Contemporary Jewish Thought*, p. 256. "In this our own time, one asks again and again: how is a Jewish life still possible after Oswiecim? . . . How is a life with God still possible in a time in which there is an Oswiecim? The estrangement has become too cruel, the hiddenness too deep. One can still 'believe' in the God who allowed those things to happen, but can one still speak to Him? Can one still hear His word? Can one still, as an individual and as a people, enter at all into a dialogic relationship with Him? Can one still call to Him? Dare we recommend to the survivors of Oswiecim, the Job of the gas chambers: 'Call to Him, He is kind, for His mercy endurest forever'?"

Note: While man pays the price of increased vulnerability to evil as the Divine omniscience is increasingly contracted, the other extreme was not without its particular severe drawbacks. The Jews at Sinai, the ultimate example of man exposed to a high level of Divine omniscience and presence, underwent agonies in the Divine presence. They beseeched Moses to shield them from overexposure to the Divine presence. In their new freedom from Pharaoh, and in spite of their God-granted freedom vis-à-vis God, the Jews of Sinai were nevertheless in a state of artificial freedom.

The Jews of the Exodus were the generation, which in spite of having witnessed God's power and munificence, trembled at the reports of the advance scouts. They were a generation doomed to die out completely; they were tainted and ultimately unworthy of entering the promised land. They were slaves within their newfound freedom. Slave mentalities in free-man bodies.

A severe price is paid by mortals coming face-to-face with Divine intervention. An entire generation, including its leaders, was doomed to preclusion from fulfilling an important potentiality. For, however great its immediate benefits, Divine intervention, even for the purpose of mundane liberation, inevitably and devastatingly decreases man's freedom and truncates his growth potential.

(See Numbers 13. With only two exceptions, the first group of twelve scouts sent out by Moses to reconnoiter the Land of Canaan returned with disheartening reports. Ten of the twelve scouts argued against any attempt to conquer the land. The Jews of Sinai grew fainthearted at the reports and lamented their fate. For their lack of confidence, the Sinai generation was doomed to die out in the desert.)

597. "[Religion] is an energy of huge potency but of ambiguous character." Professor William E. Hocking, as cited by Milton Konovitz in "Is Religion the Foundation of Morality?" *Midstream,* June–July 1985, p. 17.

598. "Men never do evil so completely and cheerfully as they do from religious conviction." Pascal.

599. See Herder, *Yet Another Philosophy of History* (1774), sec. 3, as cited in Barnard, *J. G. Herder on Social and Political Culture,* p. 219. "Liberty, sociability and equality, as they are sprouting everywhere at present, have caused, and will cause, a thousand evils to be committed in their name."

600. "Mir velen zey iberleben, iberleben, avinu shebashamayim, / Mir velen zey iberleben, iberleben, iberleben" ("We shall outlive them (the Nazis), our Heavenly Father, / We shall outlive them, outlive them, outlive them"). "The Dance of Suffering," cited in Prager, *Sparks of Glory,* p. 12.

601. Weisel, *Night* (New York: Pyramid Books, 1961), p. 78.

602. As was noted in section 1030.00, "Obscurity/Ambiguity of God, Etc." in order for man to have true freedom of choice, he must have the philosophical choice, as well, of either a secular or a religious approach to life. In this connection, it is interesting to note that the core concept of "holy quest for potential," on which our work pivots, can also be used at the heart of a powerful secular philosophy which could run roughly as follows:

Quest for potential is the underlying dynamic and spark of the universe. It is the "primal scream" of the cosmos. The potentials of life, truth, beauty, mercy, freedom, love, et al., actualized and energized a primal creative dynamic whose evolution actualized and energized matter, energy, and a chain of events leading to life itself and continuing through the present.

(This philosophical structure may, in turn, have some elements roughly in parallel with the Chinese cogmogony of P'an Ku, the creator emerging from the great chaos, and with the Chinese cogmogony of Shang-ti, the impersonal eternal element of the world order.)

603. See Midrash Bereshit Rabbah 19:3. ". . . you must not make the fence more than the principal thing, lest it fall and destroy the plants. Thus, the Holy One, blessed be He, had said, 'For in the day that thou eatest thereof thou shalt surely die' (Genesis 2:17); whereas she [Eve] did not say thus, but, 'God hath said: Ye shall not eat of it, neither shall ye touch it'; when the

serpent saw her thus lying, he took and thrust her against it. 'Have you then died?' he said to her; 'just as you were not stricken through touching it, so you will not die when you eat it.' "

604. See *Tsavoat ha-Rivosh*, as cited in Agus, *The Evolution of Jewish Thought*, p. 338. "Let no man indulge in the multiplication of additional prohibitions."

605. See Berachot 7a.

606. See Tadeusz Borowski, cited in Fackenheim, *God's Presence in History*, p. 104. "It is hope that provokes men to march indifferently to the gas chambers, and keeps them from conceiving of an insurrection . . . . Never has hope provoked so much ill as in this war, as in this camp. We were never taught to rid ourselves of hope, and that is why we are dying in the gas-chambers" (Borowski was a non-Jewish Polish writer and inmate of Auschwitz who committed suicide at age twenty-nine.)

607. This assertion is important to our study because if there is no rationally moral basis to man's interaction with the Divine, there is no point in writing studies on theodicy. At the same time, we must reconcile certain historical events, e.g., the *Akedat Yitzchak*, which seem to contradict the assertion of a rationally moral interaction.

608. According to Soloveitchik, "B'sod Ha-yachid V'hayachad," pp. 333–343, man is in one of two states: (1) random happening, and (2) deterministic. If man is in state (1), philosophical speculation is futile; if man is in state (2), then the question is inappropriate; the only question is how to best deal with and practically approach the problem at hand within the context of Halachah.

A prior book encapsulating discourses of Soloveitchik, *Reflections of the Rav*, does provide a specific theodicy with regard to the Holocaust—*Hester Panim*. Thus, the dichotomy in Soloveitchik's approach would seem resolvable by, and consistent with, our formulation.

609. See Spero, *Morality, Halakha and the Jewish Tradition*, p. 93.

610. Hirsch, *Timeless Torah*, p. 51.

611. Berkovits, "Prayer," in Stitskin, *Studies in Torah Judaism*, p. 182.

612. Spero, *Morality, Halakha and the Jewish Tradition*, p. 94.

613. *Encyclopaedia Judaica*, s.v. "Prayer," vol. 13, col. 978.

614. See Gordis, *A Faith for Moderns*, p. 258. "The English word 'prayer' is derived from the Latin verb *precare*, 'beg, entreat,' exactly like the German *Gebet*. . . . The Hebrew verb 'to pray' is derived probably from a root meaning 'to judge,' and its original meaning may therefore be 'to examine or judge oneself.' "

615. See Breuer's introduction to the *Hirsch Siddur*. "*Tefillah* (from which derives *hitpalel*) requires that we imbue ourselves *(palel)* ever anew."

616. See Gordis, *A Faith for Moderns*, p. 257. "The first prayer recorded in Scripture is that of the Patriarch Jacob at Beth-el. When, as a lad, Jacob left his father's home to go toward an unknown destiny, he found himself at nightfall in an open field. With a stone as a pillow, he fell asleep, and in a dream saw a ladder stretching from earth to heaven."

617. Berkovits notes that "theoretically it is possible for one to be a pious Jew in the strictest orthodox sense of the word without ever uttering a word of prayer." See his entire paragraph in Stitskin, *Studies in Torah Judaism*, p. 93.

The Ramban, in contradistinction to the Rambam, holds that there is no requirement for *tefillah* except *b'sh'as tzarah* *("in time of distress")*. See Nachmanides' comments on Maimonides' *Sefer ha-Mitzvot*, Positive Commandment 5.

618. See Midrash Psalms 17: "My children, return to me as long as the gates of prayer are open." As cited by Berkovits, in Stitskin, *Studies in Torah Judaism*, p. 159.

See Nachmanides on Exodus 2:25 as translated in Ramban, *Commentary on Exodus*, vol. 2, p. 25. ". . . it was only on account of the cry [of Israel in Egypt] that He and His mercies accepted their prayer."

619. See Berkovits, in Stitskin, *Studies in Torah Judaism*, pp. 96, 102, 156.

620. These are the second and third of the Divinely ordained Priestly Blessings.

621. R. Menahem Mendel of Vitebsk is reported as saying that in his prayers he was like a miserable beggar who seeks entrance to the king's palace but is thrown out again and again, yet persists in trying to gain entrance to the king. As cited in Jacobs, *Hasidic Prayer*, p. 98.

622. See also Berkovits, in Stitskin, *Studies in Torah Judaism*, p. 92, and his citations on the discussion of "the closing of the gates of prayer."

623. Gordis, *A Faith for Moderns*, p. 271.

624. See Buber, *Eclipse of God*, p. 126. ". . . prayer . . . ultimately asks for the manifestation of the divine presence, for this Presence's becoming dialogically perceivable."

625. See Heschel, *Man's Quest for God*, p. 11. "In all his prayers he begs, explicitly or implicitly, 'Do not forsake me, O Lord.' "

626. T. B. Sotah 48 records that the Levites of the First Temple recited this very psalm to awaken the slumbering God.

627. See Luban, "The Kaddish," p. 214 (juxtaposing the Kedushah and the Kaddish). "[The Kaddish] is not only a prayer to God. It is a prayer for God, for the manifestation of His presence."

628. See Heschel, *Man's Quest for God*, p. 15. "Prayer is an invitation to God to intervene in our lives, to let His will prevail in our affairs; it is the opening of a window to Him in our will, an effort to make Him the Lord of our soul."

629. Soloveitchik, "Redemption, Prayer, Talmud Torah," p. 70.

630. Nosson Scherman, "An Overview: Prayer," xii.

631. Cited by Scherman, ibid.

632. Berkovits, "Prayer," in Stitskin, *Studies in Torah Judaism*, p. 90.

633. Ibid., p. 107.

634. Ibid., p. 109.

635. T. B. Taanit 2a.

636., See Heschel, *Man's Quest for God*, p. 18. "Through prayer we sanctify ourselves, our feelings, our ideas."

Cf. Albo, as explicated by Bleich in *With Perfect Faith*, p. 240. "Prayer effects a positive change in the worshipper's state of spiritual perfection, thereby preparing the individual to receive beneficience and to avert evil. Prayer is thus efficacious in the sense that it effects a changed state of human preparation without effecting a change in divine will since the benefits associated with this state were always willed by God, but are willed by Him to be contingent upon man achieving the requisite state of preparation."

Cf. Hirsch, *Horeb*, p. 477. "He who desired to raise himself up from trouble

and darkness had to be guided by words of prayer that declared life's truth."
Ibid., p. 478. ". . . the inexhaustible source of its [Israel's] elevation to God
. . . 'tefilloth,' in which Israel of today still raises itself up to God."

637. See Heschel, *Man's Quest for God*, p. 8. "Prayer is the essence of
spiritual living. . . . Sometimes prayer is more than a light before us; it is a
light within us."

638. See ibid., p. 5. "To pray is to take notice of the wonder, to regain a
sense of the mystery that animates all beings, the divine margin in all
attainments."

Cf. Bleich, *With Perfect Faith*, p. 238. "According to kabbalistic teaching . . .
Man, through prayer and good deeds, causes the divine influence to produce
a state of harmony and balance within the *sefirot* which, in turn, enables
divine grace to flow throughout creation by providing the necessary channels
for the manifestation of divine goodness and beneficence."

639. See Heschel, *Man's Quest for God*, p. 13. "Prayer is a spiritual source in
itself. . . . But prayer goes beyond the scope of emotion; it is the approach of
the human to the transcendent."

640. See also Berkovits, "Prayer," in Stitskin, *Studies in Torah Judaism*, p.
157.

641. See Schulweis, *Evil and the Morality of God*, p. 139. "Prayer is not only
'poetry believed in' (Santayana), it is poetry acted upon."

642. See Jacobs, *Hasidic Prayer*, p. 32. "The Hasidic ideal then is contemplative prayer in which the Hasid practices self-annihilation."

Cf. ibid., pp. 17, 31.

643. See ibid., p. 28. ". . . there is no reason to doubt that the basic doctrine
of prayer for the sake of the Shekhinah is an authentic doctrine of the Baal
Shem Tov."

Cf. ibid., pp. 23–24, 29.

644. See also Soloveitchik on "prayer equals sacrifice" in "Redemption,
Prayer and Talmud Torah," pp. 71–72.

645. See Heschel, *Man's Quest for God*, p. 70, citing J. T. Berachot 4:4, 8b;
and Jacob Levy, *Neuhebraeisches und Chaldaeisches Woerterbuch*, vol. 4, p. 368b.
"A third-century scholar avers that it is improper to call upon the person who
acts as the reader of prayers for the congregation by saying, *Come and pray;*
we must rather use the words, *Come, karev . . .—bring us close to Him!*"

646. See Rivka Schatz's elaboration on the doctrine of the Baal Shem Tov,
as cited in Jacobs, *Hasidic Prayer*, p. 17.

647. See Berkovits, "Prayer," in Stitskin, *Studies in Torah Judaism*, p. 92.

648. Buber, *At the Turning* (New York: Farrar, Straus & Young, 1952), pp.
61 ff.,

649. See Jacobs, *Hasidic Prayer*, p. 21. "The logical conclusion of the Hasidic
doctrine [of loss of self in prayer] would have been to reject all petitionary
prayer as a hindrance to the attainment of self-annihilation. But such a
solution was not open to Hasidim who believed, like their contemporaries,
that the traditional liturgy, which contains numerous petitionary prayers, was
divinely inspired and divinely ordained.

"The quietistic and radical way out of this dilemma generally adopted by the early Hasidim is that petitionary prayer is not, in fact, a request to satisfy man's needs but to satisfy His own [God's] needs."

Cf. ibid., pp. 23–33.

650. See Frankl, *The Will to Meaning: Foundations and Applications of Logotherapy*, p. 145, as quoted in *Tradition* 19, no. 4 (Winter 1981):330. "I would say that God is not dead but silent. Silent, however, he has been all along. This 'living' God has been a 'hidden' God all along. You must not expect him to answer your call. If you probe the depth of the sea, you send off sound waves and wait for the echo from the bottom of the sea. If God exists, however, he is infinite, and you wait for an echo in vain. The fact that no answer comes back to you is proof that your call has reached the addressee, the infinite."

As Gordis, *A Faith for Moderns*, p. 270, notes: "One medieval thinker went as far as to declare that there is only one true prayer: 'May it be Thy will that Thy will be done.' "

651. Maimonides, *Guide* 3:51.

652. Soloveitchik, "Redemption, Prayer and Talmud Torah," p. 69.

653. Ibid., p. 70.

654. See Lamm, *Faith and Doubt*, p. 29. "God is especially immanent in Torah, and the study of Torah is therefore a means of achieving an encounter with the divine Presence. (Lamm, *The Study of Torah Lishmah in the Works of Rabbi Hayyim of Volozhin*, chap. vi.) . . . Torah, as such, is far more than a document of the divine legislation; it is in itself, mystically, an aspect of God, and hence the student's cognitive activity on Torah serves the higher end of binding him to God. (Ibid., chap. vii.)"

Cf. ibid., p. 29. "For R. Hayyim [of Volozhin], every religious performance—prayer, Torah, the *mitzvot*—is an effort to bring God out of His self-contained and impersonal Absoluteness into His Relatedness, by which alone man can achieve a personal relationship with Him. . . . whether Torah or *tefillah* is the more effective method depends entirely upon the personality of the individual in question."

655. Both *tefillah* and *karbanot* (the Temple sacrifices) are *avodah* (service); they are both expressions of dependence/humility.

656. See T. B. Shabbat 11a. "Scholars like R. Shimon bar Yohai . . . whose sole occupation was study of the Torah, would not interrupt their studies in order to pray." As noted in Jacobs, *Hasidic Prayer*, p. 18.

657. Gordis, A Faith for Moderns, p. 258.

Cf. Omar Khayyam:

The moving Finger writes, and, having writ,
   Moves on; nor all your Piety nor Wit
Shall lure it back to cancel half a Line,
   Nor all your Tears wash out a Word of it.

658. Bleich, *With Perfect Faith*, p. 238.

Cf. Gordis, *A Faith for Moderns*, p. 270. "One medieval thinker went so far as to declare that there is only one true prayer: 'May it be Thy will that Thy will be done.' "

659. Bleich, *With Perfect Faith*, p. 239.

Cf. ibid., p. 239. "Hirsch's explanation of the effect of prayer on the worshipper is based upon his philological interpretation of the Hebrew word for 'prayer,' tefillah. Hirsch regards this term as being derived from the verb 'pallel,' meaning 'to judge,' forms of which occur twice in I Samuel 2:23. Grammatically, the Hebrew word for the verb 'to pray'—le-hitpallel—is in the reflexive form. Prayer, then, for Hirsch, is a form of self-judgment. Prayer becomes the occasion for man to bring himself to trial, to engage in self-examination with a view to determining whether his conduct conforms to the norms required of a true servant of God, and to reflect upon the ways in which his conduct may be improved and brought into conformity with these ideals."

660. Ibid. pp. 238–239.

661. Hirsch, *Horeb*, sec. 618, p. 472.

662. See commentary of Shem Tov on Maimonides, *Guide* 3:28. "And it is necessary that the mass-man should believe that God is moved by human petitions and rituals of propition. Though this belief is false, strictly speaking it is necessary for the existence of society." As cited in Agus, *The Evolution of Jewish Thought*, p. 196 (see his notes on p. 429 for full citation).

663. Stitskin, *Studies in Torah Judaism*, p. 87.

664. See Yeshayahu Leibowitz, *Judaism, Human Values, and the Jewish State* (Harvard University Press 1992) Chapter: "Of Prayer"

In particular, see p. 35:

"By understanding prayer as a worshipful stance and not as an attempt to bring about God's intervention in His natural order, we are able to solve a problem which arises in religious education regarding prayer: why does not prayer—at times, even the prayer of the saintly and the just—evoke a response? . . ."

". . . The essence of the Yom Kippur experience is the consciousness of becoming purified before God and the awareness of the uniqueness of man's position before Him, even though man in himself is as nought. However, popular religiosity was unable to bear this sublimity of faith, and embellished this essential liturgy . . ."

SNAPSHOT BIOS

Abravanel, Isaac (Abarbanel)
1437–1508   *Portugal, Spain, Italy*
Medieval Jewish philosopher and biblical exegete; statesman

Agus, Jacob B.
20th century   *United States*
Jewish author and historical writer

Aristotle
384–322 B.C.E.   *Greece*
Greek philosopher

Augustine
354–430   *North Africa*
Church father, philosopher

Aquinas, Thomas
ca. 1225–1274   *Italy*
Medieval Catholic philosopher

Baal Shem Tov, Israel ben Eliezer ("Besht")
ca. 1700–1760   *Eastern Europe*
Founder of Hasidic movement

Belkin, Samuel
20th century   *United States*
Jewish scholar and writer; president, Yeshiva University

Berdyaev, Nikolai
1874–1948   *Russia*
Christian Marxist

Berg, Philip S.
20th century   *United States, Israel*
Jewish writer on kabbalistic subjects

Berkovits, Eliezer
20th century   *United States, Israel*
Orthodox Jewish thinker and writer

Bleich, J. David
20th century   *United States*
Orthodox Jewish halakhist and scholar of Jewish philosophy

Borowitz, Eugene
20th century   *United States*
Reform Jewish theologian

Buber, Martin
20th century   *Germany, Israel*
Jewish philosopher and scholar

Camus, Albert
1913–1959   *France*
Philosopher and creative writer

Cohen, Arthur
20th century   *United States*
Jewish theological writer

Cohen, Hermann
1842–1918   *Germany*
German school philosopher as well as Jewish philosopher

Epicurus
ca. 342–270 B.C.E.   *Greece*
Philosopher; founder of Epicureanism

Fackenheim, Emil
20th century   *Germany, Canada*
Jewish philosopher

Frankl, Viktor E.
20th century   *Austria, United States*
Psychiatrist, author

Gersonides (Rav Levi ben Gershon; acronym: RaLbaG)
1288–1344   *France*
Medieval Jewish philosopher, biblical exegete, mathematician, astron-
omer, and talmudist

Gordis, Robert
20th century   *United States*
Jewish thinker, writer, and biblical scholar

Greenberg, Hayim
1889–1953   *United States*
Jewish political and social thinker

Greenberg, Irving
20th century   *United States*
Jewish thinker and writer

Hartman, David
20th century   *United States, Israel*
Jewish thinker and writer

Herberg, Will
20th century   *United States*
Jewish thinker and writer

Herder, Johann Gottfried
1744–1803   *Germany*
Philosopher of history

Heschel, Abraham Joshua
20th century   *Poland, Germany, United States*
Jewish scholar, thinker, and writer

Hick, John
20th century   *England*
Philosopher and writer

Hirsch, Samson Raphael
1808–1888   *Austria, Germany*
Jewish scholar, thinker, and writer

Ibn Daud, Abraham
ca. 1110–1180   *Spain*
Medieval Jewish philosopher and historian, the first purely Aristotelian Jewish philosopher

Ibn Ezra, Abraham
1089–1164   *primarily Spain*
Medieval Jewish biblical exegete, thinker, grammarian, and poet

Ibn Ezra, Isaac
12th century   *Spain, Egypt, Iraq*
Medieval writer and poet, son of Abraham ibn Ezra; for a period, professed Islam

Ignatius of Loyola
1491–1556   *Spain, France*
Catholic thinker; founder of Society of Jesus (Jesuits)

Irenaeus
ca. 140–202   *Asia Minor, Gaul*
Catholic philosopher; a father of the Greek Church

Jacobs, Louis
20th century   *England*
Jewish thinker and writer

Jung, Carl Gustave
1875–1961   *Switzerland*
Founder: analytic psychology

Kadushin, Max
20th century   *United States*
Jewish thinker, scholar and writer

Kafka, Franz
1883–1924   *Austria*
Poet and writer of psychological and philosophical fiction

Kook, Abraham Isaac
1865–1935   *Palestine*
Neo-kabbalistic thinker, writer, and halakhist; (Ashkenazic) Chief Rabbi of Palestine

Kushner, Harold
20th century   *United States*
Conservative rabbi and author

Lamm, Norman
20th century   *United States*
Orthodox Jewish thinker and writer; president of Yeshiva University

Leibowitz, Nehama
20th century   *Israel*
Orthodox Jewish biblical exegete

Luria, Isaac (the "Ari")
1534–1572   *Palestine, (educated in Egypt)*
Founder: Lurianic kabbalistic school

Luzzatto, Moses Hayyim (acronym: "Ramhal")
1707–1747   *Italy, Germany, Holland, Palestine*
Jewish halakhist, philosopher, mystic, and poet

Maimonides, Moses (Moses ben Maimon; acronym: "Rambam")
1135–1204   *Spain, Palestine, Egypt*
Medieval Jewish philosopher, exegete, codifier, halakhist, and medical writer

Mani
ca. 215–276   *Babylonia*
Founder of Manichaeism

Merton, Thomas
20th century   *United States*
Catholic philosopher and writer

Mill, John Stuart
1806–1873   *primarily England*
Major exponent of Utilitarianism

Milton, John
1608–1674   *England*
Poet

Nachmanides, Moses (Moses ben Nachman; acronym: "Ramban")
ca. 1194–1270   *Spain, Palestine*
Medieval Jewish exegete, halakhist, and philosopher. His biblical commentaries combine rational interpretation with insistence on kabbalistic implications.

Nicholas of Cusa
1401–1464   *Germany*
Roman Catholic philosopher

Philo (Philo of Alexandria; Philo Judaeus)
20 B.C.E.–50 C.E.   *Egypt*
Hellenistic Jewish philosopher and exegete

Philoponus, John
6th century   *Egypt*
Philosopher, commentator on Aristotle, grammarian, and theologian

Rousseau, Jean-Jacques
1712–1778   *primarily France*
Philosopher and author

Russel, Bertrand
20th century   *England*
Mathematician and philosopher

Saadia Gaon (Saadyah ben Joseph)
882–942   *Egypt, Palestine, Babylonia*
Medieval Jewish philosopher, halakhist, poet, translator, and grammarian

Sartre, Jean-Paul
20th century   *France*
Philosopher

Scherman, Nosson
20th century   *United States*
Orthodox Jewish writer and editor

Schulweis, Harold M.
20th century   *United States*
Jewish thinker and writer

Schlesinger, George
20th century   *United States*
Thinker and writer

Scholem, Gershom
20th century   *Germany, Israel*
Jewish authority on Kabbalah

Socrates
470–399 B.C.E.   *Greece*
Greek philosopher; teacher of Plato

Soloveitchik, Joseph B.
20th century   *United States*
Orthodox Jewish philosopher and halakhist

Solzhenitsyn, Aleksandr
20th century   *Russia, United States*
Novelist

Spero, Shubert
20th century   *United States*
Jewish thinker and writer

Spinoza, Baruch
1632–1677   *Holland*
Philosopher, Jewish

Steinsaltz, Adin
20th century   *Israel*
Jewish writer, talmudic commentator, and religious thinker

Stitskin, Leon D.
20th century   *United States*
Jewish thinker and writer

Teilhard de Chardin, Pierre
1881–1955   *France*
Christian philosopher and paleontologist

Tillich, Paul
20th century   *Germany, United States*
Protestant theologian

Unamuno, Miguel de
1864–1936   *Spain*
Writer and philosopher

Vital, Hayyim ("Calabrese")
1543–1620   *Palestine, Syria*
(Jewish) Lurianic kabbalist

Whitehead, Alfred North
1861–1947   *England*
Mathematician and philosopher

Wiesel, Elie
20th century   *Transylvania, France, United States*
Jewish thinker and writer

Wolfson, Harry Austryn
20th century   *United States*
Historian of philosophy and authority on Jewish philosophy

Younger, Irving
20th century   *United States*
Judge, professor of law

BIBLIOGRAPHY

List of Works Cited

Abravanel, Isaac. *Principles of Faith (Rosh Amanah)*. Translated by Menachem Kellner. East Brunswick, N.J.: Fairleigh Dickinson University Press, 1982.

Agus, Jacob B. *The Evolution of Jewish Thought*. London and New York: Abelard-Schuman, 1959.

Albo, Joseph. *Book of Principles (Sefer Ha-'Ikkarim)*. Translated by Isaac Husik. Philadelphia: Jewish Publication Society, 1929–30.

Alston, William P., and Nakhnikian, George, eds. *Readings in Twentieth-Century Philosophy*. New York: Free Press of Glencoe, 1963.

Altizer, Thomas J. J. *The Descent into Hell*. Philadelphia and New York: Lippincott, 1970.

Aquinas, Thomas. *Summa Theologiae*. Edited by Thomas Gilby. Garden City, N.Y.: Doubleday Image Books, 1969.

Augustine. *Confessions and Enchiridion*. Translated and edited by Albert Outler. Vol. 7. Philadelphia: Westminster Press, 1955.

Azriel of Gerona. *Commentary on Talmudic Aggadoth*. Edited by Isaiah Tishby. Jerusalem: Magnes Press, 1982.

————. *Perush Eser Sefirot*. In Meir ibn Gabbai, *Derekh Emunah*. Warsaw, 1890; reprint, Jerusalem, 1967.

Belkin, Samuel, *In His Image*. New York: Abelard-Schuman, 1960.

Berdyaev, Nikolai. *The Destiny of Man*. Translated from the Russian by Natalie Duddington. New York: Harper & Row, 1960.

Berg, Philip S. *Kabbalah for the Layman*. New York: Press of the Research Center of Kabbalah, 1982.

Berkovits, Eliezer. *Faith after the Holocaust*. New York: Ktav, 1973.

————. *God, Man and History*. Middle Village, N.Y.: Jonathan David, 1959.

————. *Major Themes in Modern Philosophies of Judaism*. New York: Ktav, 1974.

253

————. *With God in Hell.* New York: Sanhedrin Press, 1979.

Besdin, Abraham R. *Reflections of the Rav.* Jerusalem: World Zionist Organization, Department of Torah Education and Culture in the Diaspora, 1979.

Birnbaum, Philip. *A Book of Jewish Concepts.* New York: Hebrew Publishing Co., 1964.

Bleich, J. David. *With Perfect Faith.* New York: Ktav, 1983.

Blumenthal, David. *Understanding Jewish Mysticism: A Source Reader.* New York: Ktav, 1982.

Bokser, Ben Zion, ed. and trans. *Abraham Isaac Kook.* New York: Paulist Press, 1978.

Borowitz, Eugene B. *Choices in Modern Jewish Thought.* New York: Behrman House, 1983.

Brody, Baruch A., ed. *Readings in the Philosophy of Religion,* Englewood Cliffs, N.J.: Prentice-Hall, 1974.

Bronowski, J. *The Ascent of Man.* Boston: Little, Brown, 1973.

Buber, Martin. *Eclipse of God.* New York: Harper & Row, 1957.

————. *Good and Evil.* New York: Charles Scribner's Sons, 1952.

Cohen, A., ed. and trans. *The Soncino Books of the Bible.* London: Soncino Press, 1947.

Cohen, Arthur A. *The Tremendum.* New York: Crossroad, 1981.

Crenshaw, James. *Theodicy in the Old Testament.* London: Fortress Press, 1983.

Davies, Paul. *God and the New Physics.* New York: Simon & Schuster, Touchstone Books, 1983.

Encyclopaedia Judaica. Jerusalem: Keter, 1972.

Epstein, I., ed. *Hebrew-English Edition of the Babylonian Talmud.* London: Soncino, 1976.

Fackenheim, Emil L. *Encounters Between Judaism and Modern Philosophy,* New York: Schocken, 1980.

————. *God's Presence in History: Jewish Affirmations and Philosophical Reflections.* New York: Harper Torchbooks, 1972.

————. *The Jewish Return into History.* New York: Schocken, 1978.

————. *To Mend the World.* New York: Schocken, 1982.

————. *Quest for Past and Future.* Boston: Beacon Press, 1970.

Fleischner, Eva, ed. *Auschwitz: Beginning of a New Era?* New York: Ktav, 1977.

Frankl, Viktor E. *From Death Camp to Existentialism.* Translated by Ilsa Lasch. Boston: Beacon Press. 1959.

Frazier, Alie M., ed. *Issues in Religion.* New York: Van Nostrand Reinhold, 1969.

Freedman, H., ed. and trans. *The Midrash*. New York: Soncino Press, 1983.

Gersonides. *The Wars of the Lord. (Milchamot Hashem)*. Translated by Seymour Feldman. Vol. 2. (Books 2–4) Philadelphia: Jewish Publication Society, 1987.

Ginzberg, Louis. *Legends of the Jews*. Philadelphia: Jewish Publication Society, 1913.

Glatzer, Nahum N., ed. *The Dimensions of Job*. New York: Schocken Books, 1969.

Gordis, Robert. *A Faith for Moderns*. New York, Bloch, 1971.

———. *The Book of God and Man: A Study of Job*. Chicago: University of Chicago Press, 1978.

Greenberg, Irving. "Cloud of Smoke, Pillar of Fire: Judaism, Christianity, and Modernity after the Holocaust." In *Auschwitz: Beginning of a New Era*, edited by Eva Fleischner. New York: Ktav, 1977.

———. *Perspectives: "The Third Great Cycle in Jewish History."* New York: National Jewish Resource Center, 1981.

———. *Perspectives: "Voluntary Covenant."* New York: National Jewish Resource Center, 1982.

Gruenwald, I. "Some Critical Notes on the First Part of Sefer Yezira." *Revue des Études Juives*, January–June 1973.

Hawking, Stephen. *A Brief History of Time*. New York: Bantam Books, 1988.

Hartman, David. *A Living Covenant*. New York: Free Press, 1985.

Hartshorne, Charles. *Man's Vision of God* (1941). Excerpted in *Classical and Contemporary Readings in the Philosophy of Religion*, edited by John Hick (see below).

Herberg, Will. *Judaism and Modern Man*. New York: Atheneum, 1951.

Herder, J. G. *J. G. Herder on Social and Political Culture*. Translated by F. M. Barnard. Cambridge: At the University Press, 1969.

Hertz, J. H., ed. *Pentateuch & Haftorahs*. London: Soncino, 1960.

Heschel, Abraham. *God in Search of Man*. New York: Harper Torchbooks, 1955.

———. *Man Is Not Alone*. New York: Farrar, Strauss & Young, 1951.

———. *Man's Quest for God: Studies in Prayer and Symbolism*. New York: Crossroad, 1984.

Hick, John. *Evil and the God of Love*. San Francisco: Harper & Row, 1966.

———. "The Nature of Faith" (chap. 5 of Hick's *Faith and Knowledge*).

In *Classical and Contemporary Readings in the Philosophy of Religion,* edited by John Hick (see below).

————. ed. *Classical and Contemporary Readings in the Philosophy of Religion.* Englewood Cliffs, N.J.: Prentice-Hall, 1964.

Hirsch, Samson Raphael. *Horeb: A Philosophy of Jewish Laws and Observances.* Translated from the German by I. Grunfeld. London: Soncino Press, 1962.

————. *Timeless Torah: An Anthology of the Writings of Rabbi Samson Raphael Hirsch.* Edited by Jacob Breuer. New York: Philipp Feldheim, 1969.

————. *Chapters of the Fathers: Translation and Commentary.* Translated into English by Gertrude Hirschler. New York: Philipp Feldheim, 1967.

————. ed. and trans. *The Hirsch Siddur.* Jerusalem: Feldheim Publishers, 1969.

Jacobs, Louis. *Hasidic Prayer.* New York: Schocken Books, 1978, 1972.

————. *Principles of the Jewish Faith.* New York: Basic Books, 1964.

Kadushin, Max. *The Rabbinic Mind.* New York: Jewish Theological Seminary, 1952.

Kaplan, Abraham. *The New World of Philosophy.* New York: Random House, 1961.

Kaplan, Aryeh. *If You Were God.* New York: National Council of Synagogue Youth, 1983.

————. *The Infinite Light.* New York: National Council of Synagogue Youth, 1984.

Kaufmann, Yehezkel. *The Religion of Israel.* New York: Schocken, 1960.

Kenny, Anthony, ed. *Aquinas: A Collection of Critical Essays.* Garden City, N.Y.: Doubleday Image Books, 1969.

Kook, A. I. See Bokser, Ben Zion.

Lamm, Norman. *Faith and Doubt.* New York: Ktav, 1971.

————. *The Face of God.* New York: Yeshiva University, 1986.

Leibowitz, Nehama. *Studies in Bereshit (Genesis).* Jerusalem: World Zionist Organization, 1981.

————. *Studies in Shemot (Exodus).* Jerusalem: World Zionist Organization, 1976.

Lewy, H.; Altmann, A.; and Heinemann, I., eds., *Three Jewish Philosophers.* New York: Atheneum, 1977.

Luban, M. "The Kaddish." In Stitskin, *Studies in Torah Judaism* (see below).

Luzzatto, Moshe Chayim. *The Way of God (Derech haShem)*. Translated by Aryeh Kaplan. Jerusalem and New York: Feldheim, 1977.

———. *Mesillat Yesharim (The Path of the Just)*. Translated by Shraga Silverstein. Boys Town, Jerusalem: Yaakov Feldheim, 1966.

Maccoby, Hyam. "Christianity's Break with Judaism." *Commentary* 78, no. 2 (August 1984): 38.

McKeon, Richard, ed. *Selections from Medieval Philosophers*. New York: Charles Scribner's Sons, 1957.

Maimonides, Moses. *The Guide for the Perplexed (Moreh Nevuchim)*. Translated by M. Friedland, New York: Dover, 1956.

Maslow, A. H. *The Farther Reaches of Human Nature*. East Rutherford, N.J.: Penguin Books, 1971.

Matt, Daniel C., ed. and trans. *Zohar: The Book of Enlightenment*. Ramsey, N.J.: Paulist Press, 1983.

Merton, Thomas. *The Ascent to Truth*. New York: Harcourt Brace Jovanovich, Harvest Books, 1951.

———. *The New Man*. New York: Farrar, Straus & Giroux, 1961.

Midrash Rabbah, Genesis. Translated by H. Freedman, New York and London: Soncino, 1983.

Millgram, Abraham Ezra, ed. *Great Jewish Ideas*. New York: B'nai B'rith Department of Adult Jewish Education, 1964.

Montefiore, C. G., and Loewe, H., eds. *A Rabbinic Anthology*. New York: Schocken, 1974.

Moore, G. F. *Judaism*. Cambridge: Harvard University Press, 1927.

Noveck, Simon, ed. *Contemporary Jewish Thought*. New York: B'nai B'rith Department of Adult Jewish Education, 1963.

Passmore, John. *The Perfectibility of Man*. New York: Charles Scribner's Sons, 1970.

Peli, Pinchas. *On Repentance*. Ramsey, N.J.: Paulist Press, 1984.

Prager, Dennis. *Sparks of Glory*. New York: Shengold Publishers, 1974.

Ramban (Nachmanides). *Commentary on the Torah*. Translated and annotated by Charles Chavel. New York: Shilo Publishing House, 1973.

———. Writings and Discourses. Translated and annotated by Charles Chavel. New York: Shilo Publishing House, 1978.

Saadia Gaon. *The Book of Beliefs and Opinions*. Translated by Samuel Rosenblatt. New Haven: Yale University Press, 1948.

———. *Book of Doctrines and Beliefs*. Translated by A. Altmann. Oxford: East & West Library, 1946. In Lewy et al., *Three Jewish Philosophers* (see above).

Sarna, Nahum M. *Understanding Genesis.* New York: McGraw-Hill, 1966.

Sartre, Jean-Paul. *Existentialism and Humanism.* Translated by Philip Mairet. London: Associated Book Publishers, 1948. Reprinted as "Atheistic Humanism" in Frazier, *Issues in Religion* (see above).

Schechter, Solomon. *Aspects of Rabbinic Theology.* New York: Schocken, 1961.

Scherman, Nosson. "An Overview: Prayer, A Timeless Need." In *The Complete Artscroll Siddur.* Edited by Rabbi Nosson Scherman and Rabbi Meir Zlotowitz. Translated by N. Scherman. New York: Mesorah Publications, 1984.

———. "An Overview: Kaddish—Prayer of Sanctification." in *Kaddish,* edited by Rabbi Nosson Scherman and Rabbi Meir Zlotowitz, general editors, New York: Mesorah Publications, 1980.

———. "An Overview: The Period of the Miracle." In *The Megillah (Megillat Esther),* edited by Rabbi Meir Zlotowitz. New York: Artscroll Studios, 1976.

Schlesinger, George N. "Logical Analysis and the Beliefs of an Orthodox Jew." *Intercom* 6, no. 1 (December 1963).

———. *Religion and Scientific Method.* Dordrecht: D. Reidel Publishing Co., 1977.

Scholem, Gershom. *Major Trends in Jewish Mysticism.* New York: Schocken Books, 1961.

———. *Origins of the Kabbalah.* Translated by Allan Arkush. Princeton, N.J.: Jewish Publication Society, 1987.

Schulweis, Harold M. *Evil and the Morality of God.* Cincinnati: Hebrew Union College Press, 1984.

———. "Suffering and Evil." In Millgram, *Great Jewish Ideas* (see above).

Seltzer, Robert M. *Jewish People, Jewish Thought.* New York: Macmillan, 1980.

Soloveitchik, Joseph B. "B'sod Ha-yachid v' Hayachad" (In Aloneness, In Togetherness), edited by Pinchas Peli, Jerusalem: Orot, 5736 (1975–1976).

———. "The Community." *Tradition* 17, no. 2 (Spring 1978).

———. *Halakhic Man.* Translated by Lawrence Kaplan, Philadelphia: Jewish Publication Society, 1983.

———. "The Lonely Man of Faith." *Tradition* 7, no. 2 (Summer 1965).

———. "Redemption, Prayer and Talmud Torah." *Tradition* 17, no. 2 (Spring 1978).

(See also Besdin, Abraham R.)

Sperling, Harry, and Maurice Simon, trans. *The Zohar.* 5 vols. London: Soncino, 1931–34.

Spero, Shubert. *Morality, Halakhah and the Jewish Tradition.* New York: Yeshiva University Press, 1983.

Staub, Jacob J. *The Creation of the World According to Gersonides.* Chico, Calif.: Scholars Press, 1982.

Steinsaltz, Adin. *The Thirteen Petalled Rose.* Translated by Yehuda Hanegbi. New York: Basic Books, 1980.

Stitskin, Leon D. *Eight Jewish Philosophers.* Jerusalem and New York: Feldheim Publishers, 1979.

———. *Studies in Torah Judaism.* New York: Yeshiva University Press, 1969.

Suzuki, D. T. "The Sense of Zen." In *Zen Buddhism: Selected Writings of D. T. Suzuki,* edited by William Barrett. New York: Doubleday, 1956. Reprinted in Frazier, *Issues in Religion* (see above).

Teilhard de Chardin, Pierre. *The Future of Man.* Translated from the French by Norman Denny. New York: Harper & Row, 1969.

———. *The Phenomenon of Man.* Translated by Bernard Wall. New York: Harper & Row, 1959.

Tillich, Paul. *The Eternal Now.* New York: Charles Scribner's Sons, 1956–63.

Vahnian, Gabriel. *The Death of God.* New York: George Braziller, 1967.

Vital, Hayim. introduction, *Sefer Etz Hayim: The Gate of General Principles.* Translated by Lavey Darbey. New York: 92nd Street Y, 1985.

Wells, Donald A. *God, Man, and the Thinker.* New York: Random House, 1962.

Whitehead, Alfred North. *Religion in the Making.* New York: Macmillan 1926.

Wiesel, Elie. *The Fifth Son.* Translated by Marion Wiesel. New York: Summit Books, 1985.

Wolfson, Harry Austryn. *Religious Philosophy.* Cambridge, Mass.: Harvard University Press, Belknap Press, 1961.

———. *Studies in the History of Philosophy of Religion.* 2 vols. Cambridge, Mass.: Harvard University Press, 1973 and 1977.

Wolpin, Nisson, ed. *A Path Through the Ashes.* Brooklyn, N.Y.: Masorah Publications, 1986.

BIBLICAL INDEX

261

GENERAL INDEX

Galileo, knowledge and ascendancy of
man, 111
Garden of Eden parable, 170; divine
consciousness of man, 121, 135, 145;
potential of man, 86–89, 156, 159,
161, 169
The Gate of Reward, 24–25
Gersonides, Rav Levi: divine consciousness of man, 132, 136, 138; Halachic
amendments, 171; monotheistic characteristics of Judaism, 40; origins of
universe, 58
God: eternity of, 56–60; hiding of face,
16–17, 27, 30, 63, 124, 128–30, 138–
43, 146–47; Holy potential of the divine, 61, 64–78
God and justice, 3–9; divine interaction
with man, 17–30, and permitting existence of evil, 31–36; Holocaust, dejection and discouragement, 4–8; man
and rational morality, 44–50, and
comprehension of God, 17–30
Gordis, Robert: evil as negation, 97; God
and justice, 8; Holy quest for potential,
80; man seeking fuller freedom, 107,
and infinity, 104; prayer and divine interaction with man, 181
Greenberg, Hayim, man's comprehension of God, 24
Greenberg, Irving: divine consciousness
of man, 140, 147; Holy quest for potential, 80; man seeking infinity, 103
Guide to the Perplexed, 113
Gulag Archipelago, 13

Halevi, Yehuda, logic in Judaism, 43
Hanassi, Yehudah, knowledge and ascendancy of man, 111
Hasdai ben Abraham Crescas, evil as negation, 94
Hawking, Stephen, origins of universe,
58
Herberg, Will, knowledge and ascendancy of man, 117
Heschel, Abraham Joshua: freedom of
man, 110, 160; man and God, linkage
between, 74; man seeking infinity, 102
Hester Panim, 16–17, 27, 30, 63; divine
consciousness of man, 124, 128–30,
140–41, 146; man and divine consciousness, 118, 120–22, 124, 129–33,
138–40, 143, 146–47; obscurity of

God, 158–59; prayer and divine interaction with man, 178
Hick, John: divine consciousness of man,
153, 159; divine justice permitting existence of evil, 34–35; God and justice,
man's rational morality, 47; man seeking infinity, 99
Hillel, knowledge and ascendancy of
man, 111
Hirsch, Samson Raphael; Binding of
Isaac, 173; man seeking fuller freedom, 105; prayer and divine interaction with man, 182–83
Holocaust: dejection and discouragement, 4–8; divine consciousness of
man, 120, 124, 130–31, 146–47, and
interaction with man, 10–16; man's
comprehension of God, 24, 26; moral
evil, 13–14; pain and suffering of man,
153–54, 161, 163–67

Ibn Daud, Abraham: divine consciousness of man, 136, 138; man's comprehension of God, 29; monotheistic characteristics of Judaism, 37–38
Ibn Ezra, Abraham; evil as negation, 94;
knowledge and ascendancy of man,
111–14; man's quest for potential, 72
Ibn Ezra, Moses, monotheistic characteristics of Judaism, 38
Ibn Falquera, Shem Tov, prayer and divine interaction with man, 183
Ibn Zaddik, Joseph, evil as negation, 94
Ignatius, Saint, man's rational morality,
47
"In Dust and Ashes," 24
Irenaeus: divine justice permitting existence of evil, 33–36; evil as negation,
95
Isaac, Binding of Isaac, 12, 172–73

Jefferson, Thomas, knowledge and ascendancy of man, 111
John Philoponus, origins of universe, 58
Judaism, Halachic amendments, 169–71;
logic against intellectual flaws in leaps
of faith, 9, 23, 25, 31, 36, 41–44; monotheistic characteristics, 36–41
Jung, Carl Gustave: divine interaction
with man, 11; divine justice permitting
existence of evil, 33
Justice and God, 3–9, 17–36, 44–50